PRINCIPLES

OF

POLITICAL ECONOMY

BY

FATHER MATTEO LIBERATORE, S.J.

TRANSLATED BY

EDWARD HENEAGE DERING

AUTHOR OF "FREVILLE CHASE," ETC., ETC.

A FEW WORDS BY THE TRANSLATOR.

―――

CONSIDERING what the great work of Father Liberatore's life has been, a Treatise on Political Economy from his pen would seem to be a new departure: and so it is, as compared with other economic writings, because his treatment of it is distinctly Christian and scholastic. But, for that very reason, he was just the man to write such a treatise at this time. Professed Economists may invent any number of theories about the production, distribution, and consumption of wealth; but, without the Christian principle and practice of doing as we would be done by, true Political Economy is impossible. Who, then, is better fitted for the task than he who began to teach Catholic philosophy in 1834, published his *Institutiones Philosophicæ* in 1840, and ever since has devoted his life to the study, exposition and defence of Catholic truth, as taught by the incomparably greatest of all teachers, the Angelic Doctor? In these days we go in for knowing, or supposing ourselves to know, a great many things ; but most of us need to be reminded of much that we ought to know.

The non-Catholic reader, if he has read the Holy Father's Encyclical, DE CONDITIONE OPIFICUM, can hardly fail to see in its complete accordance with this Treatise the oneness of the Catholic Church.

BADDESLEY CLINTON, *June 15th, 1891.*

TO THE READER.

FIRST of all, kind reader, I wish to explain why it was that I wrote this little work. On the one hand, I saw that our young men, not only laymen, but clerics also, had need of initiation in economic science, because it is interwoven with almost all the affairs of civil life; whilst, on the other, I found no course of instruction fitted to be a safe guide for them. The earlier writers on Political Economy had their minds misled by the sensistic philosophy of their time; and philosophy, when bad, infects, being the root of them, all the other sciences. Those who came after followed their predecessors blindly, or, if they partly differed from them, wrote nevertheless under the influence of modern liberalism. Now, modern liberalism is like a blue-bottle fly. Wherever it settles, it leaves a germ of corruption and a bad smell.

My intention, therefore, was to prepare something like a compendium of sound principles, that would suffice to put young men on the right road, along which they might proceed safely. In carrying out that idea I have, as you will see, availed myself of the theories taught by the best professors, but not without freely discussing their doctrines and refuting their errors.

This book is not addressed to the learned. That would have required greater powers and more knowledge. It is meant for aspirants and novices. *Virginibus puerisque canto.* I could have wished for more time to write it in; but my advanced age of nearly eighty years forbade me to expect that.

ROME, *January 1st, 1889.*

CONTENTS.

INTRODUCTION.

PART I.—PRODUCTION.

CONTENTS.

CONTENTS.

CONTENTS.

INTRODUCTION.

I.

ETYMOLOGY AND ORIGIN.

ECONOMY is a Greek word, from οἶκος, *house*, and νομή, *distribution*; and according to this etymology it was at first used to signify domestic administration. *Œconomus*, says St. Thomas, *vocatur procurator vel administrator alicujus familiæ.* [1] It retains this signification even to the present day; for, in colleges and seminaries, he whose duty it is to administer the income, and provide for the wants of the community, is usually called the *Œconomus*.

From the family this word was afterwards extended to the city or State (in Greek πόλις), as referring to the property of a whole people, under the name of social or public wealth: and hence Political Economy is understood to mean the doctrine which explains its nature, causes, distribution and use.[2]

---

[1] *In Primum Politicorum.* Lect. i.

[2] The first man who gave a full exposition of Political Economy and reasoned on it in detail, was a Scotchman, Adam Smith, in his famous work, *An Inquiry into the Nature and Causes of the Wealth of Nations*, which appeared in the year 1775. Many, before his time, had written about social wealth; and we find hints of it even so far back as Aristotle in the first three of his eight books on Politics. But all of them had either developed one point only, as, for instance, commerce or money, or else they considered Political Economy to be a branch of the science of Statesmanship, as did the so-called Physiocrats, headed by Quesney. The honour of having made it a distinct study, with principles, investigations, method and laws of its own, is due to Smith: and therefore he deservedly has the reputation of being its founder.

II.

POLITICAL ECONOMY IS BOTH AN ART AND A SCIENCE.

THE first question that suggests itself with regard to Political Economy is this : Is it an art or a science ? The learned disagree about that. Some maintain that it does not rise above the condition of an art, because it is entirely devoted to prescribing rules. Others affirm it to be a science purely, inasmuch as it does not of itself either command or advise, but only speculates and reasons. In our opinion both are wide of the truth. The giving of rules, or speculating and reasoning, are not good criteria for distinguishing a science from an art. A doctrine may (as in Morals) give precepts, and yet be a science. On the other hand we may speculate and reason without going beyond the range of art. A sculptor, for instance, may speculate and reason ; but sculpture is nevertheless an art, not a science. Art, like science, is a process of the intellect, and the intellect proceeds in no other way than by speculating and reasoning. Pellegrino Rossi is mistaken when, to prove that Political Economy is a science, and not an art, he puts forward the fact that it prescinds from its application, inasmuch as it would still subsist, though it were never reduced to practice.

"Science," he says, "is not required to *do* anything. Even if there were nothing in this world but poverty, ignorance and misfortune, there would still be a science of Political Economy. It would ever be true that, by applying the force of intelligence and the organic forces of man to matter in this or that way, objects fitted to satisfy human wants would be produced, and that, if things were left to their natural course, these productions would be distributed in a certain manner among the producers. If men, being informed of the conclusions of science, make use of their knowledge in the interest of social wealth and well-being, they so far do their duty : but the science remains the same,"[1]

But the not being bound to do anything is proper to art also, as art. Art does not do, but teaches to do. The hands do the work, though under the direction of the art. If, for instance, there were no more painting in the world, there would still be an art of painting ; for it would always be true that by certain arrangements of colour on the canvas, certain effects would be produced. By the quality, therefore, of the speculation or of the reasoning, are we enabled to discern the difference between art and science. Art is the result of rational rules about the making of a thing—a building, for instance, or a statue, or a harmony of sounds—and therefore St. Thomas, following Aristotle, defined it to be *Recta ratio factibilium*, or *Habitus cum ratione factivus.*[2] Art reasons out its rules, but in an empirical manner, taking them from experience, or, at the most, from *proximate* causes, without caring to reach the *highest* principles. If it rises to these, it does not indeed cease to be an art, but it assumes the dignity of a science : for science is nothing else than a system of notions deduced from the highest causes—*Cognitio rei per causas ultimas.*

Let us now apply this theory to the present subject. That Political Economy may be called an art is indisputable, because in fact it gives rules of human action about things practical, such as constitute riches. Does not Political Economy furnish us with rules for their plentiful production, just distribution and profitable employment?

But then, Political Economy does not at once furnish us with such rules. It does so by reasoning them out, not only from experience, but also from those causes that are ultimate in their own kind, and often from those that are

---

[1] *Cours d'Economie Politique.* Tome 1er. deuxième leçon.
[2] *Ethic.* Lib. vi.

absolutely ultimate. It would indeed be odd, if, while we have the science of astronomy which treats of the movements of the heavenly bodies, and the science of geology concerning the formation of the strata of the earth, there were no science to treat of the production, distribution and use of wealth. There is no object about which there may not be a science, provided that we treat it in scientific form, i.e. in virtue of certain and evident principles and by the investigation of their supreme causes.

Nor can this be disproved by pointing out that the object of science must be necessary and immutable, and that wealth is not so, being in the last degree mutable and contingent : for, if this objection were valid, theology would be the only science, because all that is not God is mutable and contingent. But, as St. Thomas wisely observes, there is nothing so contingent that it does not contain something necessary. Thus, for instance, that Socrates should run is contingent, but the fact that if he runs he must move, is a necessary truth, because running without movement is impossible :—

Nihil est adeo contingens, quin in se aliquid necessarium habeat; sicut hoc ipsum, quod est Socratem currere, in se quidem contingens est, sed habitudo cursus ad motum est necessaria; necessarium enim est Socratem moveri si currit. Est autem unumquodque contingens ex parte materiæ, quia contingens est quod potest esse et non esse. Potentia autem pertinet ad materiam; necessitas autem consequitur rationem formæ, quia ea, quæ consequuntur ad formam, ex necessitate insunt. [1]

Now science, when considering contingent things, always looks at that which is necessary in them ; and Political Economy considers wealth, not merely in this or that particular case, but in its own nature, and hence

---

[1] *Summa*, p. 1. Q. lxxxvi., a 3.

in the effects necessarily derived from it, and in the laws that universally govern it.[1] This is essentially scientific; and therefore Political Economy, though an art, is at the same time a science. We have the same thing in medicine. There is medical art and medical science. Medicine is an art, because it gives practical rules for curing the sick. It is a science, because it deduces those rules by means of reasoning from the very nature of the diseases and the virtue that is in drugs.

---

[1] The illustrious Périn says about this: "Là où l'on ne voyait d'abord que variété, divergence et confusion, on constate l'universalité et la persistance de certains faits, qui répondent évidemment à des lois générales. De ces faits persistents les uns tiennent à la constitution même de la personne humaine, les autres à la disposition des forces dans le monde extérieur. Le travail, agent nécessaire de toute production ; les bornes assignées par la nature à la puissance des agents physiques que le travail emploie ; la préoccupation naturelle à chaque travailleur d'obtenir le plus grand résultat possible avec le moindre effort ; l'accroissement de fécondité, que le travail reçoit dans la plupart de ses applications, lorsqu'il est convénablement divisé ; le haut prix des marchandises rares, le bas prix des marchandises abondantes ; tous ces faits, et bien d'autres non moins persistents, contribuent à donner un base fixe à l'ordre économique." *Les Doctrines Economiques depuis un siècle, par M. Charles Périn.* Ch. xii.

III.

Political Economy is a Practical Science.

The division of sciences into speculative and practical is well known. It applies to the highest of them ; for there is speculative and practical philosophy, pure reasoning and practical reasoning. The object by which a science is specified is always the criterion by which to judge whether that science is speculative or practical. If truth merely, apart from action, is the object, the science is called speculative. In physics, for instance, we contemplate the order of the sensible world, its phenomena, its laws, as things to be known, not as things to be done. On the contrary, if the nature of the truth contemplated shows it to be in the order of action, the science that corresponds to that truth is called practical. Such, for instance, is the science of Morals, the contemplation of which tends of itself to order well the conduct of man with regard to his ultimate end.

Now it is indisputable that Political Economy must belong to the second of these two classes ; and this is demonstrable by what we have just determined. That which is both an art and a science cannot be other than a practical science : for the object of art is practical ; and art rises to the dignity of science by ennobling the manner of regarding the object, not by changing the object. But we are not going to let this proposition depend on a premiss that some, rightly or wrongly, might dispute : and therefore we say that Political Economy, even supposing it to be not an art at all, must nevertheless be reckoned among practical sciences.

And indeed what does it consider? Wealth, as subject to the action of man.

"Political Economy, considered as a branch of the science of a statesman or legislator, proposes two distinct objects: first, to provide a plentiful revenue or subsistence for the people, or, more properly, to enable them to provide such a revenue or subsistence for themselves; and secondly, to supply the State or commonwealth with a revenue sufficient for the public services. It proposes to enrich both the people and the Sovereign."

So says Adam Smith in the introduction to the fourth book of his work on the Wealth of Nations, the work with which economic science began: and Jean-Baptiste Say gives to his own treatise on the same the title of "*Traité d'Economie Politique, ou simple exposition de la manière dont se forment, se distribuent et se consomment les richesses.* Now the procuring of wealth and distributing it and consuming it—are not these human actions to be rightly ordered? and is not the ordering of human actions for the attainment of a given end a practical object? On this point the Economists who have busied themselves with it, fall into great confusion. Pellegrino Rossi, for instance, wishing to put Political Economy among the speculative sciences, writes thus:—

"Properly speaking, science has no extrinsic end. When we think of how to employ it, its usefulness ceases to be in science, and is found to be in art. Science, whatever its object may be, is nothing else than the possession of truth, the reflex knowledge of the relations that flow from the very nature of things, a knowledge that enables us to reach principles and concatenate the deductions drawn from them. Knowledge of a certain order of truth is the object, the particular end, of a science. Enquiry into this truth, with the help of method, is the

medium. It is not the business of science to *do* anything." [1]

And further on he says :—

" Hence I boldly affirm the conclusion that the science
of Political Economy, thus regarded in its generality and
its invariability, is rather a science of reasoning than a
science of observation. This is denied by those who
confuse rational Political Economy with applied Political
Economy, the science with the art." [2]

This is indeed a jumble. First of all it is not a fact
that the end of science is never extrinsic. The preservation and restoration of health, for instance, which is the
aim of the science of medicine—is not that extrinsic to
medical science ? Nevertheless, though medicine is sometimes called an art, it is as we said before, truly a science ;
and they who would deny it that prerogative, as some do,
contradict the programme of all the Universities, in which
it is classed among the sciences. In the second place, the
fact that science consists in the possession of truth does
not forbid its being practical, if the truth possessed by it
leads to action. Jurisprudence is a science ; yet its
object, the law, is in the highest degree practical, being a
rule of action, and takes its name from the fact of obliging
us to do. *Lex dicitur a ligando, quia obligat ad agendum.* [3]
Rossi justly says that science does nothing, and that its
business is to know, not to do. But ordering to do prescribing rules for doing ; it is not doing. It is not going
beyond the province of knowledge, for knowledge, by the
very fact of being applicable, though not applied, is thence
called practical.

---

[1] *Cours d'Economie Politique,* deuxième leçon.
[2] Ibid.
[3] *Summa* 1ª. 2ªº. Q. xc. a 1

Intellectus practicus, says St. Thomas, *est motivus, non quasi exsequens motum, sed quasi dirigens ad motum; quod convenit ei secundum modum suæ apprehensionis."* [1]

But philosophizing without exact philosophical ideas is a very common defect among the Economists.

IV.

POLITICAL ECONOMY IS BY ITS NATURE SUBORDINATE TO POLITICAL SCIENCE.

POLITICAL Economy is one of the social sciences, for it regards a social *Bonum.* We say *a* social *Bonum,* not *the* social *Bonum,* because the social good, though it certainly implies wealth as necessary for supplying the wants of the population and of the State, is not restricted to that only. The social good embraces also respect for the rights of others, internal and external security, public peace, intellectual culture, virtuous habits, and generally all that is required for human well-being. The science that regards the sum of these things (generally designated by the name of social happiness) and the social organism suited to procure it, is called Political Science, or public right, or the science of Statesmanship. Now wherever a science has for its object that which is a part of the whole, it is of its nature subordinate to the science that has the whole for its object. Every whole subordinates to itself its own parts, and the sciences stand in the same order respectively as their objects do. Economy does not deserve the name of Political, unless it be considered as

---

[1] *Summa* p. 1. Q, lxxix. a. 2 ad 1.

subject to the political end, just as a part does not deserve the name of organic, unless it answers to the end of the entire organism. Hence the famous *Laissez faire, laissez passer*, which has been exalted as a fundamental axiom of economic science, is absurd when taken in its crudeness. But of this hereafter.

Economic theories should conform to the political, and in the event of a conflict between them, the economic should give way. If we were all workmen, there would no doubt be more material for wealth; but should we have a civil society? We should have nothing but a workshop. Civil society [*Civitas*], as we said before, has need of riches, because the State, like the family, cannot be well governed without the conveniences of life: but it needs other good things besides riches, and therefore, in addition to the producers of riches, has need of governors to produce order, soldiers to produce defence, magistrates to produce justice, masters to produce knowledge, Priests to produce religion—and so on.

To regard Political Economy otherwise than as a science subordinate to Political Science, leads to a most pernicious error. It leads to social corruption through an immoderate and unlimited desire of riches. A science not subordinate to another science regards its object as an end. On the contrary, a subordinate science regards its object as a means. Now the end is desired indefinitely, without restriction; but there is limit and measure in our desire for the means to an end. The reason is that the end is desirable for its own sake and absolutely, whilst the means are desirable for the sake of something else, and in proportion to their end.

Hence the greater a thing is that we desire as an end, the more does it sharpen our desire and stimulate us to procure it: but the excess of what we desire as a means is contemned as useless and sometimes hurtful. For instance we love health, knowledge, virtue, as an end;

and therefore the greater they are in our apprehension, the more do we naturally desire them. It would be rather startling to hear a man say, "I like to be healthy and virtuous, but only to a certain extent. Any more than that would be disagreeable." But medicine and clothes are desired as means, the one for the restoration of health, the other for decency and warmth : and therefore they are sought within measure. No one in his senses would say, "The more medicine you make me take, the more clothes you put on me, the better I shall be pleased."

V.

POLITICAL ECONOMY IS SUBORDINATE TO MORAL SCIENCE.

IN the first place this thesis is a corollary to the last, for once Political Economy is of its nature subordinate to Political Science, it is consequently subordinate to Moral Science, because Political Science is intrinsically and essentially dependent on Moral Science. But even if we prescind from that, evident it is that the subordination of Political Economy to Ethics can be directly proved from the fact of its being a practical science. As the true is the object of speculative sciences, so is the good the object of practical sciences. It must not be supposed however that the true when considered by speculative science is not in another respect a good, nor that the good of practical science is not in another respect a truth. The good and the true are convertible, as they say in the Schools. The true, by the fact of being desirable to the will, as being the perfection of the intellect, is a good ; and the good, by the fact of being knowable to the intellect, is true, because it is. But we say that the proper object of the speculative intellect is the true, and the proper object of the practical intellect is the good, because, as we have said, the intellect in contemplating them can either remain contemplating, or direct its knowledge to the government of actions. That God is the supreme Lord, and that the human soul is immortal, are two truths of purely contemplative science. That we owe obedience to God, as Lord, and that the good of the soul is preferable to the good of the body, because the soul is immortal and the body perishable, are two truths of practical science; for they do not tell us what is, but what ought to be done :—

Verum et bonum, says St. Thomas, *se invicem includunt. Nam verum est quoddam bonum, alioquin non esset appetibile; et bonum est quoddam verum, alioquin non esset intelligibile. Sicut igitur objectum appetitus potest esse verum, in quantum habet rationem boni, sicut cum aliquis appetit veritatem cognoscere, ita objectum intellectus practici est bonum, ordinabile ad opus, sub ratione veri. Intellectus enim practicus veritatem cognoscit, sicut speculativus, sed veritatem cognitam ordinat ad opus.* [1]

Now the most universal and practical science that regulates human actions, is the science of Morals, because it has regard to the good of mankind as such, and because in the hierarchy of the sciences each particular science is subordinate to the universal science. As every science that regards this or that particular being is under Ontology, which is the science of Being, so every science that regards this or that particular good is under the science of Morals, which is the science of the good.

On this point, the subordination of Political Economy to Morals, Minghetti speaks very well; and we shall have the pleasure of quoting two passages from him. He shows

---

[1] *Summa*, p. 1. Q. lxxix., a 2. ad 2.

that treating of wealth apart from morals, and looking on Political Economy as an independent and autonomous science, leads to most pernicious consequences. Nor is he, like Pellegrino Rossi, content to invoke Morals when applying the dictate of Economy. He justly maintains that the dictates themselves, by their own intrinsic nature, should be informed with morality and justice.

"The difference" he says, "between my opinion and Rossi's, lies in this : He will have the science and the art created pure, each cut off from every relation, like mathematics and mechanics : and only when he comes to the conclusions, does he ask advice from Morals and Politics. I argue contrariwise, that the fundamental principles of Morals and of Right circumscribe Economy within its rational limits, and, when required, furnish it with certain postulates, without which it could not rightly understand all its own laws, nor resolve all its own problems. Thus we should avoid the absurdity of supposing that a principle, acknowledged theoretically to be true and useful, may be found false and unjust in practice. Modifications may indeed be occasionally required, or we may have to proceed step by step, slowly : but to put oneself in opposition to the results of science, and annul them—Never ! . . . . Political Economy regards human activity as under the command of justice : and therefore it is circumscribed by Morals, as right is limited by duty, and duty determined by law." [1]

And elsewhere he says :—

"Economy, both as a science and as an art, is subordinate to the science of Ethics, and therefore receives from it the highest principles, and by it is circumscribed.

---

[1] *Dell' Economia Pubblica.* Libro secondo.

Hence anything whatsoever, by which wealth can be procured in opposition to justice is, as such, forbidden beforehand." [1]

Very good. But the worthy writer did not perceive that by this he contradicted himself, having previously laid down that Political Economy is a purely speculative science. It cannot be constituted in that intimate dependence on Moral Science and subordination to it which he admits, unless it be recognized as a truly practical science.

Moral Science, by the very fact that it regards the good of mankind as such, regards the end of man, as man. Now the end of man, as man, is implied in all the particular ends of man. Man cannot prescind from it in any good whatsoever that he proposes to obtain. To prescind from that, he must prescind from being a man and act like a beast.

From this follows a most important conclusion; which is, that if an economic prescription is not conformable with morals, it does not belong to economic science as a science proper to man, nor even deserve to be remembered, except for reprobation.

Political Economy is not the science of multiplying wealth anyhow. Were it so, fraud, robbery, and the pillage of the conquered would have to be included among its means. But no Political Economist would venture to recommend that; and if any one should happen to do so, alleging that Political Economy of itself prescinds from Morals, his conclusion would certainly not be accepted. What does this show? It shows that the pretended abstraction is impossible, that the one science is intrinsically dependent on the other, and that in economic teaching nothing should be admitted but what is in conformity with justice and morality. Thus, for instance, to

---

[1] Ibid. Libro Terzo.

show that working on Sunday is not an economic maxim, we have no need to fall back on the utilitarian consideration, that a day's rest once a week is conducive to the production of wealth, inasmuch as the workmen return to their work refreshed. It is sufficient for us to remember that servile work on Sundays and days of obligation is contrary to the Christian Law, and therefore cannot be lawfully enforced by any science among baptized peoples.

VI.

A DEFINITION.

Having said thus much, I feel that I may now attempt a definition of Political Economy. I say "attempt," because I have not the presumption to suppose that I shall hit the mark and put an end to the disputes of Economists on this point. Their disagreement about it is earnestly deplored by Pellegrino Rossi.

"At the cost," he says, " of having to blush for science, we must confess that the first question still to be asked is this: What is Political Economy? What is its object? What is its extent? What are its limits? On the one hand it is difficult to select the more important problems of Political Economy for the purpose of making them the subject of our labours, unless we are agreed, to begin with, about the objects and extent of the science itself. On the other, it is but too true that such agreement is wanting among Economists. The definition of this science is always one of the questions the most controverted." [1]

---

[1] *Cours d'Economie Politique*, deuxième leçon.

If we are not deceived, this disagreement is mainly traceable to the imperfect state in which Political Economy still is, notwithstanding the ardour with which it has been cultivated for more than a century by very acute minds.

To give a right definition of Political Economy we must carefully look for its proper object, because every science is specified by its proper object, and the definition does nothing more than express the specific quiddity of the thing defined. To see whether any given object be the proper object of a science, we must take it as it is regarded by that science, viz., as being its formal object. The objects, materially considered, may belong to different sciences, each of which regards it from a different point of view. Thus the living body may be the object of physiology and of medicine; the former considering it for its vital functions, the other for the diseases which it has to keep off or cure.

Now it is indisputable that the object of Political Economy is wealth, or abundance of the good things that are necessary to the life of man. As such it was conceived by Aristotle, so far as he speaks of it in the first books of his Politics. As such it was regarded by Adam Smith, who raised it to the dignity of a science. As such it is treated even by those who would enlarge its province. In their books they are compelled to speak principally of wealth, and refer thereto the other doctrines which they bring in. Now evidently the object of a science must be that on which it mainly reasons, and to which it refers everything so far as it extends.

But here we must remark that Political Economy does not treat of wealth anyhow, but as a thing to be duly ordered in its production, in its distribution, in its consumption. Moreover, the due ordering of it should not be viewed with respect to individual families, considered in themselves; for then Economy would be domestic, not political. It should be viewed as concerning the whole civil body, so far as it is for the advantage of the whole nation, people and state, subjects and sovereign. Lastly, the said ordering should be inwardly informed with the principles of morality and justice, so that wealth may answer to the nature of man, for whom it is not an end but a means.

Given what we have pointed out, it seems to us that Political Economy may fitly be defined thus: THE SCIENCE OF PUBLIC WEALTH, WITH REGARD TO ITS RIGHTFUL ORDERING AS A MEANS OF COMMON WELL-BEING. Now the word "public" distinguishes it from private economy, which belongs to the private person or the family, while that which is called public regards the whole society, government and governed. The word "wealth" points to the material object of the science—that is to say, abundance of external goods. The word "ordering" shows its formal object, viz., in what respect wealth should be considered. Lastly, the epithet "rightful" expresses its intrinsic dependence on Morals; and the words, "as a means of common well-being," express its subordination to Politics, or, as it may be called, public right.

Minghetti's definition differs little from mine. He says:—

"If we wish to include in the definition the greatest number of concepts, we may say that Economy, as a science, contemplates the laws through which wealth is produced, is distributed, is exchanged and is consumed by man freely acting in civil society, by the rule of justice and right." [1]

But whether this definition be preferred, or mine, or another like them, it is necessary to remember that we shall never clear the conception of Political Economy by defining it to be the science of wealth, as is

---

[1] *Dell' Economia Pubblica* &c., Libro secondo.

generally done   Such a definition errs gravely by per-
suading people that wealth is for mankind an end, not a
means, and by representing the treatment of it as an
autonomous science, not subordinate to a higher one.

VII.

THIS TREATISE WILL BE DIVIDED INTO THREE PARTS.

With regard to the division of our treatise we have
only to say that it must be divided under three heads,
viz. the production, distribution and consumption of
wealth ; because every possible question about wealth is
clearly reducible to these three queries :—How is it produced ? How ought it to be divided among the producers ?
What is its reasonable consumption ?

This division, as being most natural, is accepted by
nearly all the Economists. Pellegrino Rossi alone curtails
it, admitting the two first parts, but rejecting the third as
superfluous.

"In former years," he says, "I tried to lay before
you the science as a whole. We have studied it in
its great divisions, the production and distribution of
wealth, and if we have not occupied ourselves with the
third branch of it, pointed out in books under the name
of consumption, the reason is, that in our opinion it enters
into the other two.   What is called productive consumption is nothing else than the employment of capital ; and
that consumption which people have agreed to call unproductive, viz. imposts, enters directly into the distribution
of wealth.   The rest belongs to hygiene and Morals." [1]

---

[1]   *Cours d'Economie Politique.*   Première leçon.

The only truth in this passage is where he says that productive consumption is nothing else than employment of capital : but that only proves that the Economists are wrong, when in speaking of consumption they put it as a species of a genus. All the rest of the passage strikes us as inexact. That consumption, to which the Economists (wrongly, as we shall see later on) apply the epithet "unproductive," is not comprised in imposts only ; nor can imposts rightly be said to enter into the distribution of wealth. That which is different from imposts, and consists in the use of riches for the satisfaction of human wants, is certainly connected with hygiene and Morals ; but the fact of being connected with the object of one science does not prevent its belonging to another. If so, the human body could not be the object of medicine, seeing that it also belongs to physics. It is sufficient that the relation differs. Anyone who remembers that the consumption of wealth is the end of its production and distribution, will see that the consumption thereof must belong to Political Economy. No science, and least of all one of the practical sciences, can omit the consideration of the end to which all the other matters of which it treats are ordered.

Others, like Minghetti and Leroy-Beaulieu, divide Political Economy into four parts. To the three above named, viz., production, distribution and consumption, they add circulation, as the fourth. But if Rossi erred by defect, these do so by excess. Let us then keep to the mean—the threefold division, which has also the merit of being the most common. As to circulation which in fact is nothing more than exchange, we can deal with that when we treat of production.

PART I.—PRODUCTION.

1. Producing, in the philosophical sense of the word, means giving existence to a thing. Thus we say that the vine produces grapes, because it brings the grapes into being by generating them. In Political Economy, which considers wealth, the word " producing " means giving existence to wealth, or to an element of wealth. The act of producing is called *Production*. That which exercises the act is called the *Producer*. This effect resulting from it is called the *Product*.

From this it appears that in Economy, if we desire to know what production is, we must clearly understand the meaning of wealth.

CHAPTER I.

WEALTH.

WEALTH is the object of Political Economy. Therefore it seems that the Economists ought to be clear and unanimous about it. And yet it is not so. " What is value?" writes Pellegrino Rossi. " What is wealth? If common sense answers these questions easily, books answer you in so many different ways, that the spirit of criticism has had some reason for affirming that they give you no answer at all." [1] We shall endeavour to determine, as

---

[1] " Qu 'est-ce que la valeur? Qu 'est-ce que la richesse? Si le bon sens répond facilement à ces questions, les livres y répondent de tant de manières diverses, que l'esprit de critique a eu quelque raison d'affirmer qu'ils n'y répondent pas du tout." *Cours d'Economie Politique.* Quatrième leçon.

well as we can, what the concept is, declaring however
that we shall, now as always, prefer common sense to
the lucubrations of economists, whatever their authority
may be. Let us begin with the meaning of the word
" wealth."

ARTICLE I.
WHAT WE MUST UNDERSTAND BY THE WORD " WEALTH."

3. " To those readers," says Boccardo, " into whose
hands no book on Political Economy has happened to fall
before they read ours, we shall say first of all that scientifically the word " wealth" has not the meaning attributed
to it in ordinary parlance, which limits it to mean a considerable quantity of products, excluding the smaller
portions of enjoyable things. In the usual way of speaking,
he only is said to be rich who is not poor : and the meaning of the word "wealth" is purely comparative. In Political
Economy a sheet of paper worth a centime is wealth as
much as the mines of Peru or the fertile plains of
Lombardy." [1]

To say the truth, some people might be tempted to
complain of Political Economy for imposing on them, at
the outset, a species of paradox—ruling that a piece of
bread given to a starving man should be called wealth.
Fancy yourself saying to a beggar, when you give him a
penny, " Look here ! You are vulgarly said to be poor ;
but scientifically you are rich. For he who possesses

---

[1] *Trattato teorico pratico di Economia Politica*, vol. 1. Nota
sulla definizione della ricchezza.

wealth is rich : and this penny is wealth." It might be difficult, I think, to persuade the poor fellow of that.

But seriously, let us see on what arguments the Economists base this theory. Boccardo gives us no argument at all : but Say does.

" In the ordinary use of the word," he says, "wealth suggests the idea of possessions in great abundance. They who have but little are not called rich. This manner of expressing oneself is not sufficiently precise for us. The idea of more or less abundance is not necessarily required in the idea of wealth. Its being much or little is a circumstance which has nothing to do with the nature of wealth. The smallest quantity of that which we have designated by this name will for us be wealth, as much as if it were a great quantity, just as a grain of corn is grain, as much as a bushel of it is." [1]

4. That the nature of wealth prescinds from the more and less of abundance, we grant. *Plus et minus non mutat speciem.* But that it prescinds therefrom totally, so that, because a small grain of corn is called grain, we may apply the word "wealth" to the smallest object— the pen, for instance, with which we write—this, if we are not strangely mistaken, the distinguished Economist fails to show. Otherwise we, by the same reasoning, might maintain that one soldier might be called an army. We might argue thus : " The word ' army,' as commonly understood, suggests the idea of a great many soldiers : but this is not exact. The idea of a greater or less multitude is not necessarily included in the idea of an army ; and therefore a few soldiers, or even one, may be said to be an army, just as a small grain of corn is called grain." Say's mistake is this :—he uses the *collective* word in the sense of the *distributive.* " Grain " is a distributive word, and therefore, as it may be attributed to

---

[1] *Cours Complet* &c. Première partie, Ch. i.

many or to all, so may it be attributed to each individual of a given species taken separately. But "wealth" is a collective word, like "army," or "people": and therefore, as we cannot call one person or a few persons a people, nor one or a few soldiers an army, so we cannot give the name of wealth to one or a few of those things that satisfy our wants.

5. They would tell us in reply, that Political Economists precisely intended to change the meaning of the word "wealth," from collective to distributive, for their own convenience. But surely science has no right to do what it pleases with nomenclature, simply for its own convenience. It may indeed fashion new words, for the purpose of expressing new conceptions unknown to the general public:—or it may elucidate the meaning of words in common use, making them express more distinctly that which was not clear in them before. But to use them in a sense quite different from their generally accepted meaning, is, we maintain, more than it is justified in doing, especially when that new meaning presents a paradox. In the matter of language, the people (*quem penes arbitrium est et jus et norma loquendi*) should be respected even by science; and especially when its teachings have to serve in practice for the whole people, as they do in Political Economy. In such a matter convenience is not a sufficient warrant for change. There must be an absolute necessity. But that necessity is not discoverable in this case; for there is no apparent reason why singular things that are useful may not, instead of being styled *wealth*, be called *elements* of wealth — portions of wealth—constitutive or integral portions of wealth,—or simply goods, objects, products.

6. Therefore, cutting ourselves loose from the Economists in this respect, and keeping to the common parlance, let us define wealth to be A PLENTIFULNESS OF GOODS, IN EXCESS OF PURE NEED. By "good" we mean that

which answers to our desire. *Ratio boni in hoc consistit, quod aliquid sit appetibile.*[1] This plentifulness, however, may vary, according to the variation of desire through the variation of wants: and the wants of mankind vary. They are not the same in a highly civilized state and in a state of infant civilisation: nor are they the same in a literary man or in a statesman as in the artizan.

Our definition of wealth (viz. a plentifulness of goods, in excess of pure need) is like Cicero's, where he asks what is it to be rich, and answers that he is a rich man who has enough to live on with some ease. "Quem intelligimus divitem? aut hoc verbum in quo homine ponimus? Opinor in eo, cui tanta possessio est, ut ad liberaliter vivendum facile contentus sit." Wealth begins where the pure necessity ends and easy circumstances begin. He who has the necessaries of life is neither poor nor rich, but midway. "Mendicitatem et divitias ne dederis mihi, sed tribue tantum victui meo necessaria."[2]

But after all, if anyone, having made up his mind, will persist in applying the word "wealth" to every little thing possibly useful, whether it be a sheet of paper or a strip of linen rag, that somehow may serve his purpose —well! we might happen to laugh just a little, but we should not quarrel with him about it.

---

[1] *Summa*, p. 1. Q. v. a. 1
[2] *Proverbs* xxx. 8.

ARTICLE II.

IN THOSE THINGS THAT CONSTITUTE WEALTH, UTILITY MUST BE CONSIDERED.

7. Of those things that constitute wealth we may say that there are two primordial conceptions: the conception of utility and the conception of value. These are so connected with the idea of wealth that Economists take sometimes one and sometimes the other in explanation of it. Let us briefly speak of each, and first of utility.

That which is fitted to the attainment of an end is called useful. *Ea quæ sunt ad finem accomoda, utilia dicuntur.*[1] Hence utility may be defined as THE APTITUDE OF A THING FOR THE ATTAINMENT OF AN END. It is proper to means only, because only means are *used.* The end, strictly speaking, is not used, but enjoyed. A thing is loved for its own sake. *Frui est amore inhærere alicui rei, propter seipsam.*[2] Thus you would say that medicine is useful, because it is adapted for curing you if you are ill; but you would not say that your being cured is useful, unless you were considering it with reference to some higher end—science, for instance—which it serves as a means to an end. In those things, therefore, that constitute wealth, utility is apparent, insomuch as they are fitted for the end of satisfying our wants and giving us the conveniences and pleasures of life.

8. It would be difficult to point out any object, of which we cannot say that it has, or may have, some usefulness, at least by means of industry. There is nothing lower in nature than dung: and yet it serves to fertilize the soil. Stones, too, serve us in the building of houses, and the bones of animals for making many sorts of utensils.

---

[1] *Summa*, 1ª 2ᵃᵉ Q. xvi. a 3.
[2] St. Augustine. *De Doctrina Christiana*, lib. 6. c. 4.

But here we have to distinguish. For some useful things are offered to us by nature alone, and profusely, so that they are within everyone's reach—for instance, air, light, and water, where it is abundant—while others, such as tillable ground, animals, mines, &c., though offered by nature, are limited, and, therefore, being limited are exhaustible. The former (except in a few cases) may be designated by the name of goods not appropriable, but of universal use. The latter we may call goods appropriable and of particular use. The products of art and of human industry are of this kind *a fortiori*. These appropriable goods are the goods that properly deserve the denomination of wealth, because in the conception of wealth property is implied. They may be divided into natural wealth and artificial wealth, according to whether they are offered by nature only, like the earth and the animals and the mines, or come from the works of man, like houses, clothes, machines, &c.

9. Say makes another division, and so far is followed by many Economists:

"This wealth," he says, "is of two sorts; and we must distinguish them minutely. The one sort is given to us by nature gratuitously and in profusion, such as the air that we breathe, the light of the sun, the water that quenches our thirst, and a multitude of other things, the use of which has become so familiar, that we often enjoy them without even thinking about it. These may be called *natural wealth*. They belong to all mankind, to the poor as well as to the rich, and are called wealth in a general and philosophic sense. . . . The other goods are the practical result of a concourse of means, which are not gratuitous. We are compelled to buy the last (so to speak) with labour, thrift, privations—in a word with true sacrifices. Of these are the food that cannot be procured without culture, the clothes that cannot be had unless they be furnished by some one, the houses that do not exist until they are built. . . . We cannot separate from these goods the idea of property. . . . . From another point of view property presupposes a society of some sort, and agreements and laws. Consequently wealth so acquired may be called *social wealth.*" [1]

10. Neither the division nor the nomenclature pleases us. In the first place we cannot approve of his giving the name of *wealth* to the common and non-appropriable gifts of nature. Fancy anyone saying, " I am a rich man, because I enjoy plenty of fresh air and light and water." Nor can we get out of the difficulty by saying that this use of the word is restricted to philosophy. The philosophic meaning of a word should never be contrary to common sense : and the light by which we see, the air that we breathe, the water that we drink are not reckoned as wealth by common sense. Secondly, to class together under the term *"social* wealth " all the goods that are capable of appropriation, contains two faults, as it seems to us. It supposes, and in fact Say does suppose, that property proceeds from the social state. It confuses the products of nature (as for instance the fruits of the earth) with the products of art, such as a building : which, as we shall see further on, ought not to be done.

It seems more correct, therefore, to divide useful things into goods not appropriable, because unlimited, and goods appropriable, because limited ; and, applying the term " wealth " to the latter only when more or less plentiful, to subdivide them into natural wealth and artificial wealth.

---

[1] *Cours Complet,* &c. Première partie, Chap. 1.

ARTICLE III.

IN THOSE THINGS THAT CONSTITUTE WEALTH VALUE HAS TO BE CONSIDERED.

11. From the conception of utility, in those things that constitute wealth, arises ·the conception of value, in virtue of exchange : for if a thing is useful to me, it may also be useful to someone else, who would be willing to acquire it by giving me some other thing, which being useful to me I am willing to purchase. This aptitude of a useful thing, to be exchanged for another is called *value*. By giving, for instance, a certain quantity of grain, I can receive a certain quantity of sugar, or of oil, or of some other merchandise; and the aptitude of my grain for such exchange is its value. Hence the idea of value is evidently more general than the idea of *price*, inasmuch as the price of a thing is considered with respect to its being exchanged for money, while the value is considered with a view to its exchange for merchandise. The price is nothing but the value expressed in money : but since money is the equivalent of all values, what is said of value applies to price also, and the one term is used for the other. We shall have more to say afterwards about money. At present we keep to the generic concept of value.

12. Value is evidently nothing more than a relation, the relation of a thing as to its being exchangeable for other things. Hence it follows that value is mutable, because the terms between which it passes as a relation are mutable. If, for instance, you can get eight sacks of flour or a cask of wine for a sack of sugar, the eight sacks of flour and the cask of wine determine the value of the sackful of sugar, and the sackful of sugar determines the value of the eight sacks of flour and the cask of wine. But if, through one of those variations that are wont to occur in the market, you cannot get more than four sacks

of flour or half a cask of wine for your sackful of sugar, the respective value of these wares is changed. The value of the flour or the wine is doubled with respect to the sugar, and the value of the sugar with respect to the flour or the wine is halved. Say justly remarks :—

"La Valeur d'une chose est une quantité positive ; mais elle n'est que pour un instant donnée. Sa nature est d'être perpetuellement variable, de changer d'un lieu à l'autre, d'un temps à l'autre. Rien ne peut la fixer invariablement, parcequ'elle est fondée ainsi que vous le verrez plus tard, sur des besoins et des moyens de production, qui varient à chaque minute."[1]

13. Hence the value of things never can have a certain and determinate value : and the reason of this, as St. Thomas observes, is that the measure and the measured must be homogeneous, i.e. of the same genus. Thus a line is measured by a line, and time by time. Therefore the measure of values must be a value : and since every value is essentially mutable,[2] it follows that the measure is mutable. Nor can it be said that we might settle this measure by money : for though money may, as we shall see further on, be called in a relative sense the measure of the value of merchandise, it cannot be called so in an absolute sense. The reason is that money being, as we shall see, an article of merchandise, owing to the material on which it is based, has itself a mutable value, though its changes are not so rapid. A hundred crowns, for instance, have not the same value in England as in Italy, nor have they the same value in Italy now as they had thirty years

---

[1] Cours Complet, &c. Première partie, chap. 2.

[2] "An invariable measure of values," Say remarks, "is a pure chimera, because the value of a thing can only be measured by means of values, i.e. by an essentially mutable quantity." Note to Section 1 of the first chapter on David Ricardo's work.

ago. This is equally true when things are measured by their utility ; for utility, though an indisputable condition of value, because a totally useless thing is not exchangeable, cannot be its measure. If it could, the value of bread would be greater than the value of jewels, by reason of being more useful. Moreover utility is different from value. Utility is the relation of a thing to our wants ; value is the relation of the thing to other things for which it may be exchanged. Now different things, as we have already observed, cannot have a mutual measure.

14. This difference between utility and value, not only as a concept, but also in the words by which the two are expressed, is of the utmost importance in Political Economy. And yet it seems that the Economists have not, all of them and always, been zealous in guarding the distinction. Adam Smith taught it as a concept, but forgot it in practice, giving the appellation of Value to utility by speaking of the *Value in Use,* in contradistinction to the Value in Exchange. He says :—

"The word VALUE, it is to be observed, has two different meanings, and sometimes expresses the utility of some particular object, and sometimes the power of purchasing other goods which the possession of that object conveys. The one may be called ' Value in use ' ; the other ' Value in exchange.' The things which have the greatest value in use have frequently little or no value in exchange ; and, on the contrary, those which have the greatest value in exchange have frequently little or no value in use. Nothing is more useful than water ; but it will purchase scarce anything ; scarce anything can be had in exchange for it. A diamond, on the contrary, has scarcely any value in use ; but a very great quantity of other goods may frequently be had in exchange for it."[1]

---

[1] *An Enquiry into the Nature and Causes of the Wealth of Nations.* Book 1, chap. iv., p. 12.

But Say, in a letter to Ricardo, rightly disapproves of this phrase, ' the Value in use,' which indeed means no more than utility pure and simple. "Je ne saurai admettre," he says, " ce que vous appelez avec Adam Smith ' Value in use.' Q'est-ce que la valeur en utilité, si ce n'est de l'utilité pure et simple ? Le mot utilité suffit donc." [1]

15. Pellegrino Rossi, who, in the words quoted further back, had criticized other writers for their want of exactness about this, fell into the same mistake of confusing value with utility : for he says :—" La valeur, encore une fois, est l'expression du rapport qui existe entre les besoins de l'homme et des choses." [2] But this relation between our wants and the things that supply them is *utility*, not value. It is surprising that so clear-sighted a man should fall into such a mistake.

One more quotation about this. Frederic Bastiat acknowledges the importance of the distinction between utility and value in these words : " Habituons nous à distinguer l'utilité de la valeur. Il n'y a de science économique qu'à ce prix. " [3] But, distinguishing two species of utility—the one gratuitous, and found in the work of nature only, the other onerous, and proceeding from the labour of man—he attributes permutability, and therefore value to the latter alone. He says :—

" En tout ce qui est propre à satisfaire nos besoins et nos désirs il y a à considérer deux choses : ce qu 'a fait la nature et ce que fait l'homme ; ce qui est *gratuit* et ce qui est *onéreux*, le don de Dieu et le service humain ; l'utilité et la valeur." [4]

Hence he lays down the formula, that " La valeur est le rapport de deux services échangés." We shall

[1] *Œuvres diverses de J-B. Say.*   Edition Guillaumin, p. 410.
[2] *Cours d'Economie Politique.*   Tome 1.   Quatrième leçon.
[3] *Harmonies Economiques : De la Valeur.*
[4] *Harmonies Economiques : Chap. vi.*

show, when we come to it, how this theory, invented by the subtle Economist to refute Proudhon, does in fact favour him. Moreover, instead of making clear, it darkens; for by attributing value to human efforts only, it often makes the valuing inexplicable. But we shall have to speak of this theory in another chapter.

Article IV.

The cause of wealth is properly attributable to the utility of things, not to their value.

16. Say, followed by the majority of the Economists, opined that wealth consists in the value of things, and is proportionate thereto. He said: " La richesse est en proportion de la valeur. Elle est grande si la somme des valeurs, dont elle se compose, est considérable ; elle est petite, si les valeurs le sont." Ricardo, on the contrary, maintained against him, that wealth lies in the utility of things, and follows their proportion. It seems that Adam Smith held the same opinion ; for he says that a man is poor or rich according to the degree in which he can procure for himself the enjoyment of useful things. We adhere to this latter opinion, which accords with the generally accepted definition of wealth. For, indeed, what is wealth? It is that which serves to satisfy plentifully the wants of man. Now the aptitude to satisfy the wants of man constitutes utility, not value. Therefore wealth lies in the utility of things, not in their value. Only so far as it is a means and instrument in procuring for us useful things—as money does, cheques and bank notes, that represent money—can value be called wealth.

We know the mythical story of Midas, King of Phrygia,

who obtained from Bacchus in return for taking care of Silenus, when drunk, the gift of turning into gold whatever he should touch, and thus gained an unlimited command of that most valuable thing by which all other marketable things of value can be procured. Nevertheless he was practically as poor as possible, having no means of obtaining food : so that he would have died of starvation, if he had not given up his privilege. A rich man dying of hunger is in an absurd position, as Aristotle justly observes.[1]

17. Bastiat in the sixth chapter of his *Harmonies Economiques* refutes at some length Say's teaching about this proposition, and demonstrates the grave absurdities that arise from confusing wealth with value. Here is one passage : " La théorie, qui définit la richesse par la valeur, n'est en définitive que la glorification de l'Obstacle. Voici son syllogisme : La richesse est proportionelle aux valeurs, les valeurs aux efforts, les efforts aux obstacles ; donc les richesses sont proportionelles aux obstacles." [2] According to that theory, then, the way to promote wealth is to promote obstacles, as, for instance, heavy taxes, vetoes on exportation, privileges, monopolies.

If Bastiat's demonstrations about this had not rested on his favourite theory, that in exchange utility is always gratuitous, and that only efforts and services are recompensed, this would be unanswerable : but that defect weakens the force of his reasoning. Happily we do not defend it on the reasons that he gives. As we said before, it is sufficient for us to consider what it is that wealth has to do. It obtains for us the conveniences and comforts of life : and things do that by their utility, not by their value. By their value they can only do it mediately, by exchanging thing for thing, and so procuring, with the

---

[1] *Politicorum*, lib. 1, cap. 3.

[2] *Harmonies Économiques*, Chap. vi.

new acquisition, other useful things answering to our wants and desires. If diamonds could not be exchanged for the necessaries of life, a casketful of them would not save one from having to beg.

18. Another false consequence of making wealth consist in value is this :—it would make us consider value to be the sole object of Political Economy. Rossi refutes this at considerable length :

" There are many writers," he says, " for whom there is but one economic fact, the value in exchange. Value in use is by them regarded as a pure generality, to which we can accord nothing more than the honour of being mentioned at first and by the way, and then set aside. Political Economy is to them the science of exchanges, rather than the science of wealth. We cannot help saying that this is an error which attacks the foundations of the science, mutilates it, changes its nature." [1]

And he shows that by it a great number of facts in Political Economy are made inexplicable. For instance, when any one thinks of sending merchandise into this or that country, does he not regulate the price of it by its utility and by the consequent demand that may be expected? " Why," he says, " are certain markets encumbered with wares that no one will buy? Simply because the producers had not sufficiently considered their value in use." Like Adam Smith, he calls the utility of things *value* in use : but he insists on the fact that utility enters into the calculations of Political Economy. It does indeed, and still more when we are dealing with the distribution and consumption of wealth.

19. Thinking, as we do, that utility, not value, constitutes wealth, Rossi says:—

" Wealth and value are not at all the same thing; for, however small the value of a man's possessions

---

[1] *Cours d'Économie Politique*, Quatrième leçon.

are, he may be extremely rich. Thus he may have
great wealth and little that is of value. To this
Economist [we suppose him to mean Say] these
words are not even correlative. And yet, after saying
elsewhere that wealth is only a commutable value, he
goes on to say: 'Though wealth is a commutable value, the
general wealth is increased by cheapness of merchandise
and of all species of products.' If this proposition is true,
it will bear all its consequences. If the general wealth is
increased by low prices, no price at all would evidently
make it (so to speak) infinite. But if the general wealth
were infinite, there would be no more exchange. Exchange
would become impossible, because every one would have
all that he can desire. How then can wealth be a per-
mutable value, when, if it were infinite, there would be no
more value of exchange?"[1]

This hypothesis is, in fact, impossible, because the
price of things (those, at least, that depend on the labour
of man) can never come down to nothing. We must
remember, however, that in conditional proportions we
have not to consider the truth or possibility of the
condition, but only its connection with what is conditionally supposed. Now there is this connection here.

Minghetti says in reply that, according to this, there
would be no economic science.[2] But why? Because
there would be no more *value*, and therefore no more
wealth, which is the object of that science. Our answer is
that this is the fallacy of *petitio principii.* He supposes
that wealth consists in value : which is precisely what is
denied, and what he fails to prove.

---

[1] Ibid.
[2] *Dell 'Economia Pubblica*, Lib. secondo.

ARTICLE V.

MATERIALITY IS THE ESSENTIAL CHARACTERISTIC OF WEALTH, THE OBJECT OF POLITICAL ECONOMY.

20.   Absolutely speaking, the name of wealth is understood to mean material goods only. If you hear that a man is rich, you think of him as possessing plenty of money, or plenty of such things as are useful for the life of the body and obtainable by means of money. In this sense we say that Political Economy regards wealth.

But then, by the addition of some other word that carries it somewhat beyond its ordinary meaning, the term " wealth" is extended by custom to immaterial goods. Thus we say that a learned man is rich in knowledge, or an honest man rich in virtue.

This extensibility of the word has induced nearly all the French Economists to include immaterial goods within the domain of Economic Science ; and, as usual, they have been imitated by the Italian Economists. The English alone have, with rare exceptions, kept within the limits marked out by Adam Smith, who, unless our memory deceives us, gives no hint anywhere of this undue extension.

21.   Say, who in our opinion may be said to be the head of the French economic school, writes thus about it :—

" Hitherto the object of Political Economy seems to have been restricted to a knowledge of those laws that preside over the formation, distribution and consumption of wealth : and so did I consider it in my treatise of Political Economy, first published in 1803. Nevertheless, it is evident in that very work that this science links itself to everything in society. Since it had been shown that immaterial properties, such as ability and personal faculties acquired, form an integral part of social wealth, and that the services rendered by those discharging the highest functions have their analogy in the most humble labours, and when the relations of the individual to the social body, and of the social body to the individual, and their reciprocal interests, had been clearly established, it was found [by whom?] that Political Economy, which appeared to have no other objects than material goods, embraces the entire social system." [1]

This is too much for Political Economy to do.

We have the same teaching on this point from Stuart Mill, one of the few Englishmen who therein differs from the opinion of nearly the whole school. Enumerating the different species of labour, he says:

"The utilities produced by labour are of three kinds. They are, first, utilities fixed and embodied in outward objects; by labour employed in investing external material things with properties which render them serviceable to human beings. This is the common case, and requires no illustration. Secondly, utilities fixed and embodied in human beings; the labour being in this case employed in conferring on human beings, qualities which render them serviceable to themselves and others. To this class belongs the labour of all concerned in education; not only school-masters, tutors, and professors, but governments, so far as they aim successfully at the improvement of the people; moralists, and clergymen, as far as productive of benefit; the labour of physicians, as far as instrumental in preserving life and physical or mental efficiency; of the teachers of bodily exercises, and of the various trades, sciences, and arts, together with the labour of the learners in acquiring them; and all labour bestowed by any persons, throughout life, in improving the knowledge or cultivating the bodily or mental faculties of themselves or others." [2]

All these, then, are to be put on a level with artizans and tradesmen.

---

[1] *Cours complet*, &c., Considérations générales.
[2] *Principles of Political Economy*, Bk. 1, Chap. 3.

22. We abhor this confusion. We hold that it utterly materializes man and his highest faculties, and making them an object of bargain, classes physical and moral wants together. Some sort of analogy between two objects of different kinds is not enough to show that they belong to one science. There must be either a perfect likeness, or at least an analogy sufficient for bringing them under a common idea and governing them by a common law. Now under what idea can we class together the material order and the immaterial order ? Under that of relation to the wants of man ? But this relation, though nominally one, is really two-fold, and two-fold with an immense difference: for relations vary according to their terms, and the terms, matter and spirit, differ immeasurably. Indeed the discrepancy is such, that often by denying the one we express what is constituent of the other's perfection. *O ignota richezza, O ben verace !* says Dante,[1] referring to the total absence of material wealth in St. Francis, the Poor Man of Assisi. Then, as regards the laws, the reciprocal exchange of material goods is founded on equivalence: but is it so with respect to immaterial goods ? Solomon, speaking of wisdom, tells us that " *Omne aurum in comparatione illius arena est exigua, et tamquam lutum æstimabitur argentum in conspectu illius.*[2]" " All gold, in comparison of her, is as a little sand, and silver in respect to her shall be counted as clay."[3]

Material goods can be valued in money : but can money represent the value of morality or of science ? Say does not hesitate to affirm that it can. " Un médecin," he says, "nous vend l'utilité de son art, sans qu'elle ait été incorporée dans aucune matière. ... Nous l'achetons en achetant son conseil." And he says below in a note : " La science et le talent d'un médecin, d'un chirurgien, d'un professeur,

---

[1] *Paradiso.* Canto xi.
[2] *Wisdom.* vii. 9.
[3] *Douai Translation.*

ne sont ils des capitaux acquis ?"[1] According to these we had better try to ascertain how much the genius of Dante was worth, or the virtue of St. Francis of Assisi. If the doctor may be said to sell the advice that he gives to his patients, the professor may be said to sell the ideas that he puts into his pupils ; and the tutor may be said to sell the morality which he tries to inculcate in those who are under his charge ; and the magistrate may be said to sell his decisions ; and the Priest may be said to sell the sacraments which he administers to the faithful. This theory of buying and selling everything is too horrible.

These men (the doctors, &c.) do indeed receive a recompense for the service rendered by them : but what does that prove ? Not every recompense is a price, any more than every contract is a purchase. Let us here quote a Frenchman against a Frenchman :—

" Several writers," says Droz, " mean by this word 'wealth' all useful and agreeable things that man can desire. According to their theory qualities of the mind, benevolence, generosity, heroism, are wealth. It seems to me that a system which tends to confuse intellectual and moral *bona* with material objects, tends to degrade the former rather than to ennoble the latter. We can indeed say intelligibly that virtue is the most desirable wealth, because those words would be understood in a metaphorical sense : but in the proper sense they would be absurd. The wise men who reveal to us the means of happiness, make us find moral enjoyment in a higher order than that of physical pleasures : but, if we bring confusion into language by even apparently likening virtue to wealth, we impair the effect of their noble teaching. But should we not be enlarging the domain of Political Economy, and giving more splendour thereto ? The answer is, that Political Economy

---

Cours Complet, &c., tome 1, Première partie : De la production générale, Ch. v.

has no need of extending its boundaries. Its importance is sufficiently shown in the fact that wealth, which it teaches us how to diffuse, prevents or remedies sufferings, takes away the vices that are engendered by misery, and is a useful auxiliary to those most precious possessions, with which we ought to be ashamed of comparing it."[1]

23. Boccardo makes one feel quite sorry for him, when in his Dictionary, at the word "Wealth," he says: "Truly we are unable to understand why we should give the name of wealth to a steam-engine, and not to the science of Watt, who created it." According to this theory, even Almighty God is reducible to *wealth*, and therefore is a subject of Political Economy. We have only to say: "Truly we are unable to understand why we should give the name of wealth to the fruits of the earth, to animals and metals, but not to God, Who caused all these things to be, and gave them such beneficent qualities!"

The transcendental idea of wealth is not inapplicable to the science of Watt, nor even to God, Who, in a figurative sense, may be called the Supreme and Infinite Wealth, because He is the Supreme and Infinite Good. What is inapplicable to both, is the idea of wealth in its proper sense, as forming the object of Political Economy. We might say with regard to this, *Sutor, ne ultra crepidam.* Economic wealth is only matter with the qualities that are fixed and incorporated in matter.

24. And now, to sum up in a few words, we say this:

By the name of wealth we must understand a sum-total of goods, capable of satisfying the wants of man more than is purely necessary; for there is no reason why Political Economy should in this depart from the usual way of speaking.

It may refer either to individuals, or to a whole country,

---

whose wealth in fact results from the wealth of the individuals in it.

Wealth, strictly speaking, embraces appropriable things
only, not those that, owing to their inexhaustible profusion, are not the object of property.

In appropriable things we have to consider the utility
and the value, i.e. the relation of the object to the satisfaction of man, and the relation of the object to another
object with a view to exchange.

The *ratio* of wealth essentially consists in the utility of
things, not in their value. Wealth, understood as an appur-
tenance of Political Economy, is restricted to material
goods only. Immaterial goods, being incapable of exchange
and money-valuation, are outside its province.

CHAPTER II.

THE PRODUCERS OF WEALTH.

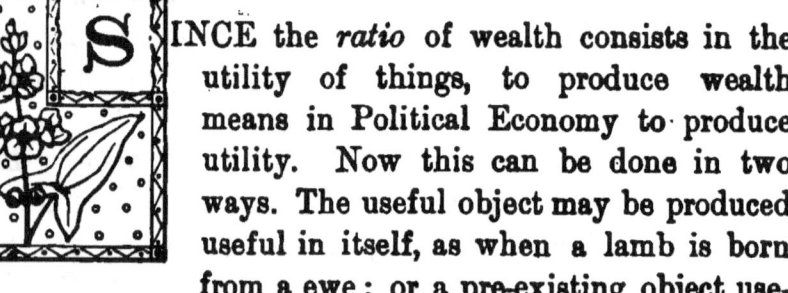

SINCE the *ratio* of wealth consists in the
utility of things, to produce wealth
means in Political Economy to produce
utility. Now this can be done in two
ways. The useful object may be produced
useful in itself, as when a lamb is born
from a ewe : or a pre-existing object use-
less in itself may be transformed either to make it useful,
or, if already useful, to give it some new sort of utility, as
when cloth is made of wool already spun, or sand made
into glass. Here we have to enquire what are the agents
with respect to such productions, or, in other words,
what the producers of wealth are.

ARTICLE I.

THERE ARE TWO PRODUCERS OF WEALTH, NATURE AND THE LABOUR OF MAN.

26. Some Economists apparently attribute the production of wealth to labour only. " Man, from the time of his birth," says Sismondi, " has wants to satisfy necessary for the support of life, desires that make him look for happiness in certain enjoyments, and industry or aptitude for work, which enables him to satisfy both. This industry is the source of his wealth."[1] Other authors say the same, and, indeed, still more explicitly. All these are wrong, at least in the manner of expressing themselves. Of what use would a man's aptitude for work be to him, without a subject to exercise it upon, or without the forces of material causes which he applies to his work ? But neither the one nor the other are created by him. They are presupposed as given to him by the Supreme Maker, and are usually expressed by the word " nature." Therefore work alone is not the producer of wealth, but nature and work, physical agents and human activity, the gift of God and the co-operation of man.

God created the earth, storing within it an immense abundance of minerals, and adorning the surface with useful herbs and fruitful trees. He peopled the air with birds, the sea with fishes, the earth with terrestrial animals. And then He created Man in His own image and likeness ; gave to him, as a patrimony, all this varied wealth. He willed, however, that it should not be idly enjoyed, but through the medium of work. He gave him power over all inferior animals' nature, but ordained that he should acquire actual dominion by intelligent industry. He allowed him to enjoy all that the earth contains or

---

[1] Sismondi. *Nouveaux Principes d'Économie Politique.* Liv. ii., Ch. i.

produces, but willed that he should subjugate it by his labour, and make its forces turn to his advantage, compelling it to disclose what had lain hidden and, as it were, in a state of potentiality within it :—

Creavit Deus hominem ad imaginem suam . . . . . masculum et feminam creavit eos. Benedixitque illis, et ait : Crescite, et multiplicamini, et replete terram, et subjicite eam, et dominamini piscibus maris et volatilibus cœli, et universis animantibus, quæ moventur super terram. [1]

27. In conformity with this divine decree, and stimulated by the wants that grew with time and civilisation, man displayed and developed his activity by degrees in an immense number of industries, works, arts and ingenious inventions. He broke up the soil, cultivated it, forced it to put forth its hidden treasures, made its productions better and more abundant. He collected the useful animals, trained them, perfected their breeds, associated them with his own labour, taught them to work in his stead. From raw material he formed objects of the greatest usefulness not merely for the preservation of life, but also for its comforts. He converted flax into linen, wool into cloth, iron into steel. He built houses, furnished them, multiplied instruments and machinery to work with. He compelled wind and water to serve him as motive powers in grinding corn, and steam to transport him from place to place. He let loose the forces of electricity, and trusting it to a metallic wire, made it transport his words to the remotest regions of the earth.

---

[1] *Genesis.* i. 27. 28.

ARTICLE II.

MUTUAL CO-OPERATION OF THE TWO PRODUCERS, NATURE AND THE WORK OF MAN.

28. The smallest consideration will suffice to show us that wealth arises from nothing else than the union of nature with work. This is verified even in those products that are the most independent of man's action: for, except those things that are diffused everywhere, as air and light, and which, not being an object of property, cannot, strictly speaking, be called wealth, there is not one that man can enjoy without some labour, at least in seeking and appropriating it. Fish and game, for instance, though supplied by nature, would be useless to mankind without fishing and shooting. *A fortiori* is this true of those natural products that require incessant care and labour to make them sufficiently plentiful. The same land that when highly cultivated suffices to feed a whole people, will hardly support a few individuals if left to go out of cultivation.

And this is equally true of industry with respect to nature. Without nature man could do nothing with his work—nothing at all. The farmer may break up the land, and plough and harrow and sow: but unless the germinative virtue in the seed, helped by the rain, by the sun's rays and by the fertility of the soil, ripened the ears, there would be no harvest. We admire the wonders of the steam engine invented by Watt: but without steam, which is a gift of nature, of what use would it be? The compass regulates navigation: but only because the needle points to the north.

29. The two agents, nature and the work of man, co-operate in turn; but their products are different. Nature produces substances. The industry of man produces modifications of substances, combinations of substances and configurations and different structures. For

instance, nature gives you the wheat, but industry forms the flour and then the bread. Nature gives you the iron and the hemp and the wood, which human industry works into a saw, or a rope, or a bedstead. And since the accidental form, the configuration, the structure, suppose the substance as subject and matter, it is rightly said that industry receives the matter of its work from nature. The matter, as supplied by nature, is called the raw material. Raw material means material not worked. The material worked by one industry may be the material of another industry. For instance, wool already spun is the material of cloth-weaving : and therefore with respect to the new work it might be called *materia secunda.* But the pure wool as it leaves the sheep-shearer's hands, the minerals as they are taken out of the mines, the cotton as it is when gathered in the cotton-fields—all these are primary materials.

Nature gives us, not only the material to work on, but also the force impressed on different substances by God. Industry avails itself of this force to obtain its diverse products. A builder builds a house : but without gravity, cohesion, impenetrability and the affinity of the different elements used in its construction, it would not stand. Iron is tempered into steel, but this is done by means of the fire, that makes it red-hot, and the coldness of the water into which it is plunged. Thus the potential and (so to speak) latent hardness and elasticity of the iron is actuated.

ARTICLE III.

NATURAL AND ARTIFICIAL WEALTH.

30. The foregoing pages have shown that wealth, as we pointed out roughly in the last chapter, is divisible into natural wealth, produced by nature, and artificial wealth, produced by art. The criterion for distinguishing

them is whether the utility of the object, or, in other words, its aptitude for satisfying our wants, is properly owing to the one or to the other of these two producers : and this criterion is usually clear in its application, but not always.

Anyone can see, for instance, that the minerals got out of the earth, the vegetables grown in it, the animals multiplied by generation, are works of nature, and therefore natural wealth ; and anyone can see that houses, carriages, ships, furniture, linen, woollen cloths, ornaments, instruments of all sorts, machinery &c., are works of art, and therefore artificial wealth. Nor can it be validly objected against this, that the utility of the former requires the industry of man, and that the utility of the latter is founded in nature, from which they receive the materials and the co-operative forces : because the truth is evident enough that the being through which the former are useful, is given by nature, and the form through which the latter are useful, is given by art. Nature gives us gold, and gold is useful as gold. A watch is useful as a watch, and, as such, is given us by art, because there are no watch mines.

Sometimes, as we said just now, the application of that criterion is uncertain, owing to a difficulty in discerning whether the utility proceeds from what nature gives, or from what is added by art. Wine, for instance, might seem to become wine in virtue of human industry ; for man it is that crushes the grapes, extracts the juice, makes it ferment, puts it into casks, and takes care of it. But evidently the strengthening virtue through which wine is useful, comes from nature ; and therefore it must be reckoned as natural wealth. Modern progress has, indeed, found ways of making apparent wine without grapes, but this is a work of pure roguery, and not wealth at all, natural or artificial.

31. Say, as we remarked in another place, calls both

kinds of wealth "social wealth."   But how can that which
belongs to individuals be called social?   We may give the
name of social wealth to anchorages, harbours, streets,
public walks, and whatever is enjoyed in common, and
also to what the State possesses as public property and
for public purposes : but to call private property social
wealth is an abuse of words, and therefore to be avoided.
When appropriable things—and they alone constitute
wealth—are possessed by a society, as such, they are social
wealth, or public, or common, if you like : but when they
are possessed by private persons, they ought to be called
private wealth, or individual, or personal, wealth.   To call
them social wealth is *miscere quadrata rotundis* with
much injury to science.   Moreover, the expression has an
unpleasant odour of Socialism, which longs to destroy
private property—at any rate, landed property—and place
it all in the hands of the State.   Let us, therefore, continue to divide wealth into natural wealth, produced by
nature, and artificial wealth, produced by art.

ARTICLE IV.

THREEFOLD DIVISION OF INDUSTRY.

32.   A little consideration will suffice to show that
industry has, broadly speaking, two tasks to accomplish.
The one is to extract the products of nature, as the miner
and the farmer do.   The other is to conform natural products in various ways so as to make them ready for our
use, as the weaver and mason do.   The former may be
called *extractive* industry, the latter *manufacturing.*
The former properly belongs to the country, the latter to
the town.

We may add a third, viz. the industry which, by
means of transport and purchase, brings to our doors

foreign merchandise that we could not personally seek. This is called *commercial* industry, or commerce.

It will clearly appear that this third member deserves to be included in the general division of industry, if we do but consider the enormous variety of human wishes that it embraces, the immeasurable extent of its developments. It now constitutes one of the principal sources of national prosperity. By exchange and transport it causes the wealth of all nations to become the wealth of each. Say speaks of it as follows :—

"Commercial industry co-operates in production as much as manufacturing industry does : raising the value [*we* should call it utility] of a product by transporting it from one place to another. A hundred weight of cotton grown in Brazil is more useful and worth more when stored in Europe than when stored in Pernambuco. This is a quality given to it by the merchant ; through which things are made useful which, if put in another place, could not be employed, and which is no less useful, complicated and hazardous than any that the other two industries give. The trader himself uses, for an analogous result, the natural properties of the wood and metals of which his ships are constructed, the hemp of which his sails are made, the wind that fills them, and all the natural agents that may contribute to his designs, just as the agriculturalist makes use of the earth, the rain and the air." [1]

If it be objected against this, that commerce does not of itself produce anything, we reply that neither does extractive industry. Its work is to seek, to excavate, to cultivate, to tend or offer the products of nature, to prepare and dispose the subject, so that by its virtue it may properly form them. Manufacturing industry alone, strictly speaking, produces—not indeed substances, but

---

[1] *Traité d'Économie Politique*, Liv. 1. Chap. 2.

modifications of substances. Commercial industry transports, and does so after overcoming immense obstacles :
therefore that also may in a way be said to produce, inasmuch as it produces for the merchandise a new situation,
by which it is rendered accessible to those who otherwise
would be unable to avail themselves of it.

From this it clearly appears that, including under the
name of industry whatever contributes anyhow to make
things useful for the satisfaction of human wants, we are
justified in dividing industry into the three principal
branches already mentioned, viz. *extractive* industry, *manufacturing* industry, and *commercial* industry.

33. The division of industry generally accepted by
Economists is that of Jean-Baptiste Say, who thus expresses it :—

" Those objects which, as supplied by nature, are not
quite fit for satisfying our wants, can be made so by our
industry. When this is limited to receiving from nature's
hands, it is called agricultural industry, or simply agriculture. When it separates, mingles and fashions the
products of nature for the purpose of adapting them to
our wants, it is called manufacturing industry. When it
puts at our disposition these objects of our wants which
without it would be unattainable, it is called commercial
industry, or simply commerce." [1]

Anyone can see that the only difference between his
division and ours is this—he calls *agricultural* industry
what we call *extractive :* and surely we have a right to
call it as we do. Surely to class together fishing, marble
quarrying, mining, the chase, &c., as agriculture, is a misuse of language.[2] On the contrary, " extractive " is a suitable word for all those industries, because all of them

---

[1] *Traité d'Économie Politique.* Liv. I, Ch. 2.
[2] Say expressly reduces all these industries to agriculture.
"A man," he tells us, " who cultivates the soil, or keeps cattle,
cuts down trees, or even catches fish that he has bred, or who,

really extract the things about which they labour, whilst, at the same time, it is not unsuitable to agriculture, because agriculture does extract the products of the earth, which it cultivates.

34.   M. Dunoyer, in his work *La Liberté du Travail*, criticises Say's division of industry, and then coins a new one.   He puts industry into two supreme categories—that which acts on things, and that which acts on persons. The former he subdivides into extractive, carrying, manufacturing and agricultural; the latter into that which is occupied in perfecting our physical nature, that which has for its object our sensible nature, that which attends to the culture of our intelligence, and that which is employed in moral education.   But this division of his found no customers in the market, and so remained on his hands.   It reduces man to economic matter, science and virtue to industrial products.   It has a strong flavour of materialism: and that alone would suffice to make us reject it.

Article V.
Capital.

35.   Droz, after setting down nature and work as agents in the production of wealth, introduces a third, viz. *capital*. " A third agent," he says, " is essential to producing. This agent is *capitalization*, that gives to labour the instru-

---

from the bowels of the earth, digs metals or stones or combustibles, deposited by nature alone, may be considered as exercising the same kind of industry. To avoid the multiplication of names, all these occupations are called agricultural industry, because the cultivation of the soil is the most important of them all." *Traité d'Economie Politique.* Liv. I, Ch. 2. note 2. But we can just as easily avoid the multiplication of names by calling it extractive industry; and besides, that name answers better to the meaning.

ments without which it could not develope its activity."[1]
Say had taught the same thing before, and the later
Economists, with very few exceptions, took it from
him :

"Industrious man," he says, "possesses products already
existing, without which, however able we may suppose
him to be, his industry would remain inactive. 1°. There
are the utensils, the instruments of the different arts.
The cultivator of the soil could not do without his spade
and his hoe, nor the weaver without his loom, nor the
sailor without his ship. 2°. There are the products that
have to supply the maintenance of the industrial man,
until he has completed his labour in the work of production.
The product of this, and the price which the man will get
out of it ought to reimburse him for the expense of that
maintenance : but he is obliged to be continually anti-
cipating it. 3°. There are the raw materials which his
industry must transform into complete products. It is true
that these raw materials are sometimes given gratuitously
to him by nature, but more often they are products already
created by industry, such as the seeds that agriculture
supplies, the metals that we owe to the industry of the
miner and the smelter, the drugs which the trader has
brought from the furthest parts of the globe. Their value
also, the industrial man has to anticipate. The value of all
these things composes what is called *a productive capital.*"[2]

Hence, in his fifth chapter, he concludes that "The
great agents of production, are three : human industry,
capital, and the agents that nature offers." In our own
days, M. Leroy-Beaulieu speaks to the same effect.   "Le
capital," he says, " est, avec la nature et le travail, l'un
des grands agents de la production humaine."[3]

Economie Politique, ou Principes de la Science des Richesses.
        Liv. I, Ch. 6.
[2] *Traité d'Economie Politique.*   Liv. I, Ch. 3.
[3] *Précis d'Economie Politique.*   Part 1, Ch. iv.

36. I had rather that capital were not called an *agent* in production, for reasons which I will give you in the next Chapter. In the meanwhile we want to have a clear conception of capital.

Capital is the fruit of saving. It is constituted by a portion of wealth not consumed. Suppose, for instance, that a man has four hundred a year from the Funds. He can spend it all, or only spend three, and save the rest. In the latter case the pounds that he might have spent, and did not spend, are his savings : and they may accumulate till they amount to a considerable sum, which, absolutely speaking, may be called capital. But the Economists have ruled that money saved is not to be called capital, unless it be destined for the production of new wealth : and we, to avoid confusion, must keep to this use of the word. Capital then may be defined as A STORE OF SAVINGS, DESTINED FOR PRODUCTION, or, WEALTH, OR A PART OF WEALTH TAKEN FROM CONSUMPTION TO SERVE FOR PRODUCTION. It must not be supposed, however, that, because this example is taken from money, therefore capital properly consists in money, as the followers of the mercantile system thought. No ;—Capital consists in all things that have utility and value, if only they be intended to produce more wealth. It may consist in money just so far as money is exchangeable for other objects that closely concern production, such as seeds for agriculture, raw material for handicraft work, means of transport, machinery, buildings, the food of labourers while they are working—all which things are reducible to these two great categories, instruments and provisions.

" It would be a great mistake," says Jean-Baptiste Say, " to suppose that society's capital consists in money. alone. A merchant, a manufacturer, a cultivator of the soil, do not, generally speaking, possess under the form of money more than the smallest part of the value that composes their capital : and, indeed, the more active their industry is, the less capital they have under the form of money, as compared with the rest. If a merchant, his funds are in merchandise on the roads, on the sea, in warehouses here and there. If a builder, they are principally under the form of primary materials in different degrees of forwardness, or under the form of tools, machines and other provisions for his workmen. If a cultivator of the soil, they are under the form of granaries, of cattle, of inclosures. All these men are careful to keep no more money than is wanted for daily expenses. What is true of the individual is also true of two, three, four individuals, true of the whole society."[1]

37. Here he evidently excludes the soil from being reckoned as capital: but other Economists include it. Indeed they include all property whatsoever that is owned by man ; and, by a gross abuse of analogy, they even include his immaterial faculties, his talents, his intellectual and moral culture. But the most notable meaning of the word " capital," is that which has been given to it quite lately by a special school of Economists, mostly Germans. They understand it to mean the *value* of things that, in any way whatever, are helpful to production—the value considered as apart from the things, and therefore as capable of being subject to the economic operations of sale, purchase, transfers, loans, and every sort of contract. This would include rents and mortgages, and those obligations of the State, or of companies, or even of individuals, which are negociated at the Stock Exchange, that great market of money and money's value.

In this sense the word " capitalist " would not mean one who owns land, or machinery, or other instruments of labour, but one who has plenty of the above mentioned qualifications, and makes use of them in lucrative business, whatever it may happen to be. In this sense they speak

---

[1] *Traité*, &c. Liv. I, Ch. 1.

of employing capital in an undertaking, drawing out capital, turning capital to account, &c. According to this, then, "capitalism" does not mean the predominant employment of utensils, machinery, workable materials and other means of production. It means the kingdom of money, and of the values therein exchangeable, that may be quickly concentrated here and there, in the possession of this or that owner, or drawn out from State loans and bonds—from the Suez Canal, for instance—in millions. Under the yoke of this economic system all society is groaning now.

38. Whenever we shall have occasion in this treatise to speak of capital, we shall understand it to mean, as we said before, the sum of those things which, remaining over and above what is consumed, are destined for the service of production. In this sense of the word we may divide capital into *fixed* and *moveable*, or, if you prefer the word, *evanescent*. The Economists call it *circulating*, or *workable*. The former has some duration, and is profitable to its owner while in his possession. Such, for instance, are beasts of burden, machines, house property, work done, and the like—all, in short, that is reducible to the category of instruments for production. The latter does not remain, but is transformed into the product intended, and brings no profit without a change of ownership. Such are the primary materials, as wool for making cloth, merchandise before sale, food stored, and, in general, all that is reducible to the category of *provisions*. But, in our opinion, the name of "circulating capital" should rather be restricted to money and whatever serves as a medium of payment.

ARTICLE VI.

CAPITAL CANNOT REASONABLY BE RECKONED AMONG THE PRODUCERS OF WEALTH.

39.　Capital is unquestionably an indispensable means of increasing wealth. A proprietor who every year spends the whole of his income, will always remain in the same economic state : and so will a workman who every week spends his week's wages. Neither can improve his finances, unless by saving he gradually forms a capital that he can apply to industry. In this sense capital may be called productive, because it helps man to produce. But to call it a producer, in the strict acceptation of the word, and put it on a level with nature and work, as the Economists generally do—telling us that the agents of wealth are the earth, capital and labour—this we cannot see our way to admit. In the first place, we cannot truly reckon among the causes of a thing that which, partly at least, supposes it. But capital does so precisely ; for inasmuch as it proceeds from savings, it supposes an unconsumed wealth. This objection was put by Dunoyer against Say, in these words : "Industry, Say tells us, would have remained in a state of inaction without the help of preexisting capital. But, if it be so, one fails to understand how the industry began ; for evidently the existence of capital could not precede the work that made it." Exactly so. Man, when he began to produce, had nothing more than natural objects and the strength of his arms. Nature and work, then, were the only primordial causes of wealth. Capital was not there, but came in later. Therefore Say's proposition, that industry without capital "*ne produirait pas*," is absurd. [1]

40.　We shall be told, that this is true if we consider capital as a primary factor of wealth, and go back to the imperfect beginnings of human labour, but not when we

---

[1] *Traité d'Economie Politique*, &c., Liv. I, Chap. 3.

are speaking of an accessory factor and of industry in a state of advanced civilisation.

Now, in the first place, if capital is not a *primitive* factor, why reckon it together with the earth (or rather, nature) and with labour, both of which are primitive factors? Are there not ambiguities enough in economic science without this?

Secondly, the idea of a producer does not agree with that of capital, but the idea of an auxiliary—a powerful means of production—does agree with it very well. The idea of a producer implies efficiency. Now efficiency is due to natural agents and workmen, but in no way to capital. Indeed, what does capital consist in? Say, in a passage already quoted, [1] assigns to it three elements—the materials for work, the sustenance of the workmen, the instruments required for the work.

Now, the material is not that which *makes* a thing, but that of which it is *made*. Therefore it may be considered as a constituent of wealth, but not as its producer: for the concurrence of the materials, as such, is purely passive, while that of the producer is active. We cannot get out of this by falling back on the active qualities that are found in materials and help to form the effect; for those qualities come in as natural agents, and so are outside the concept of materials. As materials, they only have an aptitude for receiving and retaining the form which labour impresses on them. If not gratuitously given by nature, they can enter into the expenses of production, which ought certainly to be repaid on the value of the product: but it cannot rise to the condition of a producer.

41. The same proportionately may be said about the sustenance of the workmen. The work cannot be done unless the workmen are kept alive: and the workmen cannot be kept alive without sustenance. This sustenance

---

[1] Art. v., § 35.

constitutes an expense, an expense anticipated on the future profits of the product. It does not constitute a producer. The workman is the producer, though his remuneration be anticipated. Work, or the production of wealth, is not the end for which the workman lives. He works to live, and whoever says that he lives to work, likens him to a machine, or, at the most, a brute.

The instruments, inasmuch as they truly co-operate, would apparently have some claim to be called producers : but in fact they have not. The instrument, in relation to the work, does not form an operator contradistinct from the principal or agent, but a *quid unum* with him. What would any one say, if he were told that Raphael's "Transfiguration" was painted by Raphael and his paint-brush ? Moreover, the instruments themselves are wealth, being useful and exchangeable. Therefore they cannot be rightly reckoned among the producers of wealth. Instruments are effects caused by the labour of man, to whom nature has given the human hand, called by Aristotle, the "instrument of instruments" *(organum organorum)* because it is capable of making and using all sorts of instruments. When the first instruments were made by human hands, men supplied the want of instruments, as they best could, by natural gifts. To do the work of a blacksmith, for instance, a man wanted an anvil and a sledge-hammer. But who produced the anvil and the hammer ? Man himself, by the labour of his hands, using a stone instead of an anvil, and a piece of rough iron instead of a hammer. The hand is a part of the workman. The stone with the rough piece of iron is offered by nature. Therefore it is sufficient that we enumerate nature and human labour as the true and absolute producers of wealth. All the rest comes from the one or from the other, and capital, though necessary for the increase of wealth, only deserves the name of an auxiliary, or a means, or anything you like, except that of producer in the strict sense of the word.

We say this for the sake of exactness : but if other people, unwilling to depart from the accepted language of economy, adhere to the formula—"There are three *causes* of wealth—the earth, capital, and labour"—we are not going to quarrel with them. In that case, however, the word " cause " must be understood to mean that which is in any way whatsoever required (even as a material or an instrument) in order to obtain something. In this extended sense capital is a cause of wealth ; for in the present state of industry it is evident that without capital, and large capital, almost all the production of wealth would stop, and the people would fall into frightful poverty. The word "land" must be taken to mean, not merely the tillable soil, but the whole terrestrial globe, with all the materials and forces therein contained.

CHAPTER III.

AIDS TO PRODUCTION.

WO most powerful aids to production have to be considered—the division of labour and the invention of machines. The former increases the efficiency of man, the latter the efficiency of nature. The former organizes, in order to produce the effect, the forces of the workmen. The latter organizes the forces of physical agents. We shall speak of both together in one chapter, by reason of their close connection : for the division of labour originated the invention of machinery.

ARTICLE I.

DIVISION OF LABOUR.

43. We learn something about the division of labour from nature itself by examples. In the inorganic bodies, whose end is quite simple, we find one and the same operation exercised on the whole by all the parts : but, as soon as we turn our attention from dead matter to things that have life, we at once perceive that different actions are performed by different parts endowed with different structures. The organic arrangements for taking food, for digesting it, for transmuting it into the substance of a living thing, differ from each other. The more highly organized the animal is, the more diversified is this division, and most in the most perfect animals, above whom is Man, as the link that joins the organic life of brutes to the inorganic life of pure spirits.

44. In human society, fashioned on the type of living organisms, a similar distribution spontaneously appears in the diverse branches of industry, according to the aptitudes, inclinations, hopes and intentions of each human being. The two first sons of the first pair had different occupations. Abel was a shepherd, Cain a tiller of the soil. *Fuit Abel pastor ovium, et Cain agricola.* [1] Soon after the building of the first city, called Henoch, different arts were professed by different men. Jubal was "the father of them that play on the harp and the organs." Tubal Cain "was a hammerer and artificer in every work of brass and iron." *Jubal fuit pater canentium cithara et organo ;* and Tubal Cain *fuit malleator et faber in cuncta opera æris et ferri.* [2]

Even in those early days men saw that *pluribus intentus minor est ad singula sensus :* and the division of labour went on increasing with the increase of civilized man,

---

[1] *Genesis* iv., 2.   [2] Ibid. 21, 22.

till, in our days, it seems hardly possible to divide it further.

45. This "great lever of modern industry," as Pellegrino Rossi calls it, has done wonders in every branch of human activity. Adam Smith, who considered it to be so important, that in his famous work he makes it his starting point, takes one of the smallest products, pins, as an example of its efficacy. He remarks that in making a pin there are eighteen operations. There is drawing the wire, straightening, cutting, sharpening one end, rounding the other, and putting the head on—which last requires two or three more operations. Lastly the pin is polished and put into its paper. If one man had to do all this, he would make, by a great effort, twenty pins in a day; whereas Adam Smith speaks of forty-eight thousand being made in the same time by only ten workmen, each of whom made in the day four thousand and eight hundred pins.[1] Say instances playing cards, of which, owing to the division of labour, thirty workmen make fifteen thousand, or each workman five hundred. Now if one workman had to do all this, he would hardly make two in a day. Similar examples might be taken from other branches of industry.

46. Not all industries, however, admit the division of labour in the same proportion. In some there is little or no division—in agriculture, for instance, whose diverse operations correspond with the seasons, and therefore cannot be done contemporaneously by different people :

" The nature of agriculture, indeed," says Adam Smith, " does not admit of so many subdivisions of labour, nor of so complete a separation of one business from another, as

---

[1] *Wealth of Nations*, Bk. 1., Chap. 1. Garnier takes needles for an example, and enumerates no less than a hundred and twenty operations. He tells us that he has seen manufactories where the workmen, though few in number, made a hundred thousand needles in a day. *Elements d'Economie Politique*, &c., 1ᵉʳᵉ Partie, Chap. v., § 1.

manufactures. It is impossible to separate so entirely the business of the grazier from that of the corn farmer, as the trade of the carpenter is commonly separated from that of the smith. The spinner is almost always a distinct person from the weaver; but the ploughman, the harrower, the sower of the seed, and the reaper of corn are often the same. The occasion for those different sorts of labour returning with the different seasons of the year, it is impossible that one man should be constantly employed in any one of them. This impossibility of making so complete and entire a separation of all the different branches of labour employed in agriculture, is perhaps the reason why the improvement of the productive powers of labour, in this art, does not always keep pace with their improvement in manufactures. The most opulent nations, indeed, generally excel all their neighbours in agriculture as well as in manufactures; but they are commonly more distinguished by their superiority in the latter than in the former."[1]

47. Smith gives three reasons why the division of labour so greatly increases production. First, the workman becomes more dexterous by always doing the same thing, especially when the work is very simple. Secondly, he saves time by not having to go from one sort of work to another, which usually necessitates change of place and change of tools. Lastly, there is the use of machinery, which in separate and constant works proves easier and quicker.

It is justly remarked by the Economists, that the division of labour is founded on the possibility of exchange, because no one would devote himself to one sort of work only, unless he were sure of being able to procure by exchange the necessaries of life. Nor would the mere certainty of that be sufficient. The exchange

---

[1] *Wealth of Nations*, Bk. I., Chap. 1.

must be such as exhausts his whole production; for otherwise, to avoid useless work and loss of capital, he would be compelled to limit his products according to the probabilities of exchanging them, and apply his over-time to some other sort of industry. Hence it is usually said that division of labour is founded on exchange and limited by the market; and this is the reason why in villages, and even in small towns, we often find the same person following different occupations. The carpenter often does iron work. The doctor is surgeon, dentist and druggist. The village shop supplies groceries, haberdashery and many other things, from hats and leggings to writing paper and birch brooms. But in great cities each profession, trade and business has many branches; and therefore in them the arts and industries are perfected and increased.

ARTICLE II.
MACHINERY.

48. In Political Economy the word "machine" is broadly understood to mean any sort of instrument invented by man, to help him in the work of production. Thus any tool—a spade for instance, or a hammer, or a file—would be a machine. But in a more restricted sense that name is limited to mechanical inventions, resulting from several elements ingeniously disposed for accelerating and multiplying production. [1]

---

[1] " The instruments with which he [man] arms his weakness, to act on material objects, are tools and machines. I do not separate them in my exposition, because machines and tools are, in fact, essentially and equally instruments. Both are nothing more than means, to make the power of nature serve in the accomplishment of our designs. When we knock in a nail with a hammer, we make use of an instrument that enables us to take advantage of the power resulting from a law of physics in the collision of bodies. When we employ a hydraulic wheel to raise one of those enormous hammers that flatten and lengthen a bar

49. In the invention of machinery we owe much, as I said before, to the division of labour : for no machine answers to a whole product, but to one or another of the diverse operations required. " The greatest improvements in the productive powers of labour," says Adam Smith, " and the greater part of the skill, dexterity and judgment with which it is anywhere directed or applied, seem to have been the effects of the division of labour;" [2] and he observes that men are more easily led to consider the readiest and most efficacious means of gaining an object, when their whole attention is concentrated on it. No wonder, then, that the invention and improvement of so many machines now used in manufactures, is due to mere operatives, who first conceived the idea of such machines. To illustrate this, he instances a boy who, in the early days of steam-engines, was employed in opening and shutting the communication between the boiler and the cylinder, according as the piston either ascended or descended. The boy perceived that by fastening the handle of the valve with a piece of string to another part of the machine, the valve would open and shut of itself, and leave him at leisure to play with his companions. Thus one of the most important improvements in steam-engines was discovered by a small boy.

" All the improvements in machinery, however," Smith goes on to say, " have by no means been the inventions of those who had occasion to use the machines. Many improvements have been made by the ingenuity of the makers of the machines, when to make them became the business of a peculiar trade ; and some by that of those

---

of iron, we use an instrument that enables us to take advantage of a power which nature alike furnishes. The only perceptible difference between these two instruments is, that we, in general, give the name of *tool* to a very simple machine, and call a more complicated tool a *machine*." *Cours Complet, &c.* 1ᵉʳᵉ part. Ch. 18.   [2] *Wealth of Nations.* Bk. I. Chapter 1.

who are called philosophers or men of speculation, whose trade is not to do anything, but to observe everything, and who, upon that account, are often capable of combining together the powers of the most distant and dissimilar objects." [1]

50. The usefulness of machinery lies in lightening labour and making the powers of nature wholly or partly supply for it. In ancient times corn was ground with a grind-stone by slaves and poor women. Homer tells us in the Odyssey, that in Penelope's house twelve maidens passed the whole day in grinding corn for the household. That wearisome and humiliating labour is now done by watermills or windmills, that compel nature to do the work of man, and to do it more efficiently. The force of the water that turns an ordinary watermill, is equivalent to that of a hundred and fifty men. So that machinery increases the products, and therefore diminishes their price.

51. Moreover, machinery makes the productions more perfect, and gives leisure for attending to other employments more interesting to man :

" Cheapness," Say remarks, " is not the only advantage procured for consumers by the introduction of expeditious methods. They gain generally a greater perfection in the products. Painters might execute with a brush the designs that adorn our calicoes and our wall-papers ; but the stamps and rollers employed for that purpose give a regularity to the design, a uniformity to the colours, that no artist could ever equal. If we follow out the enquiry through all the industrial arts, we shall find that most machines are not limited to supplying simply the work of man, but give a really new product by giving a new perfection. . . . . Lastly, machines do more than this. They multiply those products to whose production they are not

---

[1] *Wealth of Nations.* Bk. I. Chap. 1.

applied. One would hardly believe perhaps, without taking the trouble of reflecting, that the plough, the harrow and other such implements, whose origin is lost in the obscurity of ages, have powerfully contributed to procure for man not only the necessaries of life, but also the comfort which he is now enjoying, and of which, without those implements, he would probably have not even conceived the idea. If all the labour required for the cultivation of the soil had to be done with hoes and spades and such-like implements, that do their work slowly, and if we could not secure the co-operation of animals— which in Political Economy are considered as a species of machinery—the probable consequence would be that all the hands now employed in industrial arts would be wanted to produce the food that now maintains our present population. Thanks to the plough, a certain number of persons can devote themselves even to the less important arts, and above all, to cultivating the faculties of the Soul." [1]

The result of machinery, then, is to obtain better, quicker, more powerfully and at less cost, the products of the three species of industry—the extractive, the manufacturing, the commercial, as exemplified in windmills, weavers' looms, and vehicles. Hence more people can live and be fed on the same ground.

ARTICLE III.

DIFFICULTIES ARISING FROM THE DIVISION OF LABOUR.

52. However much the division of labour and the invention of machinery may have benefitted the production of wealth, it cannot be denied that together with these advantages there are many evils in the physical and moral order—evils deplored even by persons who are far

[1] *Traité d'Economie Politique*, Liv. I. Chap. 7.

from being adverse either to Political Economy or to modern progress. Sismondi, in a fit of indignation, went so far as to exclaim :—

"In spite of all its benefits in the social order, in spite of all the advantages that man has gained from the arts, one is sometimes tempted to curse the division of labour and the invention of manufactures, when one sees the state to which they have reduced beings who are our fellow creatures. Animals do nearly all the agricultural work of man, and machines do his work in nearly all the operations of manufacturing."[1]

Say quotes a certain Lemontey, who, in an essay entitled *The Moral Influence of the Division of Labour*, laments the evils consequent on it and on the use of machines. We shall notice the principal evils.

53. The too minute division of labour occasions two inconveniences that deserve special attention. One of them is, that it deteriorates the man's rational faculties. When a workman has to employ all his time in doing one sort of purely mechanical work, his intelligence grows dull; and the simpler the work, the worse for him. Thus the more you increase the division of labour, grinding down, so to speak, into little bits the work required for the entire product, the more does the intelligence of the individual workman deteriorate and weaken. How can you expect any mental development in one who passes all his days in polishing a piece of metal, or sharpening the point of a needle? The Economists generally, notwithstanding their zeal for the division of labour, are compelled to confess that there is truth in this. Say admits that "there is, no doubt, some deterioration in the faculties of the individual, when his *whole* occupation, his *whole* attention, his *whole* care,

---

[1] *Nouveaux Principes d'Economie Politique*, Liv. vii. Ch. 7. on "Population rendered superfluous by the invention of machines."

his *whole* time, are directed towards one particular operation constantly repeated." [1] And Garnier after repeating these words of Say literally, without quoting them, adds :—"It would be a mistake, however, to suppose that this necessity implies their being brutalized." "Cependant on aurait tort de croire qu' une operation de ce genre entraine *un abrutissement nécessaire.*" [2] Very comforting indeed—to be assured that injuring the moral faculties will not turn a man into a downright beast !

54. Another inconvenience is that it makes the workman a slave to the master or the foreman ; for, since he cannot make any entire product exchangeable in the market, his position is precarious. He is quite dependent on the proprietor of the manufactory where he works, because he can only do a particle of what is there produced as a whole : and therefore he must either starve, or accept the conditions about wages, hours of work, &c. This lowers the dignity of man.

55. Still graver difficulties arise from the introduction of machinery. We shall point out two only. It decreases the number of hands employed, and it weakens family ties. A machine worked by two or three people will sometimes do the work of a hundred, or two hundred, or even more : and thus a great many are brought to destitution. We are told that the workmen may take to some other occupation, and that machinery, by multiplying produce and lowering prices, is beneficial to them : but this change of occupation is not so easy in practice. Many of them would find it impossible. The rest would require time, and have nothing to live on in the meanwhile.

---

[1] "Il y a bien sans doute un peu de dégéneration dans les facultés de l'individu, lorsque toute son occupation, toute son attention, tous ses soins, sont dirigés vers une occupation de détail, trop constamment repétée." *Cours Complet, &c.* 1ere. Partie, Chap. 17.

[2] *Elements de l'Economie Politique.* 1ere Chap. 5.

The workman depends on his daily pay. What is the use of cheap prices to him, if, owing to want of work, he has no money in his pocket? So far as he is concerned the prices might as well be high.

56. The Economists acknowledge this difficulty: but they tell us that we must not put it in comparison with the advantages that accrue to society in general.

All very well for those who only think of the social body as a whole—which, by the bye, often means nothing more than the well-being of a few—but not for those who remember the individuals, and remember the poor, who especially ought to be protected in a well-ordered society. Moreover, the evil is not transitory. It is permanent: for the occupation of many hands is permanently taken away.

57. But this is as nothing in comparison with the loosening of domestic ties. Where machinery is used, the industry is on a grand scale, and the labour continuous. The father of a family passes his whole day in one workshop, his wife in another; and their little children are taken care of in some asylum for infants, or in what is called a *Crèche*. The members of the family are separated. They meet for a short time in the evening, but at all other times they are strangers to each other. And lest this manner of living should be interrupted by Sundays, modern civilisation has contrived that even Sunday shall be a working day![1] This is destructive to domestic union, which therein has its principle and foundation. Moreover, the introduction of machinery, by diminishing the demand for mature intelligence and practised dexterity in the workman, has opened the doors of the factories to children, boys and girls, with that injury to their education, and peril to their morals which every good man deplores, and which is tending to corrupt the whole social system through the corruption of the family.

---

[1] Happily not in England yet. (*Translator's Note.*)

58. There is another evil to be noticed—the concentration of gains in the hands of a few. Sismondi says about this :—

"Discoveries in mechanical art, have always for their ultimate result the concentration of industry in the hands of a small number of the richest traders. They teach people to make by means of expensive machinery, or in other words by great capital, that which formerly was made with much labour. They enable them to find an economical advantage in business done on a great scale, in the division of operations, in the common use of light, heat and all the forces of nature by a great number of men collected together. Hence the small traders and small manufacturers disappear, and a great contractor supplies for hundreds of workmen, whose united wealth is not equal to his." [1]

Thus modern society is tending more and more to divide off into two great classes, the class of the very rich and the class of the very poor, not unlike ancient paganism.

ARTICLE IV.

THE REMEDIES.

59. The labour question is now so difficult a knot to loosen, that our courage wavers at the idea of attempting to untie it. The difficulty of doing so arises mainly from that spirit of selfishness, that insatiable thirst for enjoyment, which in these days has taken possession of men's hearts, under the influence of the economic doctrines hitherto in vogue. If it shall please God to give us sufficient time and strength, we shall, in an appendix to this work, endeavour to solve the problem. Here we

[1] *Nouveaux Principes d'Economie Politique.* Liv. vii., Chap. 7.

shall only speak of the said remedies in the abstract, and first of all point out two things to be considered.

60. One of them is, that the above mentioned evils do not affect the division of labour in general, nor all machinery. That division of labour which answers to entire products, though they be restricted to an ultimate species, as in making an iron bed or a crystal lens, is connatural. So far from doing any harm, it is not only useful to society, but also beneficial to the workman. It makes him more expert, more highly esteemed, and puts him into a more independent position. Likewise there are machines of supreme importance—machines that harm no one, but, on the contrary, are useful to all. Such, for instance, is the plough, without which it would be almost impossible to cultivate the soil. Such is the corn-mill, which by doing a work wearisome to man, facilitates the acquirement of the most necessary food. The steam-engine often does what could not be accomplished by the hand, and is immensely useful on railways by transporting things and people. Moreover it does this without injuring, as people feared that it would, the conveyances by road; for owing to the increase in the number of passengers and the quantity of merchandise, there are more of them, and they are more profitable. We find the same result in cotton spinning, since Arkwright invented the spinning jenny. [1] The fear was, that in England most of the operatives, male and female, would be left without work: but it turned out contrariwise. Here is what Say relates about it :—

" I have been assured," he says, " by a merchant who during the last fifty years has been engaged in the sale and manufacture of cotton goods, that before the invention of the machine [the spinning jenny] there were in Great Britain no more than 5,200 female spinners at the small

---

[1] Or rather perfected, and made possible, what Hargreaves had invented. (*Translator's Note.*)

spinning wheel, and 2,700 weavers of cotton stuff, making altogether 7,900 work-people ; whereas in the year 1787, only ten years after the introduction of spinning jennies, 105,000 persons, adults and children, were engaged in spinning, and 247,000 in weaving; which makes altogether 352,000, instead of 7,900." [1]

Therefore the evils regretted concern that division only, which is characterized as a minute subdivision of labour, and those machines only, which, without being of absolute necessity, take away work from one class at least, and keep men, women and children crammed up all day long in great workshops.

61. The second consideration is, that in human affairs advantages and disadvantages are almost always intermingled. *Sunt bona mixta malis.* We have to see which preponderates. But in the case before us this inquiry would be useless ; for, whatever the result might be, these two modern discoveries, division of labour and the multiplication of machinery, when once introduced into the world, cannot be generally abolished. It might be done in this or that country : but even there, besides doing violence to the industrial freedom of the inhabitants, it would involve the ruin of the very operatives for whose protection it was done. The increase in the cost of labour, owing to the want of machinery, would cause such a rise in prices, that it would be impossible to compete with other nations where machinery is used : so that those industries must then be given up, and all the operatives discharged.

62. Let us now inquire briefly—for we shall have to speak of it again in the course of this work—how it might be possible to avoid, or at least diminish, the evils that weigh against the advantages gained through the division of labour and the use of machinery.

The first remedy is the previous instruction and education

---

[1] *Cours Complet*, &c., 1ere. Partie. Chap. 19.

of the operative.　In our opinion no child should be put
to permanent mechanical work, until his bodily strength is
developed and sufficiently consolidated by age, and his
mind by instruction, most especially in morals and
religion.　When the lad's intelligence has thus far been
developed and strengthened, there is a probability of its
not being afterwards retarded or narrowed by trivial or
monotonous labour ; especially if this culture be carried on
by the parents and clergy.　But if this caution be dis-
regarded, his mind will certainly slumber without hope of
awaking.

The second remedy is to limit the hours of labour, not
only for women and children, who ought not to work more
than six hours, but also for adults.　In no factory should
the operative work more than nine, or, at most, ten hours
in the day: so that he may have leisure for the cares and
affections of home, and raise his thoughts to things
befitting the dignity of human nature.　But above all
his freedom to abstain from material work on Sundays
and holidays ought to be kept intact, in order that he may
have time and opportunity to fulfil his religious duties and
strengthen his good resolutions.　Thirdly, the operative
should not, under any consideration whatever, be per-
petually kept at one only of those operations into which
labour is sub-divided in relation to a given product.　He
should, as far as possible, be passed on gradually through
all of them, or almost all.　This, besides not restricting
his operative powers, would greatly help to free him from
a too servile dependence on his master.　Being able to do
different sorts of work, he would be in a position to
bargain more freely and fear competition less.

63.　This will not be acceptable to the sense-worshippers
and self-worshippers, who find in human society nothing
higher than wealth, to be produced anyhow in the largest
possible quantity, and see in the operative nothing more
than a machine, to which indeed they compare him in

their treatises. [1]   But very different will be the judgment
of those who recognize in social life an end higher than
that of satisfying material wants, and who look on the
workman as a brother, equal to themselves in his nature,
and claiming their regard as belonging to the more
numerous class—the class that requires help.   "If in the
laws of labour," says Pellegrino Rossi, "you abstract
from our moral nature, you misuse analysis and lower man
to the condition of a brute.   The Economist cannot
arrogate to himself such a right." [2]   Political Economy
is, as we have already seen, a practical science, and therefore intrinsically subordinate to Morals.   It cannot consider labour without keeping in view the subject from
which it is taken : and that subject is man, who is a
person in the world, not a thing—an end, not a means.
To deprive him for one's own profit, as if he were a sheep
to be sheared, of his rights as man, is not only a most
grave injustice in itself, but also an act of treason to God :
for man is the property of God, Who has indeed decreed
that in this world he should live by labour, but not that
he should be injured by it in any way, especially as to
the upward training of his mind and the attainment of
eternal life.

The remedies for the other evils had better be considered
in the second Part, when we come to the distribution of
wealth.

---

[1] Here is what Flores Estrada says : "An operative in
Political Economy is nothing more than a piece of fixed capital,
accumulated by the country, which has maintained him during
the whole time required for learning his trade, and through the
whole development of his powers.   With respect to the production of wealth, he is considered as a machine, for whose construction capital has been employed, which begins to be repaid
and give a profit from the moment when it [the man-machine]
becomes a useful helper of industry." *Eclectic Course of Political
Economy.*   Vol. 1., p. 363.
    [2] *Cours d'Economie Politique.*   Tome 1., leçon xii.

CHAPTER IV.

CIRCULATION.

 IN Political Economy circulation means the movement of merchandise passing from one possessor to another, for the production and enjoyment of wealth. For instance, a cargo of cotton is sent from Brazil to a merchant in Europe, who sells it to the spinner, who after spinning it sells it to the weaver, who after weaving it sells it to the wholesale dealer, who sells it to the retail dealer, who sells it to the consumer. In this passing on merchandise is circulated, with successive increase of value and with profit to those through whose hands it passes. Hence it is said to be like the circulation of the blood through the different parts of the animal body, and is a necessary element in the economic life of nations. It takes place through the medium of exchange. Therefore in speaking of it we have to speak of exchange and of two other things closely connected with it. These two other things are *money*, which is the instrument of exchange, and *credit*, which in these days is generally accepted as a substitute for money.

ARTICLE I.

EXCHANGE.

65. Bartering one thing for another is called exchange. Comfort would be impossible without it, because no one could procure by his own labour all the necessaries and conveniencies of life. Man, even in a state of barbarism, or of savagery, cannot provide for his own wants without

having things done for him by others for an equivalent compensation in work or in goods. This necessity increases with the increase of culture, owing to the variety of occupations that civilisation requires. How could a tailor or a shoemaker attend to his work, if he were not sure of being able to exchange a part of his work for the produce of the earth, whence his food comes? We have seen that the efficiency of nature is much increased by the use of machines, and the efficiency of man by the division of labour: but the abundance of this or that product would be little or no use, were it not exchangeable for other things that are wanted. The variety of trades, perseverance in one sort of labour, the increase and perfection of the arts, the common prosperity, and even the exercise of noble professions would be impossible without exchange. No one could devote himself to any of these occupations, unless he were sure that his services would gain for him a suitable remuneration. Otherwise how could he live and provide for his material wants?

66. The practice of exchange constitutes commerce, which is carried out by a whole class of men, who from dealing in merchandise are called merchants. The work done by them is exceedingly beneficial to society, by freeing the consumer from a thousand annoyances and much loss of time, which would certainly come upon him, especially in buying foreign produce, if he were obliged to deal directly with the producer. Naturally, therefore, between the producer and the consumer a third person intervenes, who seeks the produce where it comes from, or where it is worked up, and conveying it to places where it is wanted, brings it within easy reach of the public.

Commerce is internal and external. The former is carried on by wholesale and by retail. The latter is divided into export trade and import trade.

It is needless to point out what commerce has done for the wealth of nations. Experience proves it by the fact that the most commercial nations are the richest : and the reason of this is plain. For wealth consists in abundance of useful objects ; and commerce greatly stimulates the activity of internal production by opening new outlets for it, while the superfluous produce is exchanged for that of foreign countries.

ARTICLE II.

MONEY.

67. Money was introduced into the social world for the exchange of things. *Primo denarii inventi sunt pro commutatione rerum.*[1] In these words does St. Thomas give us the conception of money, representing it as a discovery of man to facilitate exchanges. Such precisely is its office ; and such is its nature, defined by its end.

Man, as we have said before, provides for his own wants by means of exchange, which would be excessively tiresome and sometimes almost impossible, if he always had to exchange thing for thing. Fancy a farmer having to give a certain quantity of wheat or oats for a coat or a spade. What is to be done, if the tailor or the ironmonger should object to be paid in that way ? He must go about the neighbourhood, till he can find someone who for so much corn will give him something that will satisfy his creditor as payment for the coat or the spade. Still worse would it be for him, if, instead of corn, he had something indivisible—a bullock, for instance —to pay with. He would have to look about, with much trouble and loss of time, till he had found someone willing to give for the bullock a quantity of separate wares, out of which the creditor would consent to be paid. In foreign commerce the difficulties would be still greater. Imagine a merchant with nothing but goods to pay for tea in

---

[1] *In Lib.* 1. *Politicorum.* Lect. v. 1.

China.   He would have to load a ship with merchandise,
go to China in it, travel to the tea plantations, and there
exchange, if he could, his shipload of wares for tea.

68.   It was necessary then to find some article of merchandise with which the values of all other merchandise
could be compared, and which, therefore, would be substituted for it in exchange, as a common equivalent. This
common equivalent is money, to constitute which (for
reasons that we shall see a little further on) metals,
especially gold and silver, were chosen.

" They began," writes the Senator Lampertico, " by the
exchange of thing for thing, or, in other words, barter.
There was no money, and hence no distinction between
merchandise and price.   Everyone provided himself with
what he wanted, by giving some of that which he did not
require for use.   But since it does not always happen that,
when you have what I want, I have what you are in need
of, a material was chosen whose public and permanent
worth should remedy the difficulties of exchange by same-
ness of quantity. They agreed to choose something that
would be a common measure of the value of all, so that
the measured should be exchanged for that which measures
it, viz. that each thing should be worth so much of this
common measure, and so much of it be given and received
as payment and equivalent for each.   Thus was money
invented.[1]"

St. Thomas had said the same long ago, when commenting on Aristotle. He says :—

*Si semper homines in præsenti indigerent rebus, quas
invicem habent, non oporteret fieri commutationem nisi rei
ad rem, puta frumenti ad vinum.   Sed quandoque contin-
git quod ille, cui superabundat vinum, non indiget frumento,
quod habet ille qui indiget vino, sed forte postea indigebit,*

---

[1]   Fedele Lampertico.   *Economia de' Popoli e degli Stati.*
Introduzione cap. xii.

vel aliqua alia re. Sic ergo, pro necessitate futuræ commutationis, numisma, idest denarius, est nobis quasi fidejussor quod, si in præsenti homo nullo indiget sed indigeat in futuro, aderit sibi, offerenti denarium, illud quo indigebit.[1]

69. Till the use of gold and silver prevailed among civilised nations, as Say observes, custom varied respecting the material chosen to constitute money. "The history of the money used by different peoples," he says, "proves that it was made of many different materials. The Spartans had iron money. The early Romans had it of copper. In some countries the seed of the cocoa-nut or little shells are used for money. There was leather money in Russia, up to the time of Peter the Great. But the materials that unquestionably comprise the most advantages are gold and silver, which are often described by the denomination of precious metals."[2] The advantages are many: but it will be sufficient for us to point out the following:—1°. Gold and silver have a value of their own; for, being useful to man in many other ways, they are of themselves valuable, and as such are generally esteemed and sought. 2°. They are divisible, without loss of their proper value; so that pieces broken off answer to parts of the whole, and when reunited equal it. 3°. They are more easily transported than other things, because they concentrate much value in a small compass. 4°. They can be kept without wearing out, as anyone may see by looking at ancient coins. 5°. They are hard enough to be capable of receiving a stamp, that authenticates their goodness and weight. Money, then, as now in use among civilized nations, may be defined as METALLIC MERCHANDISE, EQUIVALENT TO THE VALUE OF ALL OTHER MERCHANDISE, AND GUARANTEED BY A WELL-KNOWN STAMP. It was used in very ancient times; for we read

---

[1] *In Lib.* V. *Ethicorum.* Lect. ix.
[2] *Cours Complet,* &c. 3me partie. Ch. vii.

in the Book of Genesis that Abraham, when he wanted a field with a double cave, to bury his deceased wife in, paid for it to Efron four hundred sicles of common current money :—*Appendit pecuniam, quam Efron postulaverat, audientibus filiis Heth; quadrigentos siclos argenti probatæ monetæ publicæ.* [1]

ARTICLE III.

WE ENQUIRE WHETHER MONEY MAY BE SAID TO BE REPRESENTATIVE OF OTHER VALUES, AND THE MEASURE OF THEM.

70. It is commonly said that money is *a representative sign* of the value of merchandise. Minghetti himself seems not to repudiate altogether this way of speaking. He says that money has been "chosen to represent the value of all other goods."[2] And further on he says : " The precious metals, like every other sort of merchandise, are subject to variation of value : but because this variation of value is little and slow, therefore they were chosen to represent that of other merchandise, in which the oscillation is more rapid and greater."[3] Say shows the falsity and the danger of this phrase. The representation of a thing is not the thing itself, nor its equivalent : but money, in virtue of the materials, gold and silver, of which it consists, has a value of its own, and is equivalent to other values. When money consisted of worthless things, such as shells and pieces of leather, it might with propriety of language be called representative, but not now, when it is made of precious metals. A sovereign, apart from its value as money, is worth in gold what it is worth in money, *minus* a trifle for the expense of coinage. Money, therefore does not represent other values, but is an equivalent

---

[1] *Genesis* xxiii. 16.

[2] *Dell' Economia Pubblica*, &c. Lib. ii.

[3] Ibid. Lib. iii., p. 208.

of other values. He who has money in his pocket may be said to have with him equipollently any other thing, because he can exchange it for any other thing. Say shows how the false idea that money is a sign has sometimes led governments to adulterate it, believing that they could do so harmlessly, because the more and the less are of little importance in a sign, while they are really inflicting a grievous injury on the country by giving it a mutilated value for the whole value. In fact it was a robbery on the part of the State.

71. Money is also called the *measure of other values.* This phrase must not be understood absolutely, but relatively. It cannot be understood absolutely, because the measure of a thing, in an absolute sense, must be invariable. A yard is rightly called a measure of the dimensions of bodies, because its length is always the same : but the value of money is liable to variations, though in a lesser degree than that of other merchandise, and not so rapidly. The value of money, like every other value, is determined by the quantity of things obtainable in exchange. A sovereign in times of scarcity will not buy as much food as it will in times of plenty. It is no answer to say that the value of the money does not fall, but the value of the goods rises ; for that only alters the phrase, leaving the case as it was. Value is a relation ; and if either of two terms in relation to each other undergoes a change, the relation changes. We have an example of change on the part of money itself, in the fact that its value began at once to fall after the discovery of silver mines in America, and gold mines in California and Australia. Why was this ? Simply because the great abundance of gold and silver thrown on the market lowered the value of both. The value of all merchandise is lowered by abundance and raised by scarcity. The lowering of the value of gold and silver necessarily lowered the value of money, which is made of gold and silver.

72. But in a *relative* sense money may be called a measure of other values, because, in respect of a given place and a given time, we are accustomed to compare all other values with it, in order to calculate and know their proportion to one another. Thus because at the present time and in this country oak timber fetches a higher price than deal, it is said to be worth more.

"When barter ceases," says Adam Smith, "and money has become the common instrument of commerce, every particular commodity is more frequently exchanged for money than for any other commodity. The butcher seldom carries his beef or his mutton to the baker or the brewer, in order to exchange them for bread or for beer; but he carries them to the market, where he exchanges them for money, and afterwards exchanges that money for bread and for beer. The quantity of money which he gets for them regulates, too, the quantity of bread and beer which he can afterwards purchase. It is more natural and obvious to him, therefore, to estimate their value by the quantity of money, the commodity for which he immediately exchanges them, than by that of bread and beer, the commodities for which he can exchange them only by the intervention of another commodity; and rather to say, that his butcher's meat is worth 3d. or 4d. a lb., than that it is worth three or four pounds of bread, or three or four quarts of small beer. Hence it comes to pass, that the exchangeable value of every commodity is more frequently estimated by the quantity of money, than by the quantity either of labour or of any other commodity which can be had in exchange for it." [1]

But then money, too, can be measured by the goods for which it is exchanged. "If," as Say remarks, "I can buy in the market for an ounce of gold money

---

[1] *Wealth of Nations*, Bk. I., Chap. 5.

fifteen times as much wheat, or some other merchandise, as I can get for an ounce of silver money, I have a right to infer that gold money is worth fifteen times as much as an equal quantity of silver money." Here we have the value of money measured by the things of which it is the measure.

73. Let us conclude this article by an observation of Droz. He says :—

"However great the importance of money may be, it is often exaggerated ; or, rather, we have long been in error about the nature of the service that it renders to society. It was regarded as the only wealth. The aim of Political Economy was to keep money in the State and attract that of foreigners. Judicious analysis has dissipated such prejudices, or at least weakened them. The precious metals are only products, and, like all other products, are not obtained without labour. This clearly appears, if we consider the people of the country that contains the metal. Mining is a kind of industry, and not so lucrative as many people suppose. It often gives false hopes, and is fruitful in ruinous results. If the profits of an abundant mine seem enormous, we find them fall afterwards to their natural measure, when the profits and losses of all the speculators who speculate in this kind of enterprise are balanced. As to the people who are not owners of mines, they by their labour are always able to procure for them-selves the metals necessary for their money, for their jewellery, &c." [1]

ARTICLE IV.

PRICE.

74. When money had once been introduced, exchanges of goods for goods were scarcely ever made in the markets. Goods were henceforth exchanged for money, which had

---

[1] *Économie Politique*, Liv. I., Chap. 9.

become the medium of exchange. The money given for anything in exchange for that money is called its price : and therefore price is nothing more than the value of a thing calculated in money. The contract for this exchange is called purchase and sale : but the contract is one. Purchase may be defined as THE ACT BY WHICH MONEY IS GIVEN, IN ORDER TO HAVE ITS EQUIVALENT IN GOODS : and sale may be defined as THE ACT BY WHICH GOODS ARE GIVEN, IN ORDER TO HAVE THEIR EQUIVALENT IN MONEY.

75. This raises the question—What is the determining cause of such equivalence ? or—How comes it that the price of one commodity is so much, and not less or more ? About this the Economists differ. Many of them say that prices are determined by demand and supply, which oscillate until they are equalized. Hence they lay down this law:—THE HEIGHT OF PRICES IS IN THE DIRECT RATIO OF THE DEMAND AND INVERSE RATIO OF THE SUPPLY.

Abundance of goods and eagerness to get rid of them increases the number of sellers. Want of those goods and wishing to have them increases the number of buyers.

76. But Ricardo, followed by many other Economists, especially those of the English school, while admitting the truth of the above mentioned fact sought a further reason of it in the cost of *production*; so that the rule for determining the price of a commodity, would be the expense of producing it. This theory of the celebrated Economist is thus summed up by Minghetti :—

"We must go back a little to examine the formula which the illustrious David Ricardo put in the place of demand and supply, wishing to substitute for generic and ideal expressions a material something capable of being easily valued. And therefore he said : 'The value of a product is equal to the cost of its production; and the cost of production is composed of the following parts :— repayment of the money invested : wages of labour :

interest of the capital invested : remuneration of the man who undertakes the business.' And therefore Ricardo argued in this form : ' No one takes to the labour of producing, except with the object of either consuming or exchanging the product. Interest is his guide. He turns whither his interest is greatest, and therefore capitalists, and projectors, and manufacturers always choose those industries that seem likely to pay best. On the other hand, the consumers acquire products in proportion to the means they possess, and no further; and they desire to go where they hope to find things cheap. From which premisses it naturally follows that when the price of a product is less its consumption is greater, and that the consumption diminishes when the price of the product goes up. If an industry did not cover the expenses of production, it would soon come to an end : but when it pays well, producers crowd into it, and soon, owing to the competition, have to be satisfied with a more reasonable profit, i.e. that which is derived from labour and capital generally.' " [1]

77. A third opinion is thus briefly and clearly put by the Senator Lampertico :—

"They considered the theory of value under another aspect. For *cost of production* they substituted *cost of reproduction* : that is they called attention no longer to the necessary cost of producing these goods, but to the necessary cost of reproducing them. 'The purchaser thinks,' they said, 'not of the vendor's efforts, but of what he himself saves by the acquisition.' Even here, therefore, they had to observe that the formula does not suffice to explain all the economic facts, and particularly the value of those goods that cannot be reproduced. Carey's theory, substituted for that of Ricardo, defended in Italy by Ferrara, was modified by distinguishing

---

[1] *Dell' Economia Pubblica* &c., Lib. II.

physical reproduction, i.e. of the identical product, from *economic* reproduction, i.e. of analagous and suppletory products." [1]

Of this theory, which appears to be only an ingenious invention of Carey, or, as some would have it, of Bastiat, we shall have to speak elsewhere. The other two, which have a better foundation, will be sufficient for us here.

78. Now which of these is true? We answer that both are true, if we consider them relatively—the one of the natural price of the article, the other of its current or market price. If we go by what nature suggests, the price of goods ought to equal the necessary cost of production, including a return for the physical agents, profit for the capital expended, wages for the work done. So understood, the cost of production is the rational term of the price in the sale of products. On this, as we shall see, the theory of distribution is founded. But if we look, not at the price dictated by reason, but at that which in fact is paid, that price is unquestionably nothing more than the result of the demand compared with the supply, and increases or decreases in direct proportion with the one and inverse proportion with the other. When the buyers become more numerous, while the quantity of goods remain the same, the price rises: and if there are more sellers, owing to a superabundance of goods, the price falls. If, *ceteris paribus*, buyers and sellers were to increase or decrease in the same proportion, then and then only would prices remain unaltered.

Nevertheless, taking the simple fact as it stands, and the natural inclinations of man, we must confess that the usual prices do, in their increase or decrease, tend always to approach the natural price, till they almost equal it. The general law is that the price of goods can neither fall below, nor permanently rise above the expenses of

---

[1] *Économia dei Popoli e degli Stati.* Introduzione, Cap. xii.

production. No man sells for the sake of selling, nor produces for the sake of producing. If he takes to a business, he does so for some gain or advantage. He may sometimes put up with a loss to get rid of goods that otherwise would not find a sale: but if he foresees that this sort of thing is likely to continue, he gives up the business and takes to another. If, on the contrary, he is able to get high prices and plenty of customers, others will take to the same sort of industry, and then competition will make the prices fall—but never below the cost of production for the reason above stated. The equalizing, however, of the effective price with the natural price will never be perfect, owing to the variable nature of the causes; and therefore contracts will always be regulated in practice by the law of proportionality between demand and supply.

"Whatever," says Minghetti, "the motives may be that induce men to act, the old formula, that the value of a thing is in the ratio of the supply and the demand, is the only formula certain in its indetermination, as being that which expresses neither more nor less than the state of mind of the two contracting parties."[1]

ARTICLE V.
CREDIT.

79. Credit, in Political Economy, means THE POWER TO DISPOSE OF CAPITAL, RECEIVED FROM ANOTHER, UNDER THE OBLIGATION OF RESTORING IT. This word is also used to signify CONFIDENCE IN THE FULFILMENT OF THE OBLIGATIONS ASSUMED BY THOSE TO WHOM THE CAPITAL IS GIVEN. And this confidence may depend either on the quality of the person under obligation, or on something agreed to as a pledge or guarantee, such as a mortgage. The former is called *personal* credit; the second *real*, because it rests on

[1] *Dell' Economia Pubblica*, &c. Lib. II.

the security of the thing, not on the honesty of the person. There are many conventional signs of restitution or payment of capital : but all of them may be expressed by the generic term, *bills of credit*, because all are equivalent to a promise of future payment, and therefore are accepted as representing money, on the assurance that, either at once, or else when they become due, they can be exchanged for gold or silver.[1] As goods are, in a manner, transported by money, so is money transported by letters of credit from one place to another, and from one time to another. The use of them has become so general that, excepting for small payments, they are used in commerce universally; so that they may be said to have almost entirely taken the place of money, and reestablished direct exchange without its inconveniencies.

80. Usually in trade, especially when it is on a great scale and between persons unknown to each other, those so-called notes are issued by banks, either public or private, which are instituted to facilitate the operations of commerce by means of conventional signs that represent money. Such banks inspire sufficient confidence, even when not guaranteed by the government, by reason of having money and great capitalists associated together in them—more confidence by far, than banks held by private persons or by a single firm : and besides offering a greater guarantee of honesty and solvency, they can dispose of greater sums of money with more facility. They are variously denominated according to the objects they have in view, but the most known are those called Circulating banks, from the notes they issue : or Discounting banks,

---

[1] The custom of representing by a paper the lending or depositing of money, on the faith of having it repaid, is very ancient. We read in the Bible that Tobias, "cum ... a Rege habuisset decem talenta argenti," lent this money to Gabelus under a bond in writing—*sub chirographo. Lib. Tobiæ* i. 16. 17.

from the discount which is given. Often the same bank carries on both sorts of business.

81. These banks have certainly rendered great services, especially to those who are in a large way of business, by giving facilities and security and by making circulation more rapid. It has been observed that raw cotton brought from India returns there woven and immensely increased in value, but in all the intermediate working it has passed through a very great number of hands, and been bought and sold over and over again. The trouble involved in all this buying and selling would have been enormous, if the payments had been made in metallic money.

82. Minghetti, after showing how credit quickens the circulation, and how the quickening of circulation increases wealth, says :—

"If we want any proof that a rapid circulation is of the utmost importance in the production of wealth, we can find it in times of public agitation and little security, when the circulation—I will not say ceases—but slackens in its course, and the producer, losing confidence, will not exchange his goods except for money, or for products of which he has present need. The consequence of this is that all classes of society suffer, as all the parts of the body become flaccid and infirm when the blood flows less quickly through the veins. Thus the production of wealth is stopped, the contractor is ruined, the capitalist no longer gets interest for his capital, and the workman offers in vain to work. This wretched condition of things is brought about by defect of circulation, particularly in nations accustomed to industry. If then circulation is of such importance, if circulation cannot work with money alone, and the supply would cost too much, it follows that exchanges should be made also between products, with the promise of future payment: and this is called working on credit. It is an operation so natural and simple, that it must have taken place in the earliest states of society, but was afterwards modified and diffused by taking away all limit, so to speak, of space and of time, and being concentrated in the institutions created to that end, acquired a marvellous power." [1]

Another benefit derived from the banks is this—they not only accumulate, through actionaries, vast sums for carrying out gigantic works, but also apply capital in advance by means of discount. Lastly, *si parva licet componere magnis*, some banks, such as Savings banks, are fruitful to the savings of the poor.

83. Against these benefits there are the evils caused by selfishness, greed and imprudence. A fatal capitalism takes its origin from credit and from the banks, in which it is embodied and personated. Minghetti says :—

" Let us suppose, amid such vicissitudes, that institutions giving credit, easy about supplying money, are many of them rivalling each other, and able to issue notes to any amount. The managers of these institutions, perceiving that the more notes they issue, and the more they restrict the metal money in reserve, the better it is for their own interest, will plunge wildly into business ; lower the rate of interest, in order to attract clients ; and by the offer of facilities will outdo each other in rashness and importunity. What happens then ? There is an artificial rise in prices : the relation between them changes unexpectedly : wages rise : speculation runs riot in the minds of all, when all have encouragement and means for the most risky enterprises. But the transient semblance of prosperity vanishes ; and the evils already pointed out, which, even within the limits of private fortunes, would be of the heaviest, then become a national calamity. Thus the institutions of credit, after having seized a power which even the Government could not resist, destroy the prosperity of a nation. Nor is the loss limited

---

[1] *Dell' Économia Pubblica*, &c. Lib. III.

to the wealthier classes. It recoils on the workman, the innocent victim of an evil that he could neither foresee nor provide against. And what shall we say of the moral ruin that follows, when honest labour and careful economy yield to a mad craving for riches— when industry is transformed into anxious and insane gambling, and commerce has become a contest of cupidity and insolence ? Of this sad spectacle North America has given us an instance—not once, but many times." [1]

Besides all this, these banks have a fundamental defect. They turn to the profit of a few private individuals that which ought to be for the advantage of society at large, and therefore of the State which represents it. The bills or notes payable to bearer issued by them, supply the place of money, which in consequence is saved and applied to other industrial operations. But for whose benefit is this saving of cash ? For the benefit of rich capitalists who keep the bank; and the advantage is excessive, owing to the privilege they have of putting in circulation a number of notes much beyond their metallic fund—for instance, two or three times as much. Certainly the banker deserves, over and above the repayment of expenses, to have some recompense for his services and a moderate profit on the capital invested. But the profit of such banks is exorbitant, without counting other lucrative affairs in which they are engaged. Some therefore think that the State should, to a great extent, and as much as possible, take to itself this credit-business, in order to make it safer and remedy the abuses.

84. Let us notice in conclusion the ambiguities to be carefully avoided. The first is the name of paper money, *papier monnaie*, which by some people is applied to Letters of Credit. This confuses two distinct and opposite concepts. A letter of credit is not money, but a representative sign of money; therefore to call it money is a

---

[1] *Dell' Économia Pubblica* &c. Lib. IV.

misuse of words, which in science is extremely dangerous :
for such misuse of words tends to false conceptions, and
false conceptions tend to bad consequences in practice.

The second ambiguity is that of confusing Letters of
Credit with the so-called *moneyed paper*, to which in times
of financial disorder governments have given a forced
currency. The difference between the one and the other
is very great. The former takes its origin from confidence, the latter from subjection to the executive that
wants effective money. The former is founded on a free
acceptance, the latter on compulsion by the government.
The letter of credit may be refused as payment : the
moneyed paper must be accepted. The one can at any time
be converted into money : the other remains as it was,
merely paper, till the government calls it in.

85. The introduction of such paper currency is always
calamitous to the country, for since the obligation to
accept it is limited to the inhabitants of that country, it
may be refused by foreigners, or only taken at a heavy
discount. The consequences are these—on the one hand,
exportation of metallic money ; on the other, an ever
increasing loss to the merchants through importation of
goods. Even home commerce is injured by it. Coining
money out of rubbish is very convenient to the coiner :
and therefore the government finds a strong temptation
therein. The value of it will fall by excess, and the price
of goods will rise.

And then—suppose a want of confidence in the
Government, owing to foreign wars or intestine commotions. Some of the mediæval rulers are justly blamed for
debasing the coinage : but surely the modern invention of
issuing paper currency, and enforcing its acceptance,
merits no less reprehension.

Nevertheless, when this paper currency has once been
introduced in a case of extreme necessity, it ought to be
withdrawn slowly and carefully. A sudden change of

that sort, for which the country is not prepared, and which would entail great sacrifices, may do more harm than good. We have an example of this in Italy. The forced currency was abolished at one stroke, leaving a debt of 640,000,000 francs, and burdening the exchequer with an annual interest of thirty millions. What was the consequence? The financial condition of the country and the government was worse than before. The loss of ten or twelve per cent discount on gold restricted at once the exportation of goods, which before, by reason of that discount, the merchants could afford to sell abroad at a lower price. A great part of the gold acquired at so great a cost has gone out of the country in payment of imported goods and of the interest on the aforesaid debt, almost all of which had been contracted abroad. Austria still enforces the currency of its notes, and its economic condition, though not prosperous, is less bad than that of Italy, where it has been suppressed.[1]

This much will be sufficient for our purpose. Those who wish to go further into these questions will consult the authors who have written specially about them.

---

[1] It may sometimes happen that the new interest which the State undertakes to pay is not a new burden, but a change of burden; that is, when the annual payment equals what was spent during the enforced currency, in procuring the gold required for paying the interest on the former debt. In which case the new expenditure would be balanced by not having to pay the previous interest, and the State would be freed from the misfortune of an enforced paper currency. But even then the sudden change is not justifiable unless all other circumstances are favourable.

CHAPTER V.

POPULATION.

 NCREASE of population is of itself good for the State, by enlarging and strengthening it. Multitude of inhabitants, rather than extent of territory, makes the great Powers great ; so that a depopulated country, though vast, is weak. Hence it is not surprising that governments, fearing a decrease of population, have sometimes given rewards for marriage. By the famous law *Papia Poppœa*, under Augustus, fathers of not less than three children were freed from the obligation of paying taxes. In modern times Louis XIV. exempted from paying taxes every man who married under the age of twenty. The celebrated Pitt proposed to bring in a bill for rewarding fathers of large families. Napoleon I. promised that whoever had seven male children should have one of them brought up at the cost of the State. But then, the mere multiplication of men and women is not sufficient. You must enable them to live in some sort of comfort, or you will only have a crowd of paupers ; so that it would be a case of *Multiplicasti gentem, et non multiplicasti lætitiam.* [1]

And this is the point of view from which Economists consider population—viz. how to provide the means of living—which however is the very point on which, generally speaking, they talk the greatest amount of nonsense.

---

[1] *Isaias* ix. 3.

ARTICLE I.

MALTHUS'S THEORY.

87. The first man who treated this question fully in the above-mentioned sense, putting forth a theory that afterwards was accepted by nearly all the most renowned Economists, was the Englishman, Malthus, in his famous work, *An Essay on Population.* "The name of Malthus," says Pellegrino Rossi, "is as much associated with the theory of population, as Galileo's is with the motion of the earth, or Harvey's with the circulation of the blood."[1] His doctrine is, briefly, as follows :

The living beings that dwell here below tend by reason of their prodigious fecundity to reproduce themselves without any limit. One species of plant, if all its germs were productive, would in a few centuries fill the whole earth : and animals would increase likewise. But this multiplication of plants and animals is checked by want of nourishment and by continual destruction ; for animals feed on vegetables and on other animals. Man, too, has this power of propagating ; so that the increase of population is always tending to exceed the means of subsistence.[2]

Malthus lays down the proportion in which the increase of population and of means to feed it stand towards each other. According to a table by Euler, he tells us, calculated on a mortality of one in 36 individuals, if the births are to the deaths in the ratio of 3 to 1, the period of doubling would be only $12\frac{4}{7}$. This, he says, is not a mere hypothesis, but a fact verified in a short time in more than one country. Sir W. Pelly thought it possible that a population, favoured by peculiar circumstances, might

---

[1] *Corso d'Économia Politica.* Primo semestre, lezione xvii.

[2] Some would say *existence*, as being a more comprehensive word, because we require clothing and shelter, as well as food : but this is a question of words.

double itself in ten years. But to be certain of not over-stepping the bounds of truth, Malthus takes a less rapid rate, as to which all evidence agrees ; and he affirms that the population, if there be no obstacle in the way of its increase, will double itself every twenty-five years, thus increasing in geometrical proportion.[1]

It is not so with the means of subsistence : for, though the progress of that is not easy to determine, slower it certainly is. A thousand million men, says Malthus, would double in twenty-five years through procreation just like one thousand ; but the food required for the greater number is not so easy to get. Man, he remarks, is necessarily limited to space : and when acre after acre is taken in until all the cultivatable soil is occupied, the increase of production must necessarily depend on the improvement of what is already in cultivation. Naturally, therefore, its productive capacity, instead of increasing, is always diminishing. Taking the earth as it is, he goes on to infer that, even under circumstances most favourable to human industry, the means of subsistence could not increase in more than arithmetical proportion.[2] He first applies this to England. Then he takes the whole earth, excluding emigration ; and supposing the population to reach a thousand millions, he concludes that the human race would increase as 1, 2, 4, 8, 16, 32, 64, 128, 256, and the food as 1, 2, 3, 4, 5, 6, 7, 8, 9. Thus, he says, in two centuries the population would be to the supply of food as 256 to 9,—in three as 4,095 to 13, and in two thousand years quite past calculation.[3]

This is called the principle of population : but a certain balance is always kept, or soon reestablished, between the population and its means of subsistence by reason of powerful obstacles that limit the former. The obstacles are of two classes, *preventive* and *repressive*. The first of

---

[1] *Essay on Population.* Bk. I., ch. i. [2] Ibid. [3] Ibid.

these checks the excess of births through abstention from too early marriage : the second increases the number of deaths through poverty, and those physical and moral evils that result from it.

88. In the two first books he shows this from history, taking all nations, barbarous and civilized. In the third he examines the remedies vainly put in force to impede the mischievous action of the repressive obstacles. Hence, in the first chapter of the fourth book, he says that in the actual condition of all societies examined by him the natural increase appears to have always been effectually checked by some repressive obstacles, while neither governments, nor emigration, nor beneficent institutions, nor the wisest direction of industry, can impede the continuous action of such obstacles, which, under one form or another, keep back the population within its proper limits. This he considers to be a *law* of nature, to which *we must submit* : so that the only thing to be done is to choose the obstacle least injurious to virtue and well-being. These obstacles he reduces to three classes,—moral restraint, vice, and poverty,—and of course prefers the first, because, given that the population must be kept in check by some obstacle, a prudent foresight is evidently better than the pressure of want and suffering. Therefore for all those who, if they married, would sink into poverty, which is a repressive obstacle to the excess of population, Malthus prescribes, as a preventive obstacle, chaste abstention from marriage, which he calls moral restraint : and he says that, till we have some means of providing for the maintenance. of a family, moral restriction will be a duty.[1] Here he pulls up : but, many of his followers, more logical or less cautious, judged that moral restraint, as laid down by him, was not sufficient, and ought to be introduced within the precincts of Matrimony ; and this is the most abominable part of the system.

---

[1] Ibid. Book IV., ch. iii.

THE PRINCIPLE OF POPULATION.

89. A little consideration will show that Malthus's principle of population is afflicted with a grave paralogism. He tells us that while the population, if no obstacle impedes it, increases in geometric proportion, the means of subsistence cannot increase in more than arithmetical proportion.

In the first member of this formula he considers the simple tendency, whilst in the second he takes the tendency as impeded by obstacles. The comparison, therefore, is illogically put. As to the effect of the pure tendency, the reproduction of man is less than the reproduction of other living beings. One apple-tree gives a great many apples in one crop, and one hen a great many eggs in the course of the year : but from one human pair, except in the very rare case of twins, only one child is produced in the same time. Therefore, taking the effect of the pure tendency in each of the terms, the proportion ought at least to be the same.

90. This objection occurred to us at once on reading Malthus, and we afterwards found it in Sismondi, though he was otherwise a Malthusian :

" Malthus tells us," he says, " that the population may be doubled in twenty-five years, or in geometric proportion, while the labour and care employed on the already cultivated soil cannot be more than quantities continually decreasing. Given that in the first five-and-twenty years the produce of the fields is doubled, in the second it will hardly produce a third more, or rather less, and then a fourth, and then a fifth. Thus the progress of the supply will be only in arithmetical progression ; and in the course of two centuries, while the population increases as 1, 2, 4, 8, 16, 32, 64, 128, the supply of food will only increase as 1, 2, 3, 4, 5, 6, 7, 8. This reasoning, that serves as the basis of Malthus's system, and to which he recurs all through his book, seems to me thoroughly sophistical. In opposition to the positive increase of animals and vegetables in a circumscribed place and under circumstances more and more unfavourable, he puts the possible increase of the human race, taken in the abstract and without regard to circumstances. But we cannot compare them so. In the abstract the geometrical progression of vegetables is much more rapid than that of animals, and the multiplication of animals is much more rapid than the multiplication of man." [1]

91. The answer to this would be, that Malthus was right but expressed himself badly—that he meant concrete multiplication, not abstract, because he put America as an example. But, even if so understood, his formula is false, and to prove this we need only take the example of North America, on which he relies.

92. This, we shall be told, was accidental, and happened so, because the people lived in a new country amid boundless tracts of tillable land. But we cannot find a country in Europe where there are not parts uncultivated and parts insufficiently cultivated. Say tells us that in his days France, where agriculture flourishes, had twenty-two million acres uncultivated, whilst of the cultivated fields the most was not made: " When you think," he says, " that in France the corn-fields do not produce, on an average, more than 5 or 6 seeds from one, whilst in the opinion of good practical farmers they ought to yield much more ; that doing away with fallows and laying down clover in the fields which even now have one year's rest out of three in the greater part of France, would marvellously multiply sheep, cattle, manure, and butcher's meat ... you will see that France, without having recourse to importation of any food, is yet very far from

---

[1] *Nouveaux Principes d'Économie Politique.* Liv. I, ch. 3.

having as many inhabitants as it would be able to feed." [1]
What he says of France is applicable to the rest of Europe,
where there is much uncultivated land. When we
remember that besides this there are enormous tracts of
virgin soil in North and South America, Australia, New
Guinea, Sumatra, Borneo, Central Asia, Central Africa,
&c., the human race is not likely to be starved out at
present. Besides which, industry and commerce can and
do supply the deficiency by the importation of food.

93. The Malthusian dogma is false at the foundation.
God said to man, *Crescite, et multiplicamini, et replete
terram.* But this has not yet been fulfilled ; for even
now three-fifths of the globe are uninhabited. Now we
cannot suppose that God, Who is infinitely wise and
prescient, and Who willed the multiplication of the human
race, did not supply the means necessary for its existence.
That in fact He did supply them is evident in the fertility
of the earth and the abundance of animals. To say the
contrary is to blaspheme Divine Providence, and attempt
to put Almighty God in contradiction with Himself.

"Assuredly," says Romagnosi, "it does not require
much wit nor much travelling to show one that, if we are
without food, we must die, and that only those who have
it will remain alive : but I am unable to see how it can be
generally supposed that nature (or rather the divine
wisdom) was so improvident as not to balance human life
with the means of subsistence. I understand of course
that if provisions run short when a ship is out at sea, the
people who are shut up within it must die of starvation :
but I do not understand why, when the human race lives
by agriculture, hunting, fishing, grazing ; gets farinaceous
food even from Africa and America ; exchanges goods for
those of every nation, and is able to go where food is, we

---

[1] *Cours d'Économie Politique Pratique*, Partie vi., Chap. 6.

must wish for a pestilence when population increases, and condemn the poor to a forced celibacy." [1]

94. Jean-Baptiste Say propounded the opinion that for every new loaf of bread a man is born. I should rather say that the more men are born the more bread there is, because there is more work to be done. The Economists, in order to show that increase of population necessarily exceeds the increase of means to supply it with food, and therefore must bring poverty, say that, while the human race is always fruitful and young, the earth is becoming barren and growing old. But the fruits of the earth are not the only food of man, but also fish, birds, sheep, cattle, game. *Omne quod movetur et vivit, erit vobis in cibum ; quasi olera viventia tradidi vobis omnia.* [2]

Now these species neither grow old, nor become barren ; and if the earth does, cultivation renews it and makes it fertile. The Dutch have shown what can be done in that way. Capital is required, of course ; but the world has never been without capital. New production makes new capital, and new capital helps to make new productions. Therefore, instead of the Malthusian formula, let us take the divine formula. *Replete terram, et subjicite eam* : " Fill the earth and subdue it," to get food out of it. These two terms are by divine ordinance proportionate. The increase of the human race has no assignable limit, though it is not the same everywhere and always : but during the interval required for doubling it the increase of vegetables and animals, if wisely promoted by human labour, can not only be doubled, but tripled. The earth will never fail to support man, so long as he is able and willing to cultivate it well. And where there is not

---

[1] *Opere di R. G. D. Romagnosi*, Vol. vi., p. 1.—*Economia Politica e Statistica Civile.* Dottrina Economica in generale, Su la crescente popolazione.

[2] *Genesis*, ix. 3.

enough, the want is supplied by exchange of goods : insomuch that manufacturing and commercial nations are very
often the best off.   What is wanting is not the produce of
the earth, but its fair distribution.   Provisions are plentiful in the market : but the money to buy them with is not
always forthcoming.   We had better think about a just
distribution of wealth and a fair distribution of wages,
instead of dreaming over weak schemes and proposing
remedies that are unnatural and cruel. [1]

Article III.

Moral Constraint.

95.   Malthus is reproached for wishing to enforce the
celibacy of the poor.   His followers call this charge a
calumny ; and he himself denies it, affirming that he had
always said the reverse, always reprobated any sort of
legal prohibition, whenever it was suggested to him.[2]
Nevertheless, his own principles unquestionably lead
thereto : for if, as he pretends, marriage were a social
crime in the poor, the government would have a right to
forbid it as a public injury.   And so we find this legal
prohibition not only recommended by various Economists, but actually put in force in some governments,
as, for instance, in Germany.   This is a tyrannical abuse
of power, which violates one of the most fundamental
rights of man—that of having a companion to share
with him the joys and sorrows of life.   But modern

---

[1] It will occur at once to the Catholic reader, that when a
whole population is truly Catholic, excessive increase is greatly
and beneficially checked by the proportionate number of religious
vocations.   The Economists are shrewd about figures, ready
with statistics, and fertile in expedients ; but they forget
Almighty God.—*Translator's Note.*

[2] Bk. III., Chap. 7.

civilisation ignores the fact that there are rights prior to the State, independent of the State—rights which the civil power cannot justifiably touch.

96. Wishing to deter the poor from marrying and consequently having children, Malthus reprobates the charitable institutions that relieve indigent fathers, or rescue foundlings. He tells us that we should leave the poor man who marries, and whom he calls culpable, to the punishment which nature inflicts on him. That man, he says, has acted against the clear dictates of reason, and cannot accuse anyone but himself. Parish relief should be closed against him; and, for the sake of humanity, private benevolence ought to be kept within bounds. He should be made to know that the laws of nature, i.e. the laws of God, have condemned him to live hard, as a punishment for having violated them, and that he has no sort of claim on society for the smallest portion of food above what he can get by work.[1] This is what Malthus says, and he is extolled by his followers as eminently philanthropical. May God preserve the faithful from such philanthropy !

97. In the first edition he had expressed himself still more savagely. He had said that when a man is born into a world already occupied, if his family cannot maintain him, and society cannot find use for his labour, he has no right to any' food, being superfluous in the world. At nature's banquet, says Malthus, there is no place for him. So nature orders him to get out of the way, and promptly enforces the order.[2] When Economists

---

[1] Bk. IV. Chap. 8.

[2] There was such an outcry against this atrocious position, that Malthus had to suppress it in the later editions, and nearly all his followers took care not to quote it. Garnier did, but only for the purpose of defending it, if possible. See his book, *Del Principio di Popolazione.* Chap. x.

talk in this way, who can wonder at the progress of socialism ?

In the second part of this treatise we shall have to speak of public and private beneficence, and see the folly of the Malthusian ideas on that point. Here we shall only say this much :—Malthus and his school, by isolating the poor man, taking from him absolutely all hope of succour from others, and holding him up to public execration as a violator of the natural and the divine law, as one who is unworthy even of commiseration, would, indirectly at least, compel him to remain in the state of celibacy.

98.   That a man, be he rich or poor, should, before he marries, think of the expenses that marriage entails, and measure his own ability to meet them, is what we knew before, without being taught by Malthus; but to make this law of prudence a rigorous obligation and a binding duty is too much.   To be that, it must correspond with some right; but what right would the poor man violate by marrying ?   Not his wife's; for she has freely consented to the marriage, and *volenti non fit injuria*.   His children's then ?   Wait till they are born, before you attribute rights to them.   Till then, their existence is uncertain.   If all marriages were fruitful, which they are not, the offspring of them would still be a *futuribile*. Now these Economists not only admit the right of one who may be in the future, but rank them before those of real living people.   If, however, it pleases them to do so, they ought to admit furthermore that this future offspring has the right of coming into existence ; and, that being admitted, what right have they to suppose that the said offspring will not prefer to have been born, in order to enjoy, if not the temporal life of the body, at any rate the immortal life of the soul, instead of for ever not being ?   At least put the question to them before you condemn their future parents to celibacy.   If not, you

take the responsibility of an unjust act, by thwarting them in the free choice of their rights. But the fact is that our Malthusians, with a few honourable exceptions, recognize no other life than the present, nor any good beyond its comforts.

Let us however assume for the moment, that a poor man is bound by the natural and the divine law not to marry, unless he foresee that he will be able to maintain a future family. How many children must he foresee, so as to be within the rule? Malthus complains of men marrying and having five or six children, when their wages will only maintain two:[1] but, according to that, the number of men who are justified in marrying would be amazingly restricted. For, if a man who has the means of supporting two children is wrong in not foreseeing that he may have half-a-dozen, another man, who could maintain half-a-dozen, has no right to marry, because he may have ten or twelve. In short the conclusion would be this : that the more or less rich would have the privilege of marrying and be freed from all obligations of charity to the poor.

---

[1] Ibid. Bk. IV. Chap. 3.

CHAPTER VI.

THE THREE ECONOMIC SYSTEMS.

E have not yet spoken of the three systems usually mentioned in Political Economy, because they apparently required the foregoing chapters; therefore we shall speak of them now. They are :—the Mercantile system, otherwise called Commercial ; the Agrarian or Physiocratical system, and the Industrial system, or system of labour understood in a general sense. We shall briefly discuss each ; and since we can judge of them by merely recurring to what has already been laid down, the present article may, in that respect, be considered almost a summary of what has preceded it.

Article I.

The Mercantile System.

100. The teachers of this system, which for a long while occupied the minds of rulers, and even now is not entirely put aside, maintain that the wealth of every nation consists in the abundance of gold and silver which it possesses. They suppose that wealth means money, and that money disposes of all industries, because industries arise from labour paid, and fall away without it. Money, they say, makes a nation powerful and feared by enabling it to feed great armies and bear the expenses of a long war ; so that every government should try to increase the money of the State as much as possible. This requires

gold or silver mines at home, or commerce with other nations, to whom it sells much and from whom it buys little. A nation without gold or silver must get money by foreign commerce, because home commerce does not increase its money, but only makes it pass from hand to hand within the confines of the country or nation itself. It may indeed enrich certain private individuals at the expense of others, but it cannot augment the quantity of national riches, which remains the same. Money must come from without, through a commerce that sends little of it out of the country and brings in much; which cannot happen unless the exports exceed the imports, because money pays for the excess. If other merchandise were given instead of money, there would not be excess, but equality. Hence the necessity of calculating what is called the Balance of Commerce, or the relation between exports and imports.

And since manufactured goods are more valuable than raw material, it follows, according to the mercantile system, that the government ought to favour manufactures in preference to agriculture, impede the exportation of raw material, and promote its importation; so that, when its value has been increased by working it up, it may be sold to foreigners.

This system was also called *Colbertism*; not that Colbert was its author, but because he applied it to France under Louis XIV.

"This system," says Minghetti, "to which the name of 'Mercantile' was improperly given, took possession of men's minds for a long time. And though we do not find it expounded methodically in any work (because Economy had no scientific form then) bits of it are found in the writers of the sixteenth and seventeenth centuries; and most of the thinkers, it seems, were convinced by it. As in private life the man who has the most money, whether in gold or silver, is considered in society to be the richest, so it was, they said, with nations; and thus they took the representative sign of wealth for wealth itself. The first consequence of this conception was the necessity of looking out for mines, appropriating them, working them on their own account, to the exclusion of others. Those nations that did not succeed in obtaining these living sources of wealth, must try to get some from others that do possess them, and therefore direct their efforts to attracting the gold and silver of other States. But how? By conquest, if you are powerful enough; and if not, by commerce. Strive to supply another nation with much merchandise, and be supplied with little. That nation must pay the difference in money, and impoverishing itself, will enrich you. Hence the famous expression, 'Commercial Balance,' which gave rise to so many other ambiguous and fallacious expressions. To bring down the balance on your own side, you must buy little and sell much, thus sufficing for yourself and producing in excess. From which premisses come the following conclusions :—1^0. To put heavy duties on manufactured goods imported. 2^0. To put heavy duties likewise on raw materials exported, so that it may not be worked up elsewhere and reduce the amount produced at home. 3^0. To put premiums on the exportation of manufactured goods. 4^0. To put premiums on the importation of raw material. 5^0. To prohibit absolutely the exportation of gold and silver. 6^0. To favour and subsidize those who found new national manufactures. 7^0. To associate and endow with privileges and monopolies private persons who, if apart, are not able to carry out certain commercial enterprises. 8^0. To possess colonies, and treat them as instruments of wealth to the mother country, retailing there our own products and keeping out the products of other countries." [1]

The above is only a paraphrase, almost a translation, of

---

[1] *Dell' Economia Politica*, &c.   Lib. I.

the passage with which Adam Smith concludes the first chapter of his fourth book, in which he examines and refutes the preceding systems of Political Economy. We have quoted it in preference to the original, as being clearer.

101. All Economists agree in rejecting this system. Its chief defect seems to be that it ignores the nature and the true office of money. Wealth, as we have shown elsewhere,[1] consists in the *utility* of things, not in their *value*. Now money, as money, is value, being exchange-able for all things as their equivalent. What utility it has is by reason of the material, gold or silver, which is valuable as such; but as money it only serves to facilitate exchanges by equivalence of value. Money is, no doubt, a part of wealth, but it is not wealth itself. Wealth con-sists in abundance of things useful to life; and that may be where money is scarce. *Ditiores sunt*, says St. Thomas, commenting on Aristotle, *qui abundant necessariis ad vitam quam qui abundant denariis.* [2] If you go into a country, and find the inhabitants well fed, well clothed and well lodged according to their condition, you say, " These people are well off," without thinking what money they have or have not; and your inference is right. For you look at the end, not at the means; and the end of wealth is consumption, because the consumption of useful things, not their exchange, is what satisfies the wants of man.

It signifies little, then, whether the balance of commerce does or does not give to the nation an excess in money, because money, as such, is good just so far as it serves to buy other things.

"Goods," Adam Smith wisely remarks, "can serve many other purposes besides purchasing money, but money

---

[1] Chap. I. "Wealth."
[2] *In Librum I Politicorum.* Lect. vii.

can serve no other purpose besides purchasing goods. Money, therefore, necessarily runs after goods, but goods do not always or necessarily run after money. The man who buys does not always mean to sell again, but frequently to use or consume ; whereas he who sells always means to buy again. The one may frequently have done the whole, but the other can never have done more than one half of his business. It is not for its own sake that men desire money, but for the sake of what they can purchase with it." [1]

102. And, indeed, it is evident that exchange is properly between goods and goods, money being the vehicle that transfers them. If you sell a bullock, you like to get your money for him, because you like to have the things that money can procure : but you might procure those things by giving other things in exchange ; and this diminishes the necessity of money.

" If," says Adam Smith, " the materials of manufacture are wanted, industry must stop. If provisions are wanted, the people must starve. But if money is wanted, barter will supply its place, though with a good deal of inconveniency. Buying and selling upon credit, and the different dealers compensating their credits with one another once a month, or once a year, will supply it with less inconveniency. A well-regulated paper-money will supply it not only without any inconveniency, but, in some cases, with some advantages. Upon every account, therefore, the attention of government never was so unnecessarily employed, as when directed to watch over the preservation or increase of the quantity of money in any country." [2]

Certain it is, that commerce, to be safe, requires plenty of money : but it ought not to exceed the amount required

---

[1] *Wealth of Nations*, Bk. IV., Chap. 1.   [2] Ibid.

for circulation. An excess would bring it down; and it would have to be exported into foreign countries, where its value is greater. To make the greatest number of exchanges with the least possible quantity of coin, is now an established maxim, because the money thus saved can be advantageously used in other ways. Gold and silver cannot be wanting where there is abundance of goods, being themselves goods and therefore exchangeable for others. " A country," says Adam Smith, "that has wherewithal to buy wine, will always get the wine which it has occasion for, and a country that has wherewithal to buy gold and silver, will never be in want of those metals. They are to be bought for a certain price, like all other commodities, and as they are the price of all other commodities, so all other commodities are the price of those metals." [1]

It is folly, then, in a government to care for nothing but the increase of money, when it should rather be trying to promote every sort of industry, and increase those products of nature and art that truly constitute the prosperity of a nation.

ARTICLE II.

THE AGRARIAN SYSTEM.

103. What we have just said was understood, but imperfectly, by Quesnay and his school, who attributed the production of wealth to the forces of nature only; and therefore, though designated at first as Economists, they were afterwards more correctly called *Physiocrats*, from φύσις, 'nature,' and κράτος, 'power.' Properly speaking, they say, the cause of wealth is to be found in the net product, i.e. in that portion of it which, after the productive work, remains beyond the expenses of production. The rest is remunerative. This net product is

---

[1] *Wealth of Nations*, Bk. IV., Chap. 1.

given by natural agents only through agriculture, which here is understood to include the breeding of sheep, cattle, &c. : and therefore they infer that agriculture is to be considered as the only source of wealth. " The earth," says Quesnay, " is the only source of wealth ; and agriculture is that which multiplies it.[1] Thus manufacture and commerce only pay back what has been anticipated for the purpose of production." " There is no increase of wealth," he says, " in the works of industry, because the value of such works does not increase beyond the price of the goods which workmen consume."[2] The same is to be said of trading ; so that the artizan and the trader do not, properly speaking, deserve to be called producers. The true producers are they who cultivate the soil. The rest are unfruitful.

" The nation," says Quesnay, " is reducible to three classes of citizens—the productive class, the class of proprietors, and the unproductive class. The productive class is that which, by cultivating the soil, revives the income of the nation, anticipates the expenses of agricultural labour, and pays the rent to the landowners. Depending on this class all the labour done there and all the expenses incurred are included, even to the sale at first hand of the produce, through which sale the value of the annual reproductions of the nation's wealth is known. The class of proprietors includes the sovereign, the landowners, and the receivers of tithes. This class lives on the rent or net produce of cultivation, which is paid annually over and above the expense and profit of production. The unproductive class is composed of all who live otherwise than on agriculture, whose expenses are paid by the productive class and by the proprietor-class,

---

[1] See his *Maxims of Economic Government*, extracted from his article on Grain. [2] Ibid.

who in their turn get their rents from the productive class."

104. If the mercantile system ignored the nature of *money*, the agrarian system ignores the nature of *economic produce*. In Economy to produce wealth is not only to produce useful things, but also to make things useful that were not so, or increase the utility of things that were useful. Now if agriculture produces useful things, other industries make or increase the utility of things. To call them unproductive is a misuse of language. We get flax from the soil and wool from the sheep; but the weavers who make linen and cloth, produce in the flax and in the wool a utility that was only potential in them, and therefore such workers cannot be called unproductive.

True it is that agriculture, by the fact of furnishing us with food, answers to the most essential of human wants. In that point of view it is pre-eminent, is preferable to every other industry, and deserves the protection of the government. Moreover it is the foundation of other industries by furnishing them with raw material. But this does not show it to be the sole producer. It gives new substances, but other industries give new modifications of substances; and modifications are true effects that before were not.

105. Adam Smith remarks that if manufacturers and traders did no more than reproduce the equivalent of what they have consumed, their industry could not be truly called productive, but only like a marriage from which a son and daughter are born, and which therefore would not increase the population, nor diminish it. Nor is it true that agriculture alone gives a net produce, or excess beyond the expenses of production. Were it so, no one would be enriched by manufactures and commerce; which is in direct contradiction to experience, as any one may see, who will take the trouble of comparing the profits derived from land with the immense fortunes made by great speculators and traders.

And this is true, not only of individuals, but of the whole social body. Through commerce and manufactures, as Adam Smith says, you can get more food than your own country can actually produce: and since a small quantity of manufactured goods will buy a great quantity of raw material, a commercial and manufacturing nation can get a great quantity of rural produce from other countries for a small quantity of its own manufactured produce, while a nation without commerce and manufacture is obliged usually to give much for little. Here there is clearly an increase of wealth, a net produce, economically considered.

Article III.

The Industrial System.

106. The mercantile system gave the first place in Economy to manufactures and trade. The rural or physiocratic system considered agriculture to be the one source of wealth. The industrial system lays down that labour, of whatsoever sort it may be, is the cause of wealth. It is called industrial because industry, in its generic sense, is nothing but human labour applied to any work that has for its end the production of wealth.

107. The origin of this system is usually attributed to Adam Smith, from whom the later Economists appear to have taken it.

"Smith," says the eminent Professor Périn, " by creating the true theory of production, caused science to make the greatest progress that it ever made by means of one man. He restored to manufacturing and commercial labour, which the Physiocrats called unproductive, the true office in the production of wealth. He established the facts that productive power is not exclusively in the soil, and that labour is the principal agent of production. He showed how labour is applied to the primary materials furnished by the earth, how it uses the forces of nature, and so directs them, that useful results proceed therefrom. He analysed the cause of labour's productive power, and pointed out with wonderful sagacity the principle and the effects of the division of labour, which before had scarcely been mentioned. Turgot had indeed perceived these things, but only touched on them at the beginning of his *Reflections*. From this fact, to which we must continually refer in the theory of exchange and distribution, Adam Smith rightly took his point of departure in his *Enquiry into the Wealth of Nations ;* and he went on to show how capital cooperates with production in supplying workmen with primary materials and means of subsistence, and how it is formed by means of saving. The theory of value was established by Adam Smith on its true basis. He distinguished the value in *use* (usefulness) from the value in *exchange,* and showed how the latter is regulated in all its fluctuations by the laws of demand and supply. He looked for the elements that compose the price of things, and showed how the variations that happen in the exchangeable value of these elements, influence the price of the products. Explaining the mechanism of exchange, he determined the nature of money and the part that it plays in economic bargains, and laid the foundations of the theory of credit."[1]

108. However true this may be, we must remark that of the two factors of wealth, nature and work, Smith takes the latter almost exclusively. He sometimes hints at natural agents ; but when they have had the honour of

---

[1] *Les Doctrines Économiques depuis un Siècle,* par Charles Périn. Ch. 3.

being named, they are noticed by him no more, as if man and his labour were everything in Economics. And yet nature has the principal share in the production of wealth; for, after all, every useful product is but an effect of the active and passive qualities of bodies made use of by the art and hand of man. Take, for instance, the bread that we eat. There is the fertility of the earth in which it grows, the hardness of the stone that grinds it, the liquid-ness of the water that mixes with the flour, the heat of the fire that makes the oven hot, &c. In all this the effect is principally and directly due to the efficacy of nature. Men work: but their work is to use the natural forces of bodies, combining them together and opportunely applying them, to secure the result required. And so it is in every other product of human industry.

109. This exaltation of work at the cost of excluding nature is a grave defect in science, which ought to look upwards for the first causes of things, and recognize their importance. It is a bad habit that makes a man forget the goodness of God, to whom we owe all the good things that we have. Moreover it leads to evil consequences in the social order, as Bastiat remarked. "What," he says, "are the means that we have to provide for our wants? It seems evident to me that there are two—nature and work—the gifts of God and the fruits of our efforts, or, if you like, the application of our faculties to the things that nature has placed at our service. No school, that I know of, has attributed to nature *alone* the satisfaction of our wants. Such an assertion is sufficiently disproved by ex-perience, and we have no need of studying Political Economy to find out that the intervention of our faculties is necessary thereto. But there are schools that have given this privilege to labour only. Their axiom is: *All wealth whatsoever comes from labour*, and *labour is wealth*. I cannot do less than point out that these formulas, taken

literally, have led to enormous errors of doctrine." [1]

Among these errors we must include Socialism, to which the exaggerated and exclusive exaltation of labour gives occasion, or at least support. But of this further on. Just now it is sufficient to have shown how the first germ of this foolish doctrine, which, ignoring God, supposes that our wants are satisfied by man alone, is to be found in Adam Smith's work. "We," says Sismondi, "profess with Adam Smith, that *Labour is the sole origin of wealth*."[2]

ARTICLE IV.

A CURIOUS THEORY LAID DOWN BY BASTIAT.

110. Bastiat, as we have just said, acknowledged the importance of natural agents in the production of wealth; but, in discussing the exchange of these products, he lays down a curious theory, which became still more curious through other people's additions. In exchange, he says, the utility proceeding from the forces and qualities of the object is always given gratuitously; but that which is paid for by money or other merchandise is only the

---

[1] *Harmonies Économiques*, Ch. 3. Hence it appears that Minghetti is deceived when he includes Bastiat among those who assert that labour is the only source of wealth. He says: "Adam Smith saw clearly this cooperation of natural forces and human labour, and pointed it out in many places: in many places he appears to consider labour only. This is the reason why some of his followers contradistinguished the school of the Scotch philosopher by this maxim, that labour is the only source of wealth. Nevertheless the men who most concisely formulated this latter opinion were Carey and Bastiat."—*Dell' Economia Pubblica*. Lib. ii. p. 140.

[2] *Nouveaux Principes d'Économie Politique*. Liv. I. Ch. 3.

effort, or fatigue, or in other words the labour, employed
to produce it. Those forces and qualities proceed from
nature; and nature does not sell, but gives. Man's labour
exacts a reward: so that the value of things is in proportion to it :

"La coopération de la nature est essentiellement
gratuite. La coopération de l'homme, intellectuelle ou
matérielle, échangée ou non, collective ou solitaire, est
essentiellement onéreuse, ainsi que l'implique ce mot
même 'Effort.'" [1]

111.   Carey, an American Economist, has the honour
of having made this discovery, seeing that he announced
it in his writings twelve years before Bastiat had done so;
but it seems hardly worth while to dispute about an
invention, which, however ingenious, is contrary to reason
and fact.

Only in the case of things not appropriable is the work
of man reckoned exclusively; as, for instance, if you were
to recompense the services of some one who had carried
water for you from a distant well, or the diver who, des-
cending into the depths of the sea, pays for the air which
some one pumps down to him. But the value of what we
call property is in virtue not only of the labour taken to
produce it, but also of its intrinsic utility, and is paid for,
as such.   He who gives what is his own, deserves to have
something in exchange for what he gives.   Certainly
nature, or rather God, the author of nature, does not
exact a recompense, because He has no need of our goods:
Deus meus es tu, quoniam bonorum meorum non eges. [2]
He only exacts obedience for His sovereignty, and gratitude
for His benefits.   But a thing of which you are justly in
possession, (a pearl for instance, that you have found in
an oyster-shell) you can justly sell as being useful, though

---

[1]   *Harmonies Économiques.*   Ch. 3. De la Valeur.
[2]   *Psalm* xv. 2.

its utility cost you no labour. Bastiat's or Carey's theory supposes that the products of nature and the forces inherent in it are not appropriable : and this favours Socialism, against which the theory was invented.

112. Besides being false, this theory becomes (*sit venia verbo*) somewhat ridiculous : for when the objection is put that sometimes things of great value cost their owners little or nothing in labour (for instance, a diamond found on the sea-shore,) Bastiat replies that in purchase we do not regard the labours of the seller, but the saving of the purchaser's labour. According to this, people are not paid for the effort of production, but for the effort of *reproduction*, and not even future reproductions, but repro ductions that might be in the future. So that if you buy a fish, you pay for saving yourself the labour that you might have had to undergo, if you had fished for it in the sea.

When it was objected that some things are not reproducible (for instance a vintage wine of unequalled goodness,) Ferrara replied that we must distinguish between *physical* and *economic* reproduction—the reproduction of products, not identical, but analagous and suppletory—according to which, and not according to physical production, the price is regulated. But anyone may see that this is mere straw splitting. Moreover, it was first said that in purchases we only pay for the seller's labour : and now, according to this doctrine, the remuneration is paid to the vendor for liberating the purchaser from the trouble of reproducing something, whether the thing reproduced be like what it reproduces, or only adapted to supply its place. These two statements differ widely.

Setting aside, then, these fantastical theories, we say that in exchanges we have to consider the proper value of the object, in relation to the utility that it brings and the wish to possess it. That utility, though resulting from forces gratuitously given by nature, is nevertheless fixed

and incorporated in a determined object, and therefore is
capable of appropriation.   We shall have to speak of this
when we come to the rights of property. Certain it is that
he who sells us anything saves us the labour of producing
it : but this is a natural effect of exchange, and not the
reason that determines its price.   The price is determined
by the value attributed to the object, and by the free consent of the two contracting parties, the purchaser and the
seller.

Part II.—Distribution.

1. Having discussed the production of wealth, we must now pass on to its distribution; which is much more important, because production without distribution would be useless. About this question the founder of economic science was silent. "Smith," says the illustrious Professor Périn, "had displayed a truly powerful mind in determining the laws of production and the laws of exchange; but he had not perceived at all the graver difficulties of the economic order, *viz.*, those that concern the distribution of wealth. To say the truth, his book was but the theory of production. The theory of distribution had yet to be founded." [1]

To this question David Ricardo, an Englishman, principally devoted himself; and all the later Economists followed in his wake.

We shall begin by treating of property, because without that we should fail to see how there could be a right to equitable distribution. Nay, we could not even conceive a cause of wealth. The idea of wealth includes that of appropriation.

---

[1] *Les Doctrines Économiques depuis un Siècle.* Chap. 3.

CHAPTER I.

PROPERTY.

PROPERTY is understood to mean that which any one possesses as a thing belonging to him exclusively, and of which he may dispose at will. This right of possessing, or right of having property, holds good with respect to those things only that are limited, and, when belonging to one person, cannot belong to another. Things that are inexhaustible, such as air and light, cannot constitute property, because they are so possessed or enjoyed by each that all can possess them equally.

ARTICLE I.

WHAT SORT OF PROPERTY IS HERE MEANT.

3. The conception of property includes personal as well as real property. The shipowner, the capitalist, the merchant, are proprietors. Indeed natural forces, and science and art, are sometimes called property. But the word is more usually understood to mean real property, and especially land. "When," says Droz, "we speak of proprietors, we almost always mean the owners of land."[1] And Rossi says : "Of natural agents, included under the name of land, that which most particularly attracts the attention of Economists is the soil. Generally the soil is private property : and this is a characteristic feature of all civilized society."[2]

---

[1] *Économie Politique*, &c., Liv. II. Chap. 2.
[2] *Cours d'Économie Politique.* Second semestre. Leçon 1.

4. Property understood in this latter. sense, *viz.*
private property in land, is what the Socialists hate the
most, calling it, as Proudhon did, a robbery : *La propriété c'est le vol.* The land, they say, with its treasures
and its fertility, was not assigned by nature to any one in
particular, but given to all in common; and he who claims
a part of it for himself, to the exclusion of others, takes
what is not his own ; which is a flagrant injustice, treason
to humanity, cries for vengeance, and will be fiercely
revenged if restitution be not made. The Socialists—not
the Socialists of the streets, who aspire to pillage, but the
cultivated Socialists who bawl out their wisdom—propose
to abolish private property and substitute collective property, regulated and administered by the State.

The Economists are almost unanimous in defending
property against the accusations and arguments of Socialism.
They maintain that to seize the property of those to whom
it belongs, through having either made its value by labour,
or bought it, or inherited it, is iniquitous and an evident
robbery. They defend a just cause : but their defence is
often unavailing for want of sound reasons.

ARTICLE II.
INSUFFICIENT DEFENCE.

5. Say derives the rights of property from the social
state of men. Against Germain Garnier, who said, "Tout
ce qui n'est pas propriétaire d'une portion du sol national,
n'y peut exister que comme étranger," he writes thus :
" This is only a specious sophism, which assumes that the
rights of property are anterior to society, whereas it exists
by reason of social agreement only, and therefore is of
later date than the political order, which alone can con-
secrate and guarantee it. The proof of this is that society
can exist without acknowledging funded property, as
numerous examples testify. Among the Arabs and the

nomad Tartars there are no owners of real property.
Their laws recognize no other than moveable property,
such as waggons and flocks; which, as we have seen,
is one of the reasons why they cannot become industrious
or very rich." [1]

6. This can by no means be admitted. True it is that
what Garnier had said was clearly wrong. Society is
formed for a higher and more extensive good than quiet
possession of property : and therefore all are members of
it who in one way or another, by wealth, ability, or labour,
help to actuate it. But in rejecting one error Say falls
into another, and a gross one. How can society give the
rights of property, when the said rights within it result
from those of the individuals therein associated ? Society
would thus give you the right to possess a part of its
land : but who gave the land to society ? Whatever can
be said to show that society has the right of possessing,
applies *a fortiori* to individuals.

7. But society, Say tells us, consecrates and protects
property. Very well : but consecrating and protecting is
not creating. Society consecrates and protects the life and
personality of the individuals in it. But does it follow
that society makes them persons and gives them the right
to live ? In short, if society creates the rights of property,
society can annul them ; and we should be silenced by
Socialism. [2]

---

[1] *Cours Complet d'Économie Politique.* Tome I., 4me. Pt., Ch. 5.

[2] Stuart Mill is not ashamed of giving society this right.
Speaking of the distribution of wealth he tells us that in the
social state, under all conditions except that of total solitude,
all disposition of wealth requires the general consent of society.
Even what a man has produced by his own labour unaided
cannot, in his opinion, be kept by that man, unless society
allows him to do so. It may even be demanded by individuals,
he says, and would in fact, if society as a whole did not oppose
it, and pay people to prevent it. See his *Principles of Political*

8. Other Economists explain otherwise the right of property. Most of them find its justification in the great advantages that it brings, being useful even to those who have not property themselves.

"When the land," says Droz, "is without owners, who will care to cultivate it carefully—devote his own toil and his own earnings to it ? A little work hurried through—which is all that men would venture on without being sure of harvesting—adds little to the spontaneous productions of the soil. The popula tion is scanty and poor. But when territorial property is established a new era begins. Products multiply, and multiplication [of the human race] increases with it. In this new state of society a great division of labour is formed between the men who get the raw materials out of the land, and those who devote themselves to the arts required for working them up. These two classes, equally laborious, see that their well-being results from their activity in labour and their exchanges. In short, material products become sufficiently common, so that certain men can devote themselves entirely to giving immaterial products. To territorial property, therefore, we owe the increase of population and of comfort and the exercise of the noblest faculties. We owe to it the development of forces, of wealth, and of human intelligence." [1]

9. All this is true : but the Socialist would say that, in spite of all this, they find society tending more and more to divide off into the two classes of the very rich and the very poor. "If," they would say, " you call private property lawful because it brings advantages, we have an equal right to call it unjust for the harm that it does."

Moreover utility does not constitute right. "They

Economy, Bk. II., Distribution, Chap. 1. To say the truth, many of our modern Economists have opened the door for Socialism to come in.

[1] *Économie Politique*, &c. Liv. II. Chap. 2.

grossly deceive themselves," as Minghetti wisely says, " who found their defence of landed property on economic reasons alone ; for, since the Socialists are wrong, not only in Economy, but also and principally in Morals and Equity, therefore to Morals and Equity must we go to refute them. Economic reasons can show us the private and public advantages—I will even say the necessity—of landed property : but they cannot go further. A higher knowledge must inform that material principle with its sanction." [1] Unless you show that the right of holding private property originates from nature, all your talking will be of no avail.

10. Other Economists try to found the right of property on the idea of labour. Every man, they say, has a right to regard as his own what he has produced by his own labour ; and this is admitted by the Socialists themselves. The effect belongs to him who is the owner of the cause : and labour belongs to the labourer. Labour is the origin of property. It has made wildernesses and marshes fruitful. Is it not just, that he who has so laboured should enjoy the fruits of his labour ?

This is true, but not the whole truth. Labour is, no doubt, the source of property, but not the original source. The house that you have built is yours : but your ownership presupposes that the land on which you built it was yours. Where (it would be said) did you get your right to call that land your own which was given by nature, not to you, but to all ? You cultivate a given number of acres : but if they belonged to the human race, they were not yours. You say that you made them fertile : but who asked you to do so ? Moreover the fertility was in the soil. You only made use of natural forces, which, like the land, were a gift of nature. How do you prove that the gift was to you ? Show us the deed of gift.

---

[1] *Dell' Economia Pubblica.* Lib. II., p. 147.

11. To ward off this attack, Carey invented a funny theory, which Bastiat developed. "Do you suppose," he said, addressing the Socialists, "that an owner of land usurps the profits that come from its natural fertility? You are in error. He only gets a return for the labour. The rest he gives you gratuitously. What constitutes the exchangeable value of an object is simply the labour of producing   No part of the value is attributable to utility."

We have already shown the falseness of this theory. [1] In purchase and sale the object is offered and sought as being useful, and sold at market price irrespective of the labour employed in producing it. If any one were to put an extra price on an article, and say that he did so because he had worked at it more than other people, the purchaser would say, "What is that to me? I mean to pay what the thing is *worth*;" and by "worth" he would mean the price at which it is commonly valued; which common valuation is relative, not to the labour that may have been bestowed on it, but to the utility and rarity of the same. When a man consents to pay twenty francs for a bottle of claret, does he reckon the labour of producing it? If so, he would value it a little more than five sous, which a bottle of Asprino costs, [2] because the labour employed is about the same for each.

12. We spoke of these things before; and it only remains for us to point out that this theory is a prop to Socialism. It admits the non-appropriability of natural agents by denying that they enter into exchange; for every one knows that what is appropriable is capable of being exchanged. Given that natural agents are not appropriable, no one would be justified in calling any land his own to the exclusion of others.

---

[1] Part I. Chap. vi. Art. iv.
[2] "Quel d'Aversa orrido Asprino
Che non so s'è agresto o vino."—Redi, *Ditirambo*.

Nor can this be evaded by saying, as if in grim fun, "I don't exclude any one from the land, considered as a natural agent, but only from the fruits of my labour. When I sell the produce of the soil I only reimburse myself for the labour. The utility that comes from the land's fruitfulness I give gratis." For the answer would be : "Very well then. If your property is not in the soil, and therefore you only charge for the labour, I will take possession of your fields, and work them, and I will sell the produce to you on the same terms." The man would protest loudly, and want to be paid for all the labour and capital put into it by himself and his forefathers ; but the grim reply would be : "Your labour and your capital have been sufficiently paid for by your annual profits. And if you will have it that the expenses have exceeded the profits (which I don't believe,) I can only say that it serves you right for expending so much labour and capital on what was naturally not your own."

But we must not lose any more time over such theories, which a little common sense would suffice to refute. We must find better arguments than these to prove the rights of property.

ARTICLE III.

PRIVATE PROPERTY IS NATURAL TO MAN.

13. We call natural, not only what nature of itself puts in action, but also what answers to its design. Thus, when we say that civil society is natural to man, we do not mean that nature put mankind in that state ; for in fact the human race originated from one pair. We mean that nature intended mankind not to be scattered about in isolated families, but to live together in civil intercourse. We can see the intention of nature in the conditions and natural tendencies of the subject (man) and the means required to satisfy them.

14. Hence it is easy to understand that permanent property is natural to man, because it is intended by nature that men should become possessors of fruitful things, where they can do so lawfully, *i.e.* without injury to others. Man needs inferior animals and plants; and nature neither leaves anything in an imperfect state, nor does anything that is useless. Therefore it is evident that nature made animals and plants for the sustenance of man. But when anyone acquires what nature has made for him, the acquisition is natural. Therefore the appropriation by which people acquire these things, which are necessary to human life, is natural.

Manifestum est, says St. Thomas in his commentary on Aristotle's "Politics," *quod homo indiget ad suam vitam aliis animalibus et plantis. Sed natura neque dimittit aliquid imperfectum, neque facit aliquid frustra. Ergo manifestum est quod natura fecit animalia et plantas propter hominem. Sed quando aliquis acquirit id quod natura propter ipsum fecit, est naturalis acquisitio. Ergo possessiva, qua hujusmodi acquiruntur, quæ pertinent ad necessitatem vitæ, est naturalis.* [1]

The holy Doctor passes from the naturalness of the acquisition of necessary things to the naturalness of the possession or appropriation of that from which those things proceed. *Ergo possessiva* (as St. Thomas usually expresses property), *qua hujusmodi acquiruntur, quæ pertinent ad necessitatem vitæ, est naturalis.* Man, as a rational being, is a provident being. Now a man cannot be rightly called provident, unless he supplies not only for present wants, but also for future wants; which cannot be done without permanent possession of fruitful things. If the wants of mankind ceased when satisfied once, this possession would not be in nature's design. But man, being so constituted that he has daily wants, reasonably

---

[1] *In Lib. I. Politicorum.* Lect. vi.

seeks to appropriate the fund from which those wants are supplied ; so that the permanence of the want leads to the permanence of the possession. This is the more apparent when we consider, not the isolated man, but the domestic man, who has children to provide for. Moreover the land and the animals on it require care and labour, which no one would give, unless he were sure of keeping his own ; so that labour is intended in the appropriation of land, but, as we have said before, is not the origin of property.

15. There are things to be distinguished in this matter—the efficient cause, the end, and the concrete determination. The efficient cause of property is nature, which has produced the fields, not for the absurd and mischievous purpose of their belonging to all men in common, but in order that they might become the legitimate property of individuals. The concrete determination of this generic concession from nature proceeds from the first occupation, through which this or that portion of land becomes the property of this or that man, who, by an act of free will externally manifested, makes t his own. The end of this natural ordering is, that what nature produces should become abundantly fruitful by means of labour. God said to man in the person of Adam, "Fill the earth, and subdue it." [1] Now, subjugating the earth means compelling it to give abundantly the fruits required by man, which cannot be done without labour.

16. To show that private property is natural, St. Thomas makes the following remarks : In the first place, men are more careful of what is their own, than of what they have in common with others ; for their inclination to avoid labour prompts them to put their work on other people. Secondly, things are ordered better when

---

[1] *Genesis* i. 28.

each man has the care of his own. Thirdly, it is easier to preserve peace when each man is contented with his own. We know from experience that when property is held in common, people claim too large a share, and quarrels arise. [1]

17. Evidently, then, the argument of the Economists, that private property is necessary to human civilization, can become demonstrative, if rightly used.

" History," says Pellegrino Rossi, " teaches us that the appropriation of land is unknown to none but savage populations and nomadic tribes. Fixed abodes, appropriation of the soil, and regular society are three ideas that never have been separated in the mind of man—three facts that history always presents united. . . . Without appropriation of the soil there is no regular society, no civilization. Uncertain property and barbarism are facts deducible from each other always and everywhere." [2]

True : but to prove the right, we must connect it with the intentions of nature. We must reason in this sort of way : Neither a well-ordered and peaceful society, nor civilization are possible without private property. But nature intends that society should be well-ordered and peaceful and civilized. Therefore nature intends private property to be. But that which is intended by nature is a natural right. Therefore private property is a natural right. Or we might argue thus : That which has the consent of all civilized nations must proceed from nature. But private property has the consent of all civilized nations. Therefore it must proceed from nature. This will appear more clearly when we examine the objections.

---

[1] *Summa*, 2ᵃ. 2ᵃᵉ Q. LXVI. a 2.

[2] *Cours d'Économie Politique*, Second Semestre. Leçon i.

ARTICLE IV.

ANSWERS TO SOME OBJECTIONS.

18. *First Objection.*—The old jurists taught that property does not appertain to Natural Right, but to the Right of Nations. Therefore it does not proceed from the order of nature.

Answer.—This objection comes from not rightly understanding what the difference is between Natural Right and the Right of Nations in the teaching of the old Jurisconsults. They distinguished the one from the other, not by origin, as if they had not both of them proceeded from nature, but by the object. According to them, Natural Right is that right which regards things corresponding to animal instinct, and therefore common to human beings and brutes; while the Right of Nations regards things that correspond to the discourse of reason, and therefore are proper to man alone. Such is property.

" Jus naturale," we read in the *Institutes* of Justinian, " est quod natura omnia animalia docuit ; nam illud non humani generis proprium est, sed omnium animalium, quæ in cœlo, quæ in terra, quæ in mari nascuntur. Hinc descendit maris atque feminæ conjunctio, quam nos matrimonium appellamus ; hinc liberorum procreatio, hinc educatio ; videmus etenim cetera quoque animalia istius juris perita censeri. . . . Quod vero naturalis ratio inter omnes homines constituit, id apud omnes peræque custoditur, vocaturque Jus Gentium, quasi quo jure omnes gentes utuntur." [1]

Here the Right of Nations is attributed to nature— " quod naturalis ratio inter omnes homines constituit." That which is an institute of reason is an institute of nature, because reason is in the nature of man.

But of these things,—*viz.* what the distinction between

---

[1] *Institutionum* Lib. I. tit. ii.

Natural Right and the Right of Nations is, and how property, while appertaining to the latter, is rightly said to proceed from nature—we shall have to speak in the next Chapter.

19. *Second Objection.*—Property would thus be derived from occupation. But occupation is a fact: and fact does not constitute a right.

Answer.—We must distinguish. That it would be derived from occupation, as a determining principle, I grant. That it would be derived from occupation as an authorizing principle, I deny. Its authorizing principle is nature, which gives dominion to man over inferior things, as being for him, and makes him provident and social, and therefore capable of permanent possession. The occupation determines the possession with regard to something that may be taken without injury to anyone, inasmuch as it does not belong to some one else. And this is proper to every right. Every right comes from nature in an undetermined and abstract manner. To become concrete and individual it needs a fact. The consent of a bride and bridegroom is a fact, that determines concretely the conjugal right. Generation is a fact, that determines in particular instances the paternal right. And so it is with property. Occupation is a fact that serves to determine a right, given indeterminately to man by nature. If the lawfulness of the occupation be denied, all property, personal as well as real, falls to pieces.

20. *Third Objection.*—The earth was endowed by God with fertility, so that all might live on its produce; and therefore it is, by divine institution, common patrimony. He who appropriates it to himself, commits a crime against the order willed by God, and robs the human race. By excluding only one man from his possession you deprive him of his right to life, because you deprive him of the fruits of the earth, which are to preserve it.

Answer.—There is a great confusion of ideas in this discourse. Let us distinguish them in a few words. Unquestionably God made the earth fertile, in order that it might furnish food for man; but He did not intend it to do so without its becoming the private property of individuals. Were it so, neither nations nor individuals could have appropriated any part of it; and foreigners would have a divine right to invade their neighbours. The invaders might say : "We are not doing you any wrong. The earth is the heritage of all." People had better take care ; for we cannot deny the right of private property without implicitly denying the right of national property : the reasoning for the one and for the other is the same, and for each we must acknowledge the lawfulness of the occupation.

The earth, as St. Thomas says, may be said to be common patrimony in a negative sense, inasmuch as no part of it was appropriated by God to this or that person; but not in a positive sense, as if He had commanded that it should remain in common. Indeed, by making it tillable He made it appropriable ; for if its cultivation is to be efficacious, well-ordered, and peaceful, it must be divided into permanent properties of individuals. Therefore property is not against the primitive right of nature, but added thereto by discourse of human reason :

Communitas rerum attribuitur juri naturali, non quia jus naturale dictat omnia esse possidenda communiter, et nihil esse quasi proprium possidendum; sed quia secundum jus naturæ non est distinctio possessionum . . . Unde proprietas possessionum non est contra jus naturale, sed juri naturali superadditum per adinventionem rationis humanæ. [1]

It is calumnious to say that property takes from non-proprietors their right to live ; for many landowners are poor, while men in business are rich without possessing a

----

[1] *Summa,* 2ª 2ᵃᵉ· Q. LXVI. a. 2. ad 1.

rood of land. Certain it is that man cannot live without bread; but he can have it without the land on which it grows. When God said *In sudore vultus tui vesceris pane,*[1] by "the sweat of thy brow" He meant labour. This is the true means of living, common to all; and workmen not unfrequently rise to wealth by labour. If all merchandise is bread, because it can be exchanged for bread, *a fortiori* the labour that produces the bread gives the right to receive it in return. Land supplies nourishment; but possession of land is not a necessary condition of participating in that supply. Work of all sorts enables people to participate in it; and there is, as we shall see further on, a moral obligation to support those who cannot work.

21. *Fourth Objection.*—But it cannot be denied that property causes inequality between men; and this is against the intention of nature, which requires all men to be equal.

Answer.—Property brings inequality between men just as industry does, and commerce, and everything else in which a man can exercise judgment and energy. He who works more, exerts himself more, helps himself more, gains more; and by gaining more, if he is thrifty, honest, and intelligent, he can save more, and so make a fortune that will be the source of more wealth. There is inequality in that; and the inequality is not caused by possession of land. Shall we, then, for the sake of equality, abolish thrift, skill, temperance, and good conduct? It is curious to hear the partisans of equality glorifying freedom, not perceiving that freedom and equality are quite incompatible. Two free beings could not remain equal for one day. Their actions by the fact of being free would be different, and cause differences in the effects resulting from them, whether in the moral order, the juridical order, or the economic order.

---

[1] *Genesis* iii. 19.

It is evident, then, that equality is not natural. If it were so, men would be naturally equal, whereas in fact they are by nature unequal in the powers of body and of mind. Moreover, if nature required equality of conditions, man would not be by nature fitted for society, which, as every one knows, is essentially unequal, because it is not an accumulation of parts, but an organism, and therefore a result of dissimilar parts. The only equality required by nature is that which regards personal dignity and the inviolable rights of every one. But that is a juridical, not an economic question.

CHAPTER II.

WHAT THE CATHOLIC DOCTORS TEACH ABOUT THE RIGHTS OF PROPERTY AND PARTICULARLY LANDED PROPERTY.

AN Irish periodical, the name of which I prefer to omit, published in October and November, 1887, two articles entitled *The Theology of Land Nationalization.* These articles were intended to show that Catholic Theology nowhere denies the right of the State to abolish private property and be the only landowner. This is of the utmost importance by reason of the socialistic conclusions deducible from it ; and since the question is treated subtly in these two articles, we shall take them as the matter of our discussion.

ARTICLE I.

IN WHAT SENSE THE ANCIENT CATHOLIC DOCTORS DISTINGUISHED THE RIGHT OF NATIONS FROM NATURAL RIGHT.

23. The theological Schools, says the author of the said articles, not having heard of the modern theory that makes the land question exceptional, have not explicitly treated of territorial property. They only mention property in general, and especially the *jus stabilis proprietatis.* Their conclusions are as follows : The right of private property (or the property of individuals) belongs to the

Right of Nations—*jus gentium;* the Right of Nations is quite distinct from Natural Right, and is a positive human law : therefore it is the doctrine of the Theologians that the *jus gentium* owes its obligatory force to the free will of mankind ; and its dictates, though suggested for the most part by the wants of our nature, are only suggested as useful and expedient, not as binding. Hence, they argue, it follows that they can in certain cases, be validly and justly abrogated, revoked, or modified ; and this consequently holds good with regard to private property, which, as being a result of positive human legislation, can by the same be abolished.

24.   Let us examine successively these assertions.   It is true that, after the apparition of Socialism, people began to make a special question of landed property, because landed property is what Socialism attacks most.   It is also true that the earth, as including animals, terrestrial, aerial, and aquatic, was given immediately by God to the whole human race, in order that they might inhabit it, and get therefrom food and work.   But it is false to say that the Catholic Schools, being ignorant of what modern writers were going to say, passed over the question. If, as the author of these two articles admits, the Catholic Doctors spoke of the right of permanent property, they by the fact of doing so spoke not only implicitly, but explicitly, of the rights of landed property.   When we say that any property is permanent, we understand it to be made of what is immoveable, and there is nothing so immoveable as land.   Houses are said to be immoveable, because the land on which they are built, is immoveable.   Moreover, the Catholic Doctors, when treating of private property, exemplified it almost always by the division of fields— *divisio agrorum, proprietas possessionum*—and from territorial dominion took the objections that had to be solved. But let us now proceed to examine the meaning of *jus gentium.*

25. The old jurists divided private right into three species, *viz.*, Natural Right, Right of Nations, and Civil Right. " Privatum jus tripartitum est ; collectum etenim est ex naturalibus præceptis, aut gentium aut civilibus." That right which regards actions common to man and brutes, they called Natural Right :

" Jus naturale est quod natura omnia animalia docuit. Nam jus istud non humani generis est proprium, sed omnium animalium, quæ in terra, quæ in mari nascuntur, avium quoque commune est. [1] Hinc descendit maris atque feminæ conjunctio, quam nos matrimonium appellamus ; hinc liberorum procreatio ; hinc educatio."

If the right regards actions proper to man only—such as the duties of religion, obedience to parents, love of one's native country, defence against unjust aggressors, division of goods, commercial intercourse, and the rest, it is called the *Right of Nations*:

" Jus gentium est, quo gentes humanæ utuntur ; veluti erga Deum religio, ut parentibus et patriæ pareamus, ut vim atque injuriam propulsemus. Ex hoc jure gentium introducta bella, discretæ gentes, regna condita, dominia distincta, agris termini positi, ædificia collocata, commercium, emptiones, venditiones, locationes, conductiones, obligationes institutæ."

Lastly, Civil Right is that which each nation sanctions for its own benefit and government : " Quod quisque populus ipse sibi jus constituit, id ipsius proprium civitatis est, vocaturque jus civile, quasi jus proprium ipsius civitatis." [2]

This gives to the Right of Nations a very wide meaning ;

---

[1] It should be remembered that here, as some Theologians have wisely remarked, the *jus naturale* is called common to man and the brutes materially, *not formally*, i.e. as to the *thing* which it regards, not as the *reason* in right or law, which belongs to reasonable beings only.

[2] *Pandects*, Lib. I. tit. 1.

for it attributes thereto not only commerce, contracts, obedience to parents and to the laws of one's native country, (all of which are dictates of nature,) but even religion, which is chief among the natural duties of man: *Diliges Dominum Deum tuum... Hoc est maximum et primum mandatum.*[1]

26. The Catholic Theologians did not *substantially* reject this doctrine, but only explained and distinguished it better. They regarded the formal reason of the three species of right, and hence presented the criterion for discerning more precisely and exactly what each prescribes.

It will be sufficient to see this in St. Thomas, the perfector and master of all the other Theologians, and therefore called the Angel of the Schools. He first separated the *jus naturale* from the *jus positivum*, inasmuch as the former regards what is just or adequate to any one by the very nature of the thing, whilst the latter regards that which becomes just, either through private agreement or through a public order, *ex condicto, sive ex communi placito.* Here is the passage : " Right, or the just," he says, " is that which is adequate to others, according to some mode of equality. Now a thing can be adequate to a man in two ways. One is by the nature of the thing, when, for instance, anyone receives as much as he gave : and this is called *jus naturale.* Another way of being adequate or commensurate is by agreement, or by common consent, as, for instance, when anyone is satisfied to receive so much. And this can be done in two ways : one by private contract between private persons ; the other by public agreement, as when a whole people agree that a thing should be considered adequate or commensurate to another, or when it is so ruled by the prince who has the care of the people,

---

[1] *Matt.* xxii. 38.

and impersonates them. And this is called *jus positivum.*"[1]

27. Having thus determined the difference between the just as Natural Right, and the just as *Positive* Right, he puts the question, whether the Right of Nations is one with Natural Right : *Utrum jus gentium sit idem cum jure naturali;* and he says in reply that the one is distinguished from the other as part from part of the same whole; for the name of *jus naturale* is given to that species of Natural Right which is absolutely such—as, for instance, marriage and the education of children : while the name of *jus gentium* is given to that species of Natural Right which is so, not absolutely considered, but relatively to some good that is a consequence of it, such as the appropriation of the soil. Hence it follows that the former, requiring mere apprehension of the object by immediate judgment, can embrace things common to the brutes, when they answer to the generic part of man, *viz.* animality ; while the latter, always requiring a more or less lengthy discourse of reason, can only embrace those things that are proper to man, because reasoning is proper to man only.

This is so important, that we had better have it in the words of the Angelic Doctor. " *Jus* or *justum naturale,*" he

---

[1] *Jus sive justum est aliquod opus adæquatum alteri, secundum aliquem æqualitatis modum. Dupliciter autem potest alicui homini esse aliquid adæquatum. Uno quidem modo ex ipsa natura rei ; puta cum aliquis tantum dat ut tantumdem recipiat, et hoc vocatur* JUS NATURALE. *Alio modo aliquid est adæquatum vel commensuratum alteri ex condicto, sive ex communi placito, quando scilicet aliquis reputat se contentum si tantum accipiat. Quod quidem potest fieri dupliciter : uno modo per aliquod privatum condictum, sicut quod firmatur aliquo pacto inter privatas personas ; alio modo ex condicto publico, puta cum totus populus consentit quod aliquid habeatur quasi adæquatum et commensuratum alteri, vel cum hoc ordinat Princeps qui curam populi habet et ejus personam gerit, et hoc dicitur* JUS POSITIVUM.—*Summa,* 2ª. 2ªᵉ. Q. LVII. a. 2.

says, " is that which from its nature is adequate or commensurate to some one else.   This may happen in two
ways.   One way is according to the absolute consideration
of it, as the male is commensurate to the female in the
order of generation, and the father to his children, whom
he is bound to support.   The other way of being naturally
commensurate to another [i.e. naturally just] is not according to its absolute reason, but according to its relative
reason, i.e. with respect to what follows it, such as the
ownership of possessions.   For this or that field, if we
consider it absolutely, has nothing in itself whereby it
should belong to this man rather than to that ; but if we
consider it with respect to the cultivation and peaceful use
of it, then we find therein a certain fitness for belonging to
a determinate person and not to another, as the Philosopher
shows in his *Politics*, ii. 3.   Now apprehending a thing
absolutely does not belong to man alone, but also to the
brutes.   Therefore the Right which is called *natural*
according to the first way is common to us and the other
animals.   From Natural Right thus understood, the Right
of Nations differs (as the Jurisconsult says in the first
Book of the Pandects, *De Justitia et Jure*), because the
former is common to all animals, the latter to man only
among themselves.   To consider a thing in comparison
with what follows from it is proper to reason, and therefore is natural to man, in accordance with the natural
reason that dictates it.   Hence the Jurisconsult, Caius,
says, (lib. 9. ff cod.) : 'That which natural reason constitutes among men is observed equally by all, and is
called the *jus gentium*.' " [1]

---

[1]   JUS, *sive* JUSTUM *naturale, est quod ex sui natura est adæquatum vel commensuratum alteri.   Hoc autem potest contin-
gere dupliciter : uno modo secundum absolutam sui considera-
tionem, sicut masculus ex sui ratione habet commensurationem
ad feminam ut ex ea generet, et parens ad filium, ut eum nutriat.
Alio modo aliquid est* NATURALITER *alteri commensuratum, non*

28. This distinction between the *jus gentium* and the *jus naturale* shows that many things, attributed to the *jus gentium* by the old Jurisconsults, are attributable to the *jus* which retains the name of Natural, and not only those which they called *effectus juris gentium primarii*, such as divine worship and obedience to parents, but also many of those which were called *effectus juris gentium secundarii*, such as self-defence and not plotting against other people,[2] for these dictates are apprehended by us absolutely, as immediate consequences of the first principles of the Natural Law. Therefore, to say that the Right of Nations is distinguished from Natural Right insomuch as Natural Right regards things common to the brutes also, must be understood as the principal difference, not the only difference. This is expressly stated by St. Thomas. *Jus gentium*, he says, *distinguitur a lege naturali*, MAXIME *ab eo quod est omnibus animalibus commune*.[3] What is

---

secundum sui absolutam rationem, sed secundum quod ex ipso sequitur, puta proprietas possessionum. Si enim consideretur iste ager absolute, non habet unde magis sit hujus quam illius : sed si consideretur per respectum ad opportunitatem colendi et ad pacificum usum agri, secundum hoc habet quamdam commensurationem ad hoc quod sit unius et non alterius, ut patet per Philosophum in ii. Polit. cap. 3. Absolute autem apprehendere aliquid non solum convenit homini, sed etiam aliis animalibus. Et ideo jus, quod dicitur naturale secundum primum modum, commune est nobis et aliis animalibus. A jure naturæ naturali sic dicto recedit jus gentium, (ut Jurisconsultus dicit Lib. i. ff. De Justo et Jure) quia ILLUD omnibus animalibus, HOC solum hominibus inter se commune est. Considerare autem aliquid, comparando ad id quod ex ipso sequitur, est proprium rationis ; et ideo hoc idem est naturale homini secundum rationem naturalem, quæ hoc dictat. Et ideo dicit Caius Jurisconsultus (Lib. ix. ff. cod.) quod naturalis ratio inter omnes homines constituit, id apud omnes peræque custoditur, vocaturque JUS GENTIUM.—Summa, 2ª 2ªe. Q. LVII, a. 3.

[2] See *Pandects*, where above quoted.
[3] *Summa*, 1ª. 2ªe. Q. XCV. a. 4. ad. 1.

distinguished *maxime* is clearly not distinguished *unice*. Hence the first principles of Morals and their immediate consequences are ascribed by the Theologians generally to Natural Right. The mediate and more or less remote consequences they ascribe to the Right of Nations; yet both are from nature, because both regard, though in different ways, that which is naturally just: *Utrumque horum comprehenditur sub justo naturali.*[1]

29. But, it is said, Theologians, including St. Thomas, call the Right of Nations *positive;* and Positive Right is mutable, because it proceeds from the free will of man; and indeed, the Catholic Doctors called the Right of Nations mutable. This is the argument contained in the two Irish articles. Our answer is as follows :

As the Right of Nations is midway between Natural Right and Civil Right, and partakes of both, as being deduced on the one hand from the principles of the Right of Nature, strictly so called, and on the other as involving the assent of nations, we need not be surprised at its often coming under the name of both. But when we call it *positive,* we do not take the epithet "positive" in the sense of *ex condicto, sive ex communi placito,* but only in the sense of being *put* by man, not by free will, but by deduction from the Natural Law. If any Theologian, (or more than one,) said the contrary, he is not to be followed. St. Thomas, as we have remarked before, expressly denies that the dictates of the Right of Nations proceeds from human institution or the good-will and pleasure of human beings : *quia ea quæ sunt juris gentium naturalis ratio dictat, puta ex propinquo habentia æquitatem, inde est quod non indigeat aliqua speciali institutione, sed ipsa naturalis ratio ea instituit.*[2] And elsewhere, objecting from the

---

[1] St. Thomas, *In Lib. V. Ethicorum,* lect. xii.

[2] *Summa,* 2ª. 2ᵃᵉ. Q. LXVII. a. 3 ad 3.

text of Aristotle, that *justum legale est, quod principio qui-dem nihil differt utrum sic vel aliter fiat*, and therefore pro-ceeds from the will and pleasure of those who make it to be so, he replies that this is understood of things belong-ing to the civil law: *Philosophus loquitur de illis quæ sunt lege posita per determinationem vel specificationem quamdam præceptorum legis naturæ.* And, on the other hand, putting the objection that *ea quæ derivantur a prin-cipiis communibus legis naturæ pertinent ad legem naturæ*, he answers that *ratio illa procedit de his quæ derivantur a lege naturæ, tamquam conclusiones ;* [1] which, as he him-self had said, is proper to the Right of Nations. There-fore according to him the Right of Nations is not positive in the sense of proceeding from human will.

Bellarmine, in order to show that ecclesiastical exemp-tion is of divine right, argues that it is of the Right of Nations, and that the Right of Nations is Natural Right, not primary, but secondary : *Exemptionem clericorum non esse de jure naturæ primario, quod nos supra in duos gradus distinximus, sed esse de jure naturæ secundario, quod etiam jus gentium appellari diximus. Nam, ut St. Thomas recte docet, in 2ᵃ. 2ᵃᵉ. Q. lvii. a. 3. jus naturæ pri-marium respicit rem absolute consideratam, jus naturæ secundarium, sive jus gentium, respicit rem in ordine ad certum finem, et ideo pendet ex discursu rationis.* [2]

30. With regard to the mutability, I admit that some Theologians without explaining themselves clearly have called the *jus gentium* mutable ; but others have explicitly said that it is immutable. Bellarmine speaks of it, as follows : "Things that are *de jure gentium*, being in some degree natural, are prohibited as being bad in themselves ; on the contrary, those that are *de jure civili*, being positive, are bad because they are prohibited. Again, those things

---

[1] *Summa*, l. 2. Q. XCV. a. 2. ad 1. et ad 2.
[2] *Controv.* Tom. II. Lib. i. De Clericis, cap. xxx.

that are *de jure gentium*, being in some manner natural, cannot be abrogated or changed by princes or magistrates ; while, on the contrary, those that are *de jure civili* are of themselves positive ; and as they were established by princes or magistrates, so can they by princes or magistrates be abolished."[1]   Others, like Suarez, say that the *jus gentium* is mutable, so far as it depends on human consent : *jus gentium esse mutabile, quatenus ex hominum consensu pendet.*[2] Others say that some parts of it are mutable, but not every part : and this they take to be one of the principal differences between the *jus gentium* and the *jus civile. Hinc*, says Suarez, speaking of them, *intelligitur alia differentia, quæ in hoc constitui solet inter jus gentium et civile : nam civile dicitur esse mutabile in totum, jus autem gentium non in toto sed in parte.*[3] He substantially adheres to this ; and so does Silvius in the text quoted by the writer of the two articles : *Potest jus gentium, si secundum se spectatur, abrogari : quoddam quidem absque peccato, quoddam quidem vero non sine peccato.*[4] And that which cannot be changed without sin is not mutable. In this sense we should interpret any one who may have happened to express himself thereon in equivocal or indeterminate words. If they cannot be so interpreted,

---

[1] *Quæ sunt* DE JURE GENTIUM, *quia sunt aliquo modo naturalia, ideo prohibentur quia sunt mala ; contra autem quæ sunt* DE JURE CIVILI, *quia sunt per se positiva, ideo sunt mala quia prohibentur. Rursus sequitur ut ea quæ sunt* DE JURE GENTIUM, *quia sunt aliquo modo naturalia, non possint a principibus vel magistratibus abrogari vel immutari ; contra autem, quæ sunt* DE JURE CIVILI, *quia sunt per se positiva, sicut a principibus vel magistratibus constituuntur, ita possunt a principibus, vel magistratibus abrogari.*—*Controversiarum*, Tom. II. De Clericis, cap. xxx.

[2] *De legibus.* Lib. ii. cap. 20.   [3] Ibid.

[4] In 2. 2ae. Q. LVII. a. 3. ad 3.

what he says is of little importance ; for his suffrage is of no value.

The above mentioned opinion, which, when all has been said, is the most common, is also most just; for it is not credible that all the dictates of the *jus gentium* have connection with the first principles of the Natural Law. Some are more connected with them, and some less. Therefore some are more, and some less immutable, and some absolutely so. Certain it is that commerce among men and good faith in contracts are generally attributed to the *jus gentium*. Now could you conceive such things mutable, so that buying and selling might lawfully be forbidden, and breaking faith be lawfully permitted ? But the right of property, as we shall show later on, is similar to these.

ARTICLE II.

WHETHER ACCORDING TO THE CATHOLIC DOCTORS PRIVATE PROPERTY CAN BE ABROGATED BY THE CIVIL POWER.

31.   In the first of the two articles above mentioned the writer discoursed on the Right of Nations. In the second he applied his conclusions to the right of property.

What he says is substantially as follows : Catholic Theologians are unanimous in teaching that the right to acquire *personal property* is given to us, not by Divine or Natural Law, but by the Law of Nations. The Natural Law, according to most Theologians, recommends private possession under the present circumstances of society, even protects it by forbidding robbery, supposes it to be legally established ; but it does not of itself impose any moral obligation to establish the same, and still less does it prescribe the forms and modes thereof. Such obligation, where it exists, is determined by the wants of each society. This is, he tells us, undoubted by the traditional

doctrine of the Catholic Schools. They even, he says, go
further; for they say this not only with respect to landed
property, but of all material property whatsoever, whose
right they seek from positive human law merely. The
consequences of this doctrine are that the right of private
property in land, being derived from the Law of Nations,
which is positive and human and therefore lawfully
revocable, can be abrogated by the legislative authority,
if the public good requires it, and common property
established instead.

The greatest Theologians, he goes on to say, considered
this hypothesis, and saw nothing in it essentially immoral
or contrary to the teaching of the Catholic Church; nor
could they, having before their eyes the example of the
Primitive Church, and that of the Religious Orders, and
the efforts made by the Jesuits in Paraguay to establish
it.

So much for the abstract question. In the concrete,
he tells us, the determining in particular cases whether,
and how, and on what conditions we can take the leap
from private to common property in land, and whether the
public good requires it or not, or in what measure—this
belongs to the prudence of legislators. It is enough for
us to know that the tradition of the Catholic Church does
not put any obstacle in the way of such legislation where
it is for the common good of the people. For many
centuries, he says, the Catholic Schools taught, and they
still teach, that man may have mastership over his fellow
creatures, and that private property in land and private
property in human slaves are equally founded on the *jus
gentium*. Now the Church made no difficulty when
slavery was abolished, whether with compensation to the
masters as under the English government, or without
compensation as in North America; and it will make
none against the abolition of private property in land,
when such a measure is for the public good.

His conclusion is this : 1°. Common ownership of all material things may be ordained by the State, if such is for the common good. 2°. The State's ownership of land —*Land Nationalisation*—if it be judged opportune for the common good and decreed by a competent legislative authority, is in perfect accord with the traditional principles of Catholic theology.

32. We must begin by remarking that he alters the state of the question by speaking of private property as a duty. He says that the Natural Law does not of itself impose on man any obligation of appropriating the land to himself individually. But this is not the question. When we ask whether man has a natural right, *jus*, to personal possession of land, we take the word "right" to mean what is commonly meant by it—not a *moral bond*, but a *moral faculty* ; an authorization, not an obligation that comes from nature. Now, that this moral faculty, this authorization, is given naturally to man, not through an absolute dictate of reason, but through a dictate relative to human well-being, is a doctrine of all Theologians ; for they explain the division of land *jure gentium*, as having been introduced *per hominum rationem ad utilitatem humanæ vitæ ;* [1] . . . and, *tum ad pacem, tum ad meliorem rerum administrationem.* [2]

Therefore the examples of the early Christians and the Religious Orders, &c., are quite beside the question ; for any one may give up his own right, provided that it does not proceed from a previous duty. Men have an evident right to marry ; but a man may renounce the right and bind himself to a life of celibacy.

From this it by no means follows that the State may suppress private property, and make itself the proprietor of all the land, on the plea that such a step is conducive

---

[1] *Summa*, 1. 2ᵃᵉ., Q. XCIV. a. 5. ad 3.

[2] Lessius. *De Justitia et Jure*, Lib. XV., Chap. 5.

to the common good. The reason why this cannot be justly done, is that the right of property arises in us as an individual and domestic right, and therefore as substantially prior to civil society and independent of it ; just as the human person and the family are prior to civil society and independent of it. The State has authority over the rights that come from itself. It has no authority over rights that come from nature—rights that precede the State in history and in reason. The State can only harmonize such rights, invest them with legal forms, modify, temper, and determine them, as the common good may require. It has no authority to abolish them under any pretext whatsoever, but is in duty bound to acknowledge them, protect them, and facilitate the use of them.

33. It is no answer to say that the right of private property, being given by nature *propter utilitatem humanæ vitæ*, fails with the failure of utility, and that the State is the judge of such failure. The objection solves itself; for the utility of *human* life is not the same as the utility of *civil* life. It is a larger thing and more intrinsic to our nature, and refers to the subjects of the State, not as such, but as *men*, and as bound together, not in this or that civil community, but in the universal society of the human race under the government of God. Hence no State is competent to decide about that utility ; and therefore private property cannot be abolished by any political legislation, even if all the States in the world, *as States*, agreed together to do so. [1] Only by the Divine Legislator could it be abolished, or by the spontaneous renouncement of it by all men, taken one

---

[1] God has, on the contrary, confirmed it by a positive commandment, forbidding us even to covet other men's property, not only personal, but real and productive. *Non concupisces uxorem proximi tui : non domum, non agrum, non servum, non ancillam, non bovem, non asinum, et universa, quæ illius sunt.—Deuteronomy*, v. 21.

by one. If such abolition were forcibly imposed by the State, it would be a tyrannical violation of man's rights, and must, as such, meet with the reprobation of the Church.

34. Nor is the example of slavery, as attributed to the *jus gentium* by the old Jurisconsults, of any value at all. First, as we have already shown, not all the dictates of the *jus gentium* have an equal participation of immutability, because they are not equally connected with the first principles of the Natural Law. Therefore there is nothing remarkable in the fact that slavery, being one of its mutable dictates, was abolished. In the second place, slavery, if we consider the formal reason of it, is not derived from the Right of Nature, as a *deduction*, but only as a determination of one of its principles. Slavery took its origin from war, and was so called *a servando*, because the conqueror having power to kill the conquered, saved their lives and enslaved them. "Servi," says Justinian, "ex eo appellati sunt, quod Imperatores captivos vendere, ac per hoc servare, nec occidere solent; qui etiam mancipia dicti sunt, eo quod ab hostibus manu capiuntur.[1]" Now, assuming that the conquered were guilty, it is a dictate of nature that some punishment was due to them. Reason does not say what punishment; but use, or rather abuse, determined it among the nations to be the loss of their natural freedom. *Servitus est constitutio juris gentium, qua quis dominio alieno contra naturam constituitur.*[2] It therefore rested on Natural Right, not as an inference,—for that, as we showed in the preceding article, is proper to the Right of Nations, *jus gentium*, properly so-called—but as a free determination of a dictate of nature, which is proper to civil right and purely positive and therefore mutable. No

---

[1] *Institutionum*, Lib. I, tit. iii. § 3.
[2] Ibid., § 2.

wonder, then, that slavery was abolished, though it was
said to be a right of nations as to the fact—a fact generally
admitted in heathendom, through want of clear ideas
about human personality.   In short, the right to deprive
the conquered of their freedom was conceived as resulting
from the rights of war.   Now the rights of war are
rights, not individual, but social, and therefore subject in
many of their consequences to the national will.   Not so the
rights of property ; for they, as we have said, are individual,
as resulting from the right that every individual person
has to secure permanently his own maintenance and that
of his children.

The writer's remark that no objection was made by the
Church against the abolition of slavery, is curious.   How
could the Church object to it after having helped and
inspired it by her preaching, by her law, and by her
example ?   The same cannot be said about the abolition
of private property ; for the Church has never been
adverse to its possession, but, on the contrary, defended
the right of Clerics to have it, as a guarantee of their
not being obliged to depend on the civil power.

ARTICLE III.

A DOCTRINAL SUMMARY.

35.   In conclusion we shall sum up under distinct
heads.

1⁰.   The *jus gentium*, according to Catholic Theologians, is midway between the *jus naturæ*, strictly so-
called, and the *jus civile ;* for its dictates come from the
natural law as consequences, more or less mediate,—not as
determinations of general principles.

2⁰.   When the Catholic Theologians called the *jus
gentium* positive, they spoke of Positive Right in contradistinction to Natural Right strictly so-called, whether

Natural Right be understood in the sense intended by the old jurists (*jus naturale est quod natura omnia animalia docuit*) or in the Scholastic sense, as containing the first principles of the Natural Law and their immediate consequences. Assuredly the *jus gentium*, not being natural in this sense, must be called positive, if we wish to divide rights into natural and positive. But if the epithet "positive" is understood strictly, as expressing a right given by human will *ex condicto aut ex communi placito*, the *jus gentium* cannot be called positive, because *quæ sunt juris gentium, non indigent aliqua speciali institutione.*[1] It must be called a natural right, *quia ipsa naturalis ratio ea instituit*; but that Natural Right, be it remembered, is *secondary*, not primary. The dictates of reason are dictates of nature, because reason in us is nature. *Homo est animal rationale.*

3⁰. The *jus civile* is, in the strict sense of the word, positive, being derived from Natural Right, not as an *illation*, but as a *determination* of universal principles by public authority. Whence it follows that while the *jus naturale* strictly so-called is entirely immutable, and the *jus civile* is entirely mutable, the *jus gentium* is partly immutable and partly mutable, according to whether its dictates are more or less connected with the principles of Natural Right, strictly so-called.

4⁰. Private property belongs to the *jus gentium*, because it is suggested by nature, not according to the absolute consideration of it, but relatively to human well-being, which follows therefrom. This is manifestly taught by St. Thomas, for in one of the passages above quoted, where he is speaking of the *justum naturale* in the sense pointed out, he instances private property—*puta proprietas possessionum.*[2]

---

[1] *Summa*, 2ª. 2ᵃᵉ. Q. LVII. a 3. ad 3.
[2] *Summa*, 2ª. 2ᵃᵉ. Q. LVII. a 3.

5⁰. Private property comes from nature, not by way of command, but of authorisation, and therefore as a moral power, not as a moral obligation. In other words, private property comes from nature as a right, not as a duty; and therefore, though it exacts the respect of others, because the right is inviolable, yet the possessor is free to renounce it, because every one may yield *jus suum.*

6⁰. The State has no right to abolish private property, because private property is not a social right, but an individual right derived from nature, not derived from the State. Nay, the State is in duty bound to acknowledge, respect, and guard private property, just as it is in duty bound to acknowledge, respect, and guard all the rights of the subject that come from nature, and are in reason anterior to the formation of the State.

7⁰. Not even the consent of all the States could sanction the abolition of private property; for the universal, or almost universal, consent implied in what is of the *jus gentium,* must be understood with regard to men *as men,* not as members of a State. Moreover, this consent is not the cause, but the effect, of that dictate of reason which gives that right *propter utilitatem humanæ vitæ,* not *civilis vitæ.* The only case in which it could be abolished would be if all men, taken individually one by one, consented thereto, as for instance in a society formed of shipwrecked people cast on an uninhabited island, who agreed to possess it in common. But that compact would only bind those individuals who had consented thereto. It would not be binding on their sons and grandsons, for the sons and grandsons would receive the right of having property, not from them, but from nature.

8⁰. In questions of right we must diligently guard against attributing too much power to the State. There are three things with respect to man that are of immediate divine institution, and therefore have laws independent of the State. These are individual personality, the family, and the universal society of all men under the direct but invisible government of God.[1] Now the right of property flows from the two first, though with essential relation to the third, by which, as we shall see when treating of beneficence, it comes to be limited.

9⁰. False, therefore, are both of the conclusions drawn by the writer of the two articles : *viz.* that the State, judging it to be expedient, may force people to have property in common ; and that this, when done by the legislative authority, would not be in opposition to the principles of Catholic Theology. Nothing of the sort. No State, no legislative power, is of itself competent for that. To claim such a right would be to oppose not only the doctrine of sound Theologians, but the evidently natural rights of man.

ARTICLE IV.

A QUESTION.

36. It may be asked why, since the old Scholastics did not hesitate to say that private property is of positive and human right—*rerum divisionem et appropriationem, ex jure humano procedentem,*[2]—we should not use the same language.

My answer is that I should not advise it, because in the distribution of the laws, and therefore of rights and duties, the epithets " positive" and "human" are not used in the same sense now as formerly. The Scholastic Doctors, treading in the footsteps of St. Isidore, divided right and likewise law (it comes to the same thing) first into natural

---

[1] See the author's *Trattato di Diritto Pubblico Ecclesiastico,* Cap. IV. a 1.

[2] *Summa,* 2ᵃ. 2ᵃᵉ. Q. LXVI. a. 7.

and positive.   By Natural Right they meant the immediate
dictates of reason in the practical order : by Positive
Right they meant the dictates that man derives from these
immediate dictates of reason, either in the way of conclusion or in the way of determination.   Hence Positive
Right was divided into the *jus gentium,* which is derived
from Natural Right as conclusions from principles, and *jus
civile,* which is derived therefrom as a determination.
*Dividitur jus positivum in jus gentium et jus civile, secun-
dum duos modos quibus aliquid derivatur a lege naturæ.
Nam ad jus gentium pertinent ea quæ derivantur a lege
naturæ sicut conclusiones ex principiis, ut justæ emptiones,
venditiones et alia hujusmodi, sine quibus homines ad
invicem convivere non possent; quod est de lege naturæ,
quia homo est naturaliter animal sociabile.   Quæ vero
derivantur a lege naturæ per modum particularis deter-
minationis pertinent ad jus civile, secundum quod quæ-
libet civitas aliquid sibi accommode determinat.*[1]

"Both of these Rights," says the holy Doctor, "are
contained in human law, but very differently ; for the
jus civile takes its force from human law only, but the
ius gentium takes its force from the Natural Law also.
Utraque igitur inveniuntur in lege humana posita.   Sed
ea quæ sunt primi modi, continentur in lege humana, non
tamquam sint solum lege posita, sed habent etiam
aliquid vigoris ex lege naturali.   Sed ea quæ sunt secundi
modi, ex sola lege humana vigorem habent.*[2]   And the
reason of this is evident from what has been said.   For
things belonging to the *jus gentium* are derived from the
Law of Nature as conclusions, and conclusions participate in the virtue of their principles.   But things
belonging to the *jus civile* are derived from the Laws of
Nature as determinations : and, since determinations may

---

[1] *Summa,* 1ª. 2ª. Q. XLV. a. 4.
[2] *Summa,* 1ª. 2ªe. Q. XCV. a. 2.

differ, they are made by the will of the determinator. Hence the axiom of the old Jurisconsults : *Quod Principi placuit, legis vigorem habet.*

37. But all this has been changed. By *jus naturæ* modern writers mean all that is dictated by practical reason, whether as principles or as conclusions; so the *jus naturæ* is made to include the *jus gentium* in the sense meant by the Scholastics. By the *jus positivum* modern writers understand that which is dictated by the mere will of the legislator—as, for instance, penalties for this or that crime, taxes &c.—which the Scholastics attributed to the *jus civile.* Lastly, these same moderns call *jus gentium* (the Law of Nations) that which regards international relations, whether it proceeds from the Natural Law, or whether it springs from the universal, or almost universal, custom of civilized peoples.

38. This being so, it seems to me imprudent and dangerous in these days to call the right of property "positive and human" in the old sense of these words. We should only be helping the Socialists to play tricks of sophistry and confuse the question, by maintaining that because in modern language the right of having property is not given by nature, but by man, therefore private property may be abolished. It is better, I think, to use phrases not liable to false interpretation but easily understood, and call property a *natural right* in the sense now in vogue,—a sense that substantially corresponds with the old sense when brought into modern parlance. Moreover, this use of the epithet "*natural*" was not unknown to the Scholastics. Having seen this before, we need only remark that St. Thomas, when he puts the question whether the possession of external things is natural to man—*Utrum naturalis sit homini possessio rerum exteriorum*—replies in the affirmative, appealing to the authority of Aristotle : *Philosophus probat in Lib. I. Polit. c. 5. quod possessio rerum exteriorum est homini*

naturalis.[1]   And, indeed, if the right to have property is a dictate of reason, it may well be said to be a dictate of nature ; for man's reason flows from his essence, inasmuch as the essence of man is that of a rational animal.

Now-a-days the question of property has passed from the Schools to the streets, and writers, therefore, should take the greatest care to avoid words that may be misused ; for, as St. Jerome says : *Ex verbis temere prolatis incurritur hæresis.*

---

[1] *Summa,* 2ª. 2ᵃᵉ Q. LXVI. a. 1.

CHAPTER III.

INHERITANCE.

B Y the right of inheritance we mean THE RIGHT OF GIVING AND OF RECEIVING PROPERTY,—the right of choosing a successor to one's possessions, and the right of that person to have them. The right of the testator and the right of the heir are correlative; so that to speak of the one is pretty much the same as to speak of the other.

The right of inheritance is closely connected with that of property. He who possesses nothing cannot have an heir, and he who is incapable of being an heir is incapable of possessing. Inheritance and property are mutually affirmed or denied. The Socialists, therefore, are logical in attacking inheritance for the purpose of destroying property; and they who wish to save property, but care not to defend inheritance, are very bad reasoners.

There are two ways of inheriting—by will, or as being next-of-kin. We shall speak of each in turn.

ARTICLE I.

INHERITANCE BY WILL.

40. A last will and testament is defined in the *Digests* as being a just decision of the will about that which any one wishes to be done after his death. "Testamentum est voluntatis nostræ justa sententia, de eo quod quis post mortem suam fieri velit." [1] Taken so it has a very large

---

[1] *Digestorum*, Lib. xxviii., tit. i. n. 1.

meaning, and regards all that depends on the will of man, whether it concerns his property, his dead body, his grave, the manifestation of his thoughts, or in general, anything whatsoever of which he can dispose. But here we have to consider it in the first sense alone, *viz.*, as constituting an heir to succeed the testator in the possession of the property that he relinquishes by dying.

Now that such a right is natural to man, or arises in him from nature, is quite evident, being a pure corollary from the right of having property. Property is an absolute power over the things to which it corresponds. He who possesses anything has the right of consuming, exchanging, relinquishing, or destroying it, and therefore has the right of giving it. Is the destroying of a thing a lesser exercise of dominion than giving it to some one to be enjoyed by him? If a proprietor may do that during his whole life, he can do so at its end. The right of having property, then, brings with it the right of making a will, or, in other words, appointing an heir. Therefore inheritance by will is just, and proceeds from nature.

41. The right of constituting an heir reduces itself after all to the right of giving. A will, substantially regarded, is not distinguishable from a pure donation, except so far as this—that it does not come into effect till after the death of the donor, and that it transfers to the donee the property and the obligations of the deceased. But these may well be considered as conditions of the gift, and therefore as mere accidents that do not affect the substance. "There are," as Steccanella rightly says, "two ways of disposing or giving, *viz.* absolute, and conditional. The testator makes use of the second, seeing that under certain conditions the heir shall enter into possession after his (the testator's) death—that the testamentary act may be revoked by the testator, and that this or that charge attached thereto be satisfied. The will, therefore, considered in its being, agrees perfectly

with the gratuitous conditional disposition. It has been shown above that not only the right of disposing or giving absolutely, but also the right of disposing or giving conditionally germinates from the very nature of man; whence it follows that the right of bequeathing does not receive its vitality from the Civil Law, but has its root in nature itself." [1] A will, therefore, may well be considered as a conditional donation.

42. Minghetti also deduces testamentary right from the idea of property and the idea of donation. "The right of property," he says, "carries with it that of property and of donation, and the reason of contracts is derived entirely from the guarantee of that right. Without secure possession and free use the stimulus of labour would cease with the consumption; there would no longer be a motive for division of labour and exchanges. And if you allow the gift and the transmission among the living, how can you reject inheritance, when the one is a corollary of the other?" [2]

43. Some people, in order to maintain that the right of bequeathing is not from nature, but from civil laws, object that man, losing by death all right over material things, cannot dispose of them in favour of a survivor. They seem to think that the act by which the testator gives his possessions to his heir, is to be considered as having been done by him, after he was dead. But the act of making a will is considered as having been done by the testator at the last moment of his life; and therefore that will, not having been retracted, is called the last will of the dying man, who certainly up to that time enjoyed all his rights.

"Never mind," they reply: "Anyhow this act does not meet with the donee's acceptance, which, except in a few rare cases, takes place when the will has been notified

---

[1] *Del Communismo*, &c., Lib. II., Chap. 23.

[2] *Dell' Economia Pubblica*, Lib. V., p. 479.

to him after the testator's death.   Is not the donation
a contract?   And does not every contract require the
simultaneous will of the contracting parties?"

Our answer is this : The concurrence of two wills does
not require that both co-exist formally—that is, in their
own being.   It is sufficient that the one co-exists with the
other virtually—that is, in some fact determined by it,
and in which it is as represented.   Otherwise two people
at a distance from each other could not contract either in
writing or by commission, especially when the man who
writes or reads, happens to change his mind in the meanwhile.   Now it is a fact that when the heir accepts his
inheritance, the testator's will does not co-exist with his
formally, because the testator is dead ; but it does co-
exist therewith virtually, inasmuch as it is expressed in
the written last will and testament, or is affirmed by
competent witnesses.

44.   And here we must point out a legitimate sense of
Leibnitz' words, where he says that the validity of a will
is founded on the immortality of the human soul.   From
such immortality he infers that a man, by reason of not
entirely ceasing to live, continues to be the proprietor of
what he had, and therefore, in appointing an heir, does not
appoint an owner, but simply an administrator of the
property which he, the testator, still possesses.[1]   This
illation is false.   The deceased, though he does not
entirely cease to be, because his soul survives, quite
ceases to be in the quality of a proprietor and the aptitude
for it.   Property does not belong to the soul, but to the
compositum.   Now the *compositum* perishes, though one
of its component parts, i.e. the soul, survives.   And then

---

[1] "Testamenta vero meo jure nullius essent momenti, nisi
anima esset immortalis.   Sed quia mortui revera adhuc vivunt,
ideo manent domini rerum ; quos vero hæredes reliquerunt,
concipiendi sunt procuratores in rem suam."—*Nova methodus
Jurisprudentiæ*, Pars II. § 20.

the soul, no longer having anything to do with the visible world, can no longer have any right in it. Moreover that which the right of property presupposes, *viz.* the need of providing for the maintenance of organic life by material means, would here be wanting. The right of property ends, *ipso facto*, with the ending of our mundane existence : and therefore the words, *quia mortui adhuc vivunt, ideo manent domini*, have no rational meaning. Neither is it reasonable to say that the heir is nothing more than the administrator of another man's property. He is its true owner, and therefore may do what he likes with it. But we may say that the validity of the will is founded on the immortality of the soul, inasmuch as the wish of the testator continues after death, being an act that springs from an immortal substance. Though the willer is the man, his soul is that from which the act of volition proceeds, and in which it resides. Therefore the act of this faculty, considered in itself, is not within the corporeal order and its consequences. If man's wishes were only affections of pure matter, they could not reach beyond the grave. That, and that alone, which proceeds from a being intrinsically not subject to time, is not measurable by time.

45. That the right of making a will does not arise from a legislative statute, is clear from its being, as we have shown, a necessary sequel to the right of property. If the right of property is from nature, as we have shown it to be, and not from civil laws, whatever is necessarily derived from the right of property must be from nature also. One and the same cause originates a thing and its consequences. *Qui dat esse, dat et consequentia ad esse.* When Abraham left his whole patrimony to Isaac and only gifts to the sons of his secondary wives—*Deditque Abraham cuncta quæ possederat, Isaac : filiis autem concubinarum largitus est munera* [1]—in virtue of what laws

---

[1] *Genesis*, xxv. 5, 6.

did he do so? Of what political body was he a member? He lived in a state of patriarchal independence, and acted according to the Law of Nature. The right to possess, and therefore to dispose of one's possessions, is an individual right in man, because it is relative to the wants of the individual as such; and therefore by its nature it precedes the social state. As society supposes the individual and comes after the individual, so does it suppose and come after the right of property and its consequences. Therefore society cannot make laws injurious to the right of property, or injurious to its consequences, without doing violence to nature, and indeed to human reason.

ARTICLE II.

DYING INTESTATE.

46. In the case of dying intestate the inheritance falls to the next-of-kin: as such, children come first, and therefore, not to be too long, we shall speak of them only. We say, then, that children naturally succeed; so that to deprive them of succession is manifestly to violate the laws of nature.

The son is a natural continuation of the father, who in a way transfuses himself into him by generation, and survives in him. Therefore, since he inherits his father's name, reputation, teaching, and more or less the same physical disposition, so ought he to inherit his goods. [1]

---

[1] From the *quasi-identity* of the father and the son, Taparelli wisely deduces the rule of preference respecting the property to be inherited. "Should the son succeed," he asks, "or the daughter? The title of unity with the deceased is the same in both; but the perpetuity of the father is more lasting in the son than in the daughter. Should the wife or the son succeed? Unity of action is greater in the wife than unity of being in the son. Therefore the use may go to the wife, but the power over it should go to the son. . Should a friend succeed, or society (the exchequer)? The unity of the friend is all mental, in the

What the father had acquired, was intended according to the order of nature, not only for his own advantage, but also for that of his children, whose future he ought to secure as well as he can, maintaining them in the state wherein they were placed by his giving them life and education.

47. St. Thomas, putting the question whether the son is bound to assist his father, says: "Since the father has the quality of a cause, and the son is an effect, therefore *per se* it is the father's duty to assist his son, not only for a time, but for his whole life; which implies laying by. But a son helps his father *per accidens*, by reason of some urgent necessity, in which he is bound to succour him;—not, however, to lay by for him; because parents do not naturally survive their children, but children survive their parents." *Quia pater habet rationem principii, filius autem habet rationem a principio existentis, ideo per se patri convenit ut subveniat filio; et propter hoc non solum ad horam debet ei subvenire, sed ad totam suam vitam, quod est thesaurizare. Sed quod filius aliquid conferat patri, hoc est per accidens, ratione alicujus necessitatis instantis, in qua tenetur ei subvenire, non autem thesaurizare quasi in longinquum; quia naturaliter non parentes filiorum, sed filii parentum sunt successores.* [1]

This reasoning clearly shows the son's right of succession to his paternal inheritance without needing a will. The father, having given existence to his son, is in duty bound to provide for him permanently. *Non solum ad horam debet ei subvenire, sed per totam suam vitam.* Hence the father's duty of laying by: *Quod est thesaurizare.* Now if this property is to supply his wants permanently—*ad totam vitam*—and children naturally live

case of a man dying intestate; but social unity is real and external, and therefore has the preference in the social order."—*Saggio Teoretico di Diritto Naturale*, Vol. I., § 783. Nota a.

[1] *Summa*, 2ª. 2ᵃᵉ. Q. CI., a. 2. ad 2.

longer than their parents—*naturaliter non parentes filiorum, sed filii parentum sunt successores*—who can fail to see that it is naturally due to them, in virtue of the rightful end for which it was laid by?

And this again shows that the right of having private property is a natural right; for if it is the father's natural duty to lay by for his children, and yet he could not leave what he has laid by unless he had power over it, clear it is that the right of acquiring such dominion is from nature; for otherwise nature would contradict itself by imposing a duty while denying the right to have the means of fulfilling it.

48. Nor can we make an exception against landed property, as some people do. The reasoning that shows the right of ownership, regards generally all useful things whatsoever; and especially the soil, as being permanently fruitful, and therefore more adapted for the end intended. And, besides, every man of intelligence knows that this restriction of the clamour against property to landed property alone, is nothing but a trick of the Socialists. They begin with an assault on landed estates for the purpose of going on to attack house-property, and manufactures, and every sort of private possession. For if ownership of land were contrary to human right, there is no intelligible reason why the ownership of manufactures, or of anything else, should not be contrary to it also. Man requires lodging and clothes, and the means of acquiring them, as much as he requires food. Moreover, by reason of buying and selling, all goods are nearly equal in comparative importance; and therefore to have landed property is more or less the same as having any other property. The war against landed property is a war against all property. There is no reason whatever for making a difference between them. But we must go on.

49. The idea of the family necessarily leads us to acknowledge the right of inheritance. The family is a

true moral body, of which the father is the head, and the children the members. It constitutes a whole, endowed with true unity, a unity supreme in a collective being, because it results from bonds interwoven by nature itself. Hence the paternal property is individual, so as to be also domestic. Therefore the subject of it does not quite cease to be, when the father dies ; for the children remain, who had already participated in it as a thing that concerned them also. " The spirit of inheritance and of perpetuity," says Guizot, " is inherent in the family spirit. Hence there is a sort of identity between the actual possessor and the whole series of future possessors." [1] And Paul, the Jurisconsult, said : " In his hæredibus evidentius apparet continuationem dominii eo rem perducere, ut nulla videatur hæreditas fuisse : quasi olim ii domini essent, qui etiam vivo patre quodammodo domini existimabantur. Unde etiam filius familias appellatur, sicut pater familias, sola nota hac adjecta, per quam distinguitur genitor ab eo qui genitus sit. Itaque post mortem patris non hæreditatem percipere videntur, sed magis liberam bonorum administrationem consequuntur ; hac ex causa, licet non sunt hæredes instituti, domini sunt." [2] These words of the distinguished jurist are very beautiful. He appeals to the unity of the family, which in a manner is the subject of the property, of which the son partakes in a way as soon as he is born, so that, on the death of his father, he does not so much inherit, as freely administer.

50. A similar argument is philosophically worked out on high principles by Taparelli.

"Every society," he says, " is an association for the common good, with common use of material goods ; and since this association could not take place without an authority to combine its efforts, in every society there

---

[1] *Civil. Europ.*, Leçon iv.
[2] *Digestorum*, Lib. xxviii., tit. ii., § 2.

exists an authority that regulates these efforts ; and the society and the authority have a certain right over the temporal goods of the associated, *resulting from the very nature of the association*, and therefore strong in proportion to the strength of the associating principle, because every effect is proportionate to its cause. The publicists thought little of this right in the family, because, for the most part, they considered society as public, an aggregation of detached individuals. But if the hypostatic theory already explained by us is admitted, there subsists in the family a species of *eminent* right, subordinate to the public right in order to the public good, but regulating the right of individuals for the domestic good. Now, given these principles, already demonstrated by us in the third dissertation, does death always and truly take away the owner? Yes, if the deceased was an isolated individual, independent of any particular society whatsoever. Death has cut off every thread of that solitary existence. But if the individual belonged to a family, what was he in that family? He was a member of a society in which there existed a principle of unity, constituted by nature. He formed with these individuals one being, whose means were to be employed for the common good, and the members of the family had a positive right to have enjoyment of his goods (according to certain laws which we need not explain here,) as he had to enjoy theirs. Therefore they had in a way already occupied those possessions with consent of the co-lord, and the domestico-social authority had a species of *eminent dominion* over those social means. And therefore the death of the master did not leave the property ownerless. The family is the same all the while. The change from one owner to another, though a leap in the individual order, is a continuation in the domestic order. Nay, since domestic unity has more of the individual in it than any other society, it can hardly be said in that case that the owner is quite changed." [1]

Hence the profound philosopher traces the permanence of the deceased man's possessions from the idea of domestico-social unity, and therefore from a species of *eminent* right above that which belongs to the individuals who compose it, even including the father.

51. Minghetti also bases his defence of inheritance on the idea of family, almost reproducing Taparelli's argument a little watered.

" If," he says, " we consider man as he is, not solitary, but in the midst of his family, and if we have regard to the sentiments of veneration and tenderness that link its members together, we shall see the domestic gift and the transmission of property proceed spontaneously, even without a will. For the family is not a simple aggregation of individuals, but an organic whole, that leaves the personality of each distinct; and yet it has its proper unity, from which there arises a species of co-participation of goods, as there arises a reciprocal protection and support. Hence the Jurisconsults profoundly say that heirs continue the person of the deceased, and call the sons *hæredes sui*, i.e. not of their things only, but also of themselves. Nay, inheritance tempers whatever is narrow and selfish in personal freedom, and converts all private progress into civil progress. People often identify their own good with the good of those who are dear to them ; and, indeed, industry is more stimulated by the desire of enabling their children to be prosperous than by the hope of gain." [2]

This is very well put. We remember hearing a man say to an extravagant friend, "Remember that you have children."

---

[1] *Saggio Teoretico di Diritto Naturale appoggiato sul fatto,* Vol. I. § 780, 781.

[2] *Dell' Economia Pubblica,* &c., Lib. V., p. 480.

CHAPTER IV.

BENEFICENCE.

ENEFICENCE is that virtue which induces us to do good to others. *Beneficentia nihil aliud importat quam facere bonum alicui.*[1] It proceeds from love, because love includes benevolence, i.e. desire of good in favour of the loved—for loving people and wishing well to them are convertible phrases—and the will effects what it wills, where there is power to do so. *In actu dilectionis includitur benevolentia, per quam vult aliquis bonum amico ; voluntas autem est effectiva eorum quæ vult, si facultas adsit.*[2]

Strictly speaking, love means more than benevolence; for simple benevolence is an act of the will, by which we wish well to some one, while love implies an effective union of the person who loves with the person loved, because the one who loves, regards the one who is loved as being one with himself, or as belonging to himself. *Amor ... differt a benevolentia: importat enim quamdam unionem secundum affectum amantis ad amatum, in quantum scilicet amans æstimat amatum quodammodo ut unum sibi vel ad se pertinens ... Sed benevolentia est simplex actus voluntatis, quo volumus alicui bonum, etiam non præsupposita prædicta unione affectus ad ipsum.*[3]

Love, benevolence, beneficence, are three conceptions closely connected.

---

[1] *Summa,* 2ª. 2ªᵉ. Q. XXXI. a. 1.   [2] Ibid., a. 1.
[3] *Summa,* 2ª. 2ªᵉ. Q. XXVII. a. 2.

ARTICLE I.

THE DUTY OF BENEFICENCE IS INSEPARABLE FROM THE RIGHT OF PROPERTY.

53. We have defended private property, real as well as personal, and strongly defended it. We spoke of it as necessary for the order and peace of society and for the abundance of production, and affirmed it to be a natural consequence of the right that man has to provide for his own and his children's future.

Here a difficulty comes in the way. Permanent appropriation of land and of its contents implies the distinction between owners and non-owners, between rich and poor, between those who have plenty and those who have not, while God has clearly given to all of us, with our existence, the right of preserving that existence through the products of land. To say that work supplies the want of possession is no answer : for work is the universal means of living, given by God to man. Work is sometimes impossible through infirmity or old age. Not unfrequently the supply of workmen exceeds the demand for them, or the wages are not enough to live on.

The objection would be unanswerable, if the right of property were not accompanied by the duty of beneficence : but it is not so when the two are combined. Unquestionably every man born here below has by a divine decree the right to live on the fruits of the earth. *Secundum naturalem ordinem, ex divina Providentia institutum, res inferiores sunt ordinatæ ad hoc, quod ex his subveniatur hominum necessitati.*[1] But for the actuation of this decree, it is not necessary that the earth should remain in common : which indeed would not bring universal wealth, but universal poverty, because plentiful production is not possible without careful cultivation, nor careful cultivation without the stimulus of private interest. What really is requisite

---

Summa, 2ª. 2ᵃᵉ. Q. LXVI. a. 7.

is that no one should be excluded from the enjoyment of what the land produces : and this is fulfilled when those who have, give what they can afford for the use of those who have not.

54. Let us see what St. Thomas says about it. He distinguishes the *possession* of temporal goods from the *use* of them : and he teaches that private possession is lawful. *Licitum est quod homo propria possideat.* Nay, he says that such possession is necessary to human life— *Est etiam necessarium ad humanam vitam*—for the reasons that we gave elsewhere.[1] But with regard to the use of them he adds that we should not have them *as* our own, but as common in the sense that we should willingly give a part of them to the indigent, as St. Paul teaches in the first Epistle to Timothy, vi.17. *Aliud, quod competit homini circa res exteriores, est usus ipsarum : et quantum ad hoc non debet homo habere res exteriores ut proprias, sed ut communes, ut scilicet de facili aliquis eas communicet in necessitate aliorum. Unde Apostolus dicit,* (1. ad Timoth. ult. 17.) *Divitibus hujus sæculi præcipe . . . facile tribuere, communicare de bonis, &c.*[2]

And in another place he says that temporal goods, which man receives from Divine Providence, are his to possess, but that they should also be used for the support of others : *Bona temporalia, quæ homini divinitus conferuntur, ejus quidem sunt quantum ad proprietatem : sed quantum ad usum, non solum debent esse ejus, sed etiam aliorum, qui ex eis sustentari possunt ex eo quod ei superfluit.*[3] And this is just what our Lord expressly commanded in the Gospel : *Quod superat, date pauperibus.* A proprietor, by the fact of being a proprietor, is bound to be a benefactor. He is as a minister of Divine Providence, which operates in the world and governs the world by means of

---

[1] See the two first Chapters of this second Part.
[2] *Summa,* 2ª. 2ᵃᵉ. Q. LXVI. a. 2.
[3] *Summa,* 2ª. 2ᵃᵉ. Q. XXXII. a. 5. ad 2.

secondary causes. In this way property escapes the assaults of Socialism, and appears as benefitting, instead of injuring, those who have it not.

55. All is connected in the Divine System, and shows itself to be admirable, unless man by an abuse of freedom spoils the harmony. If property made it impossible for a part of the human race to be maintained, certainly there would be a disorder and a crime ; but it does not do that, being united by God to the duty of beneficence, in virtue of which we are bound to give out of our abundance, if we have it, to those who are in want. *Mendicus est qui ab alio petit ; et pauper qui sibi non sufficit.*[1]

In this way the two elements, wealth and poverty, which at first sight seem opposed, are quite reconcilable ; for, while maintaining diversity of conditions, without which civil society could not subsist, they prove to be a mutual help and support. Without the labour of the poor, wealth could not be kept up ; nor could the poor find a refuge in distress, if there were no wealth. The relation of the giver and the receiver is a mutual bond, and they are coordinate in the purpose of God, Who willed that the poor should respect the property of the rich, and that the rich should be beneficent to the poor. *Dives et pauper obviaverunt sibi : utriusque operator est Dominus.*[2] Thus understood, there is nothing in landed property for Socialists to lay hold of.

ARTICLE II.
THREE EXPLANATIONS.

56. Three points have to be cleared up. We shall explain them with the help of St. Thomas. The first is the meaning of *superfluous*. The holy Doctor teaches us that it must be taken in a sense relative to the person,

---

[1] Capiodorus, quoted by St. Thomas, *Summa*, 2ª. 2ᵃᵉ. Q. CLXXXVII. a. 5. [2] *Proverbs*, xxii. 2.

regarded in his social state and his obligation to provide
for those of whom he has special care, such as the
members of his family : *Dico superfluum non solum respectu sui ipsius, quod est supra id quod est necessarium
individuo, sed etiam respectu aliorum quorum cura sibi in-
cumbit : respectu quorum dicitur necessarium personæ,
secundum quod persona dignitatem importat.*[1] Clearly the
excess is different in different classes ; nor is it the same
for an unmarried man as it is for one who is married and
has a large family. The difficulty is to determine the
superfluous, considering the uncertain extension of the
idea and the intellectual confusion that results from
selfishness, ambition, and immoderate love of our own ;
but it is made easy by the religious idea, as we shall see
in the next article.

57. The other point is the nature of the obligation.
We say plainly that it is a *grave* obligation, because it
proceeds from a strict law of nature. The things that a
man has beyond and above his wants are owed for the
maintenance of the poor. *Res quas aliqui superabundanter
habent, ex naturali jure debentur pauperum sustentationi.*[2]
And the reason of this is evident. The right of every
man to live on the fruits of the earth is *primary*, being
one of those rights that proceed immediately from nature,
and therefore are said to be *iure naturali*. The right of
property is *secondary*, being one of those that proceed
from nature mediately, and therefore are said to be *de jure
gentium :* so that if they clash, the right gives way in
that part of the income which exceeds the wants of the
owner. Nature gave the right of appropriation, not
absolutely, but with respect to an end ; and that end is to
secure for the future peacefully, certainly, and abundantly
the fruits of the earth, which are necessary to maintain
oneself and those for whom one is bound to provide. But

---

[1] *Summa*, 2ª. 2ᵃᵉ. Q. XXXII. a. 5.
[2] *Summa*, 2ª. 2ᵃᵉ. Q. LXVI. a. 7.

if these fruits of the earth exceed that measure, while there are people wanting the necessaries of life, the owner has no right to the excess, because by not giving it he clearly would be injuring others, who, having an absolute right to live, have no means of supporting life. To them it should be dispensed as their natural appanage. He who keeps it for himself, gravely violates a divine decree, and claims a right not given to him by any one ; for the right of property was conferred by God under the condition of giving the excess to the poor. And therefore St. Basil says against a man who had unjustly withheld it : " Art thou not a despoiler,—thou who thinkest thine own what thou didst receive to dispense ? The bread which thou keepest, belongs to the famishing ; thy locked-up clothes to the naked ; thy rotting shoes to the shoeless ; thy hidden money to the indigent. Wherefore thy wrongdoing is in proportion to what thou art able to give, and dost not give." *Nonne spoliator es tu, qui, quæ dispensanda accepisti, propria' reputas ? Est panis famelici, quem tu tenes ; nudi tunica, quam in conclavi conservas ; discalceati calceus, qui penes te marcescit ; indigentis argentum, quod possides inhumatum. Quocirca tot injuriaris, quot dare valens es.*[1]

58. But if, it may be said, that superfluity belongs to the poor, any poor man can take it against the will of the owner without stealing. We answer by denying the consequence. That superfluity is owed to the poor in general, not to this or that poor person. And since it cannot suffice for all, the owner has the right of choosing. *Quia multi sunt necessitatem patientes, et non potest ex eadem re omnibus subveniri, committitur arbitrio uniuscujusque dispensatio propriarum rerum, ut ex eis subveniat necessitatem patientibus.*[2]

59. In such a decision, however, the order of reason

---

[1] *Hom. super illud Lucæ xii.* "Destruam horrea mea."
[2] *Summa*, 2ª. 2ªe. Q. LXVI. a. 7.

must be kept: and this is the third point that we have to clear up. Beneficence, as we have said, proceeds from the love that we owe to our neighbour; and that love is greater or less in proportion to the nearness of the person. This is the rule which, when the circumstances are equal, should guide us in the distribution of relief. Relations, therefore, according to the degrees of relationship should be preferred to friends; friends to neighbours; neighbours to fellow-countrymen; fellow-countrymen to foreigners. *Exhibitio beneficiorum,* says St. Thomas, *est quædam actio charitatis in alios. Et ideo oportet quod ad magis propinquos simus magis benefici.*[1] This rule, however, is not invariable for every case, because the greater poverty of a more distant kinsman, or a closer relation to the public good, may counsel us to act otherwise; and therefore prudence is required in its application: *Si autem duorum unus est magis conjunctus et alter magis indigens, non potest universali regula determinari, cui sit magis subveniendum; quia sunt diversi gradus et indigentiæ et propinquitatis: sed hoc requirit prudentis judicium.*[2]

60. There is an exception in the case of very grave necessity, so urgent as not to admit delay. Moralists call this necessity *extreme,* or *almost extreme.* In such a crisis a man may take what is required to relieve the want that he cannot supply otherwise: *Si tamen adeo sit evidens et urgens necessitas, ut manifestum sit instanti necessitati de rebus occurrentibus esse subveniendum (puta cum imminet personæ periculum et aliter subveniri non potest), tunc licite potest aliquis ex rebus alienis suæ necessitati subvenire, sive manifeste sive occulte sublatis.*[3]

Nor can this taking be properly called theft, though it

---

[1] *Summa,* 2ᵃ. 2ᵃᵉ. Q. XXXI. a. 3. ad 1.

[2] *Summa,* 2ᵃ. 2ᵃᵉ. Q. XXX. a. 3.

[3] *Summa,* 2ᵃ. 2ᵃᵉ. Q. LXVI. a. 7.

be done without, or against the will of the owner ; for the pressing gravity of the need determines it as due to that individual : *Non habet rationem furti proprie loquendo, quia per talem necessitatem efficitur suum id, quod quis accipit ad sustentandam propriam vitam.*[1]

ARTICLE III.

THE RELIGIOUS IDEA.

61. It has, I think, been clearly shewn that the rich are naturally bound to give out of their superfluity to the poor, and that we may call superfluous what exceeds a man's own wants and those of his family, according to his social position. But here we are confronted by a knotty question : What is this excess ? Respecting the necessary, understood in relation to the social degree of the man and of those who belong to him, there is no term placed in the indivisible. The addition of much does not make it go beyond, nor does the subtraction of much take it away : *Hujusmodi necessarii terminus*, says St. Thomas, *non est in indivisibili constitutus. Sed multis additis, non potest dijudicari esse ultra tale necessarium ; et multis subtractis, adhuc remanet, unde possit convenienter aliquis vitam transigere secundum proprium statum.*[2]

Add to this that selfishness, ambition, and luxury have a powerful influence in confusing the judgment by making people think necessary for their condition what is not so in fact : so that the superfluous is either not found at all, or is quite out of any just proportion. This is most evidently the case in the present social order, or rather *disorder ;* for now the position of each man is measured by his wealth, and he who has the most, is credited with the

---

[1] *Summa,* 2ª. 2ᵃᵉ. Q. LXVI. a. 7, ad 2.
[2] *Summa,* 2ª. 2ᵃᵉ. Q. XXXII. a .6.

highest position. Here the superfluous cannot be found, because the measure is confused with the measurable.

62. In this difficulty religion comes to the rescue, converting the act of beneficence into an act of love towards God, closely connecting it with the ordinate love that man owes to himself. Thus it gives a most powerful stimulus to the exercise of beneficence, and deprives of all force the deceitful calculations of selfishness.

St. John the Apostle says in his First Epistle : "He that hath the substance of this world, and shall see his brother in need, and shall put up his bowels from him, how doth the charity of God abide in him?" *Qui habuerit substantiam hujus mundi, et viderit fratrem suum necessitatem habere, et clauserit viscera sua ab eo, quomodo charitas Dei manet in eo?* [1] Here the holy Apostle plainly teaches us that he who does not practise beneficence to his neighbour, does not love God. The reason is clear, because beneficence is a necessary sequel to the love of our neighbour, and the love of our neighbour is a necessary sequel to the love of God. *Hoc mandatum habemus a Deo ut, qui diligit Deum, diligat et fratrem suum.* [2] And therefore Theologians teach that among Christians the love of God is the reason of loving our neighbour, and that the two loves have a specifically identical act. *Ratio diligendi proximum Deus est. . . . Idem specie actus est, quo diligitur Deus et quo diligitur proximus.* [3]

63. Moreover, religion puts almsgiving before us as an indispensable means of obtaining eternal life. To begin with, it terrifies the rich : "Woe to you, rich men, who have your consolation here below." *Væ vobis divitibus, quia habetis consolationem vestram.* [4] "It is easier for a camel to pass through the eye of a needle, than for a rich man to enter into the Kingdom of Heaven." *Facilius est*

---

[1] 1 *John* iii. 17.   [2] Ibid. iv. 21.
[3] *Summa*, 2ᵃ. 2ᵃᵉ. Q. XXV. a. 1.   [4] *Luke* vii. 24.

*camelum per foramen acus transire quam divitem intrare
in regnum cœlorum.*[1] To the rich man who wishes to save
his soul, it is a condition *sine qua non* that the poor be
under obligation to him for beneficence. It is of immeasurably greater value to him than accumulating
treasure. *Bona est . . . eleemosyna magis quam thesauros
auri recondere.*[2]

With these criteria, therefore, we can easily find the
superfluous to be given to the poor. The beneficent act
becomes an act of love to God and a price for obtaining
eternal salvation.

64. Both motives our Lord Jesus Christ rendered
sensible and concrete, elevating the poor man to be a
representative of His Divine Person. This would be hard
to believe, if Christ Himself had not made it clear. In the
twenty-fifth chapter of St. Matthew we find His own des-
cription of the Last Judgment. To the good (He tells us)
He will say, "Come ye blessed of My Father, possess you the
kingdom prepared for you from the foundation of the world.
For I was hungry, and you gave Me to eat : I was thirsty,
and you gave Me to drink : I was a stranger, and you took
Me in : naked, and you covered Me : sick, and you visited
Me : I was in prison, and you came to Me. Then shall
the just answer Him, saying : Lord, when did we see
Thee hungry, and fed Thee ; thirsty, and gave Thee
drink ? And when did we see Thee a stranger, and took
Thee in ? or naked, and covered Thee ? Or when did we
see Thee sick, or in prison, and came to Thee ? And the
King answering, shall say to them : Amen I say to you,
as long as you did it to one of these My least brethren,
you did it to Me." [3]

---

[1] *Matt.* xix. 24.   [2] *Tobias* xii. 8.

[3] *Venite benedicti Patris mei, possidete paratum vobis regnum
a constitutione mundi. Esurivi enim, et dedistis mihi manducare :
sitivi, et dedistis mihi bibere : hospes eram, et collegistis me :
nudus, et cooperuistis me : infirmus, et visitastis me : in carcere*

Such a sublime conception as this could only be introduced into the world by God Himself, come among men in assumed human nature. In the light of these words all the sophisms of selfishness disappear from the rich man's mind like shadows. It opens his heart. He will easily find the superfluous, or, if need be, find that he can even deprive himself of what is necessary. To him the human creature without food is Christ starving. To him the insufficiently clothed is Christ in want of clothing. To him the destitute man, sleeping on a door-step, is Christ deprived of bed and lodging. Oh, God! How can a believer think of this, and not feel his heart touched—not take at once the bread from his table and the money from his purse, to relieve that Divine indigence ? Is there anything that Christ does not deserve ? Let us offer to Christ all that we can do. Moreover, if Christ is in the poor, the rich man by gaining the friendship of the poor gains the friendship of Christ, which means the friendship of his Judge.

No wonder, then, that among Christians we often see the rich giving immense alms to the poor, so that frequently through relief of the poor they are poor themselves. Of the celebrated Donoso Cortes, in whom noble blood and genius were united to unbounded piety, it is related that he only kept a sixth of his income for his own use, and gave the other five parts for the relief of the poor. Certainly there is no selfishness in that way of measuring the superfluous.

---

eram, et venistis ad me. Tunc respondebunt ei justi dicentes: Domine quando te vidimus esurientem, et pavimus te: sitientem, et dedimus tibi potum? Quando autem te vidimus hospitem, et collegimus te ; aut nudum, et cooperuimus te? Aut quando te vidimus infirmum, aut in carcere, et venimus ad te? Et respondens Rex, dicet illis : Amen dico vobis, quamdiu fecistis uni ex his fratribus meis minimis, mihi fecistis.—Matt. xxv. 34-40.

ARTICLE IV.

THE BUSINESS OF THE STATE WITH REGARD TO BENEFICENCE.

65. Man does not live apart, but in civil society ; and society not only insures the enjoyment of his rights, but also helps him to practise his duties. It does this even in the order of beneficence.

It seems to us that the duties of the civil government in this matter are two, protection and supply—guardianship of the charitable institutions that are : supply of those that cannot be supplied by private effort.

The rich, when informed with Christian charity, are not satisfied by doing good during their life, but carry on their beneficence beyond. The charitable foundations in the Catholic Church are enormous. Not only does she by her doctrine infuse charity into the minds of the faithful and regulate it by laws, but also to a great extent she executes it by means of the different pious works and religious institutes devoted thereto. Beneficence is to her a part of religion, because Christ has willed that He should be represented by the poor ; and being by her nature immortal, she impresses immortality on the effects of which she is the cause. To such institutions, which have their origin not from the State, but from the Church, either immediately through herself or mediately through her faithful children, the civil government owes protection, security of rights, defence against all injuries, and, above all, freedom of action. If these be sufficient, the civil government may justifiably dispense itself from all exercises of beneficence, and be contented with promoting them indirectly.

66. We are glad to find Minghetti agreeing with us about this. " I think," he says, " that if private persons, families,

the Church, or corporations instituted for the end of helping the poor, are sufficient for the purpose, the government has no right to meddle with them.   It would be unfortunate, because free and private charity is ennobled by infinite worth.   Private charity waits not for destitution to knock at the door and lay bare its wounds before the eyes of the profane, but goes in search of it and prepares the remedy.   Moreover it is accompanied by that sagacious and foreseeing judgment which knows how to distinguish the false from the true.   Lastly, it arouses in the benefactor a pleasant feeling of content, in the benefitted a feeling of gratitude, and improves the heart and intellect of both."[1]

These words from an Economist of such liberal principles are a just reproof to our governments [2] for taking to themselves the administration of the *Opere Pie*, to make beneficence a monopoly of the State.   Setting aside the violation of the founder's rights, they inflict a grave injury and a cruel outrage on the poor themselves, whose protectors they pretend to be.   They injure them not only by subtracting a considerable part of what is their due, and paying place-men therewith—to say no worse— but also by drying up the very sources of almsgiving, because the minds of men are alienated from it through want of confidence in the State and its officials.   They outrage the poor in two ways.   Firstly they enforce a painful humiliation.   The modern atheistic State represents man alone, while the Catholic Church directly represents God.   Now we are all mendicants before God, and beg from Him our daily bread.   *Panem nostrum quotidianum da nobis hodie.*   The poor man, therefore, does not consider himself degraded by applying to a minister of the Church in his need : but he does feel lowered by holding

---

[1] *Dell 'Economia Pubblica*, Lib. V.
[2] *Scil.* in Italy.

out his hand for relief to a paid servant of the government. In the second place, poverty is often connected with hidden sorrows. These the poor man has no difficulty in telling to a Priest, but is justly indignant at revealing them to a government official.

67. Besides the duty of protecting beneficence, the civil government has, as we have said, the duty of supplying : which means that it should come in with public money when the Church and private effort are insufficient. Here again we are glad to find Minghetti in agreement with us. After enumerating the evils usually noticed in State beneficence, he goes on to say : " These reasons and these examples are, as it seems to me, of great weight ; but not so as to exclude altogether legal charity, when private and free charity is not sufficient, especially in certain extraordinary calamities and in those dolorous crises to which industry is subject." [1]

We think that in such, or similar, times of trouble, the government may even impose a tax on the possessions of the rich. The Economists generally exclaim against such expedients ; but whatever they may choose to say, society would not be justified in suffering one part of the population to perish through hunger, while another part is enjoying every comfort. The Economists bring against us the example of England, where the poor-rate, they say, has done more harm than good ; and they describe the unpleasant spectacle of the Relieving Officer [2] sitting at a

---

[1] *Dell 'Economia Publica*, Lib. V.

[2] Given the dissolution of the monasteries and the loss of religious unity, the Relieving Officer must be employed, and, with all due respect to M. Droz, must have a table. Outdoor and indoor relief through the Relieving Officer do *not* prevent or *impede*, but merely supplement the work of private charity and charitable institutions—the latter being in England remarkable in number and munificence—but the said outdoor and indoor relief *do* prevent the necessity of starving. Poor laws must

table to distribute loaves and shillings. But England now
is not a Catholic country; and we are speaking of Catholic
countries, where all this can easily be avoided, and
especially by intrusting the relief of the poor, not to
people paid by the government, but to those that are
moved to do it by the love of God. Droz, who disapproves
of the English Relieving Officer, adds that where a tax
is raised for the poor, the best means of making it as bad
as possible is to have it distributed by paid persons.
" Since the foundation of numerous schools," he says, " I
see nothing more useful for ameliorating society than
putting in contact with the poor enlightened and beneficent persons, [1] who know how to give advice and revive
courage, and, while bringing relief, teach them how they
may suffice for themselves." But above all, we must add,
they should be able to cure the wounds of the soul with
the balm of religion.

68.   Poverty, which never since original sin can be
quite banished from the world,—*semper pauperes habetis
vobiscum*,[2]—needs permanent relief; and for this purpose
permanent foundations are more useful than casual alms.
Where the faithful who have only moderate fortunes, and
the Church, now despoiled almost entirely by modern
civilization, cannot give much, the government should
bring help out of its own money, which could not be more
justly and usefully employed; and since the government
has no source of riches except the purses of the subjects,

---

always leave much to be desired and much to be regretted : but
unhappily we cannot do without them, circumstanced as we
are.—*Translator's Note.*

[1]   This is just what Henry VIII. did away with by the dissolution of the monasteries, when men, truly " enlightened
and beneficent," had in England the entire care of the poor ; and
this is what " regenerated Italy " is now making impossible by
stealing the property of the *Opere Pie.*—*Translator's Note.*

[2]   *Matt.* xxvi. 11.

it may by prudent laws burden the possessions of the more wealthy to relieve the distress of the destitute. True it is that to convert into legal compulsion what ought to be an effect of spontaneous liberality, is deplorable. We acknowledge how odious and violent it is. We admit that it might be regarded by some, and not without cause, as a step towards Socialism. But what is to be done? If hearts are warmed no longer by the love of God and consequent charity to our neighbour, force naturally comes in. When man resists the gentle impulse of the Divine Law, everything is disordered and upsidedown. We must understand that between Christian charity and Socialism there is no medium. When you turn away from the one, you hurry on towards the other.

69. Among the manifold wants of the poor, the three most dependent on beneficence are infantine weakness, infirmity and old age. The followers of Malthus, wishing to prevent the marriage of the poor, which they hate *cane pejus et angue*, would like to see the suppression of such and such-like public establishments. Malthus reprobates especially the foundling hospitals, where babies, abandoned by sinful or inhuman parents, are received; but what would become of those poor little innocent creatures, if there were no such places? One shrinks from the thought.

It is objected that most of them die very soon: but would they be likely to live longer, if they had no help at all? The objection, at the most, would only shew that the institutions might be better than they are. To do away with these and other institutions, regardless of the consequences, is a stupid and cruel remedy.

70. The hospitals, they say, loosen family ties, because the sick are thus intrusted to strangers, instead of being nursed by parents, children, husbands, wives, &c. Unquestionably it is a more pious work to relieve the sick in their own homes; but, inasmuch as it is very difficult for the poor to attend on them at home with due skill and

care, even when generously helped, it is always necessary
to have public hospitals well regulated and provided.
Above all things it is important that the care of the sick
should not be entrusted to mercenaries, but to persons
informed by the true spirit of charity, as Religious are.
The objection would then have no force; for in respect of
loving care, the compassionate sons of St. John of God
and the heroic Sisters of Charity will bear comparison
with any relation whomsoever. Yet Liberalism, with a
bestial want of intelligence, not only does not seek for
such helpers, but drives them away from the places where
it finds them, and puts hired nurses in their place.

71. Lastly, it is requisite that superannuated work-
people should be taken care of. If we give pensions to
officials and soldiers, are we to leave destitute the veterans
of labour, when they have used up their strength in procuring the necessaries and comforts of life for the
community?

But these and similar institutions (they would say) are
an encouragement to matrimony. The poor often reckon
on them when they marry. Be it so. But what of that?
Have we not shown that by a natural and divine law the
superfluous money of the rich is the appanage of the
poor? and what are these institutions but permanent fruits
of that superfluous money? Certainly the poor men should,
before they marry, put themselves in a position to maintain a family; and this is usually done by trying to
become expert in some sort of work that promises a sufficient remuneration. But there is no reason why they should
not, in view of possible accidents, calculate on those
institutions which Christian charity has created for their
comfort and relief. Nay, they have a right to do so.

72. Our opinion is quite contrary to that of the Malthusians. Not only do we say that no existing institution
of beneficence ought to be suppressed, but even that the
number and variety of them should be increased, so that

there might be a remedy, as far as is possible, for every misfortune—a balm for every wound, help for every need. We only ask that such charitable works be intrusted, not to officials who know nothing about charity, but to the Church, which is animated by the love of Christ, administers in the name of God, enjoys the full confidence of the faithful, and is in a position through intimate knowledge of them to distinguish the genuine poor from impostors, and can add to the corporal works of mercy the spiritual, of which poverty has often the greater need.

CHAPTER V.

THREEFOLD DIVISION OF WEALTH PRODUCED.

 IN the division of products among those who have co-operated to produce them, lies the chief idea of the distribution of wealth. Now these co-operators, as we have already seen, are three, *viz.* the proprietor who furnished the natural agents, the capitalist who anticipated the necessary expenses, and the workman who contributed his labour. Between the proprietor, therefore, the capitalist, and the workman, the wealth produced is divided, so that it may repay according to justice the entire work of its production. That part of it which belongs to the proprietor is called *rent*, the capitalist's part *profit*, the workman's part *wages*. The produce of the earth, says Ricardo, all that comes out of its surface, is through the combined application of labour, machinery, and capital, distributed among three classes of society, *viz.* the proprietors of the soil, the proprietors of the value or capital required to cultivate it, and the workmen who labour.[1]

Sometimes these classes are only two; for the proprietor is sometimes the capitalist, as when a land-owner farms the whole or a part of his land; and sometimes the capitalist (a small farmer, for instance) is also a workman. They are even reducible to one, as in the case of a

---

[1] See his *Principles of Political Economy*, Preface.

very small freeholder who is his own tenant and his own labourer. But the three functions are different, and cause a difference in the relative remuneration—of rent, profit, and wages. We shall discuss each of them separately.

ARTICLE I.
RENT.

74. Though the word "rent" is commonly used [but not in English] to mean any annual income that comes from the possession of a proprietor, the Economists restrict its meaning to income from land. Ricardo defines it to be that portion of the products of land which is paid to the proprietor for the use of the original and indestructible forces of nature.[1] He points out that in this sense it must not be confused, as it often is, with the whole sum paid by the farmer to the landlord, part of which corresponds to the capital employed; and he says that, when speaking of rent, he wishes the word to be understood as meaning the remuneration which the proprietor of the soil receives for allowing the primitive and indestructible forces of the soil to be used.[2] Most of the Economists, especially in England, say the same. McCulloch thinks that rent is that part of the gross sum which is paid for the land in compensation for its inherent natural qualities, and which would be paid, even if it were in a state of nature, without any improvement. Whatever is beyond that, he says, is profit, not rent.[3]

---

[1] *Principles of Political Economy*, Chap 2.

[2] Ibid. If these Economists had practised the trade of a landlord, they would know that, besides the "indestructible forces of the soil" (which, by the bye, are seriously diminished by bad farmers,) there are the very destructible buildings, gates, fences, &c., the repairing of which reduces the income of the landlord to less than two thirds of the whole rent received, when he *does* receive it.—*Translator's Note.*

[3] *Principles of Political Economy*, Book II. Chap. 16.

Stuart Mill says that land is the chief agent among those that can be appropriated, and that the compensation paid for it is called rent.[1]

75. On this conception of rent Ricardo bases his theory about its origin. He derives it from the superior quality of some land, its nearness to a market, and its consequent capability of being more profitable. He remarks that when people take up their abode in a new country, where good land is abundant and only a small part requires cultivation for the support of the inhabitants, which part can be cultivated with a small capital, there will be no rent, because nobody would pay for the use of what is no better than the unoccupied land which any one may have. If all land, he says, were equally fertile and unlimited, none would fetch any rent except for some peculiar advantage of locality; so that rent is paid by reason of its being limited in extent, and not uniform in quality, and because, as the population increases, second-rate land, less advantageously situated, is put under cultivation. When, in the progress of society, the second-rate land is cultivated, the rent of the better land rises in proportion to the difference in quality between the two.[2] Clearly so. To make the worse land as fruitful as the better, more money must be laid out; and the owners have to make up the difference by demanding higher prices, which the inhabitants owing to the increase of population have to pay. Whereupon the owners of the better land raise their prices too, getting thereby a return over and above their expenses. This excess over their expenses constitutes rent.

Ricardo adds that the employment of new capital on already cultivated land for the purpose of making it produce more will sufficiently explain the origin of rent, without having recourse to the cultivation of inferior

---

[1] *Principles of Political Economy*, Chap. 5.
[2] Ibid., Chap. 2.

land ; for this extra produce must be sold at a higher price, because it cannot equal in quantity the former produce, and therefore will raise the price of the former. This increase of price will constitute rent. He tells us that often and usually before cultivating the less fertile parts of the country (which he designates by the numbers 2, 3, 4, 5) we can employ capital more profitably than heretofore in the already cultivated land. It might happen, he says, that by doubling the capital first employed on number one, *viz.* the first-rate land, the produce, though not doubled—not 100 per cent, for instance—may be 85 per cent, and so be more than the same capital would bring out of number three, the third-rate land. In that case people will prefer to invest their capital in the old land, and this alike will constitute a rent, because that is always the difference between the products obtained from two equal quantities of capital and labour. . In this case also, he says, as in that of cultivating inferior land, the capital employed last pays no rent. [1]

76. This theory was hailed by most of the Economists as a most valuable discovery in economic science.[2] To us

----

[1] Ibid.

[2] McCulloch thinks that this explains the true origin of rent, but attributes it to Dr. Anderson. He tells us that soon after the publication of Smith's *Wealth of Nations*, the true theory of rent was first discovered by Dr. James Anderson, who showed that rent is not the reward of nature's work, nor a consequence of private property in land, but is due to the varying fertility of the soil, and the impossibility of applying unlimited capital thereto without entailing, as a rule, a gradual diminution of produce. The passage that he quotes from Dr. Anderson expresses Ricardo's meaning with little variation of words, but more clearly. In all countries, says Dr. Anderson, the fertility of land varies, and therefore the cultivators of the better land can afford to sell in the market at a lower price than others whose land is not so good. But if the produce of the better land is not sufficient to supply the demand, the price will rise naturally, and thus indemnify the cultivators of the poorer land. Consequently, those who cultivate the better land will be able to get

it seems an ingenious speculation, but very far from being true or even plausible.   First of all, it is founded on an hypothesis.   It supposes that a great number of people have come to live in the same neighbourhood at the same time ; that there is an abundance of land there, all equally fertile ; that the new comers have settled near this good land ; that the good land is cultivated first, in preference to other land less good but nearer ; that all are provided with capital ; that all, or nearly all, incline to agriculture, rather than to manufacture or commerce.   One can hardly believe that all these conditions would be verified, and apply to the whole human race.

77.   In the second place, the theory would serve to explain the origin of rent, but not the reason of its origin—its historical, not its juridical origin.   Indeed, it would be dangerous to the latter ; for a Socialist might say that if rent was occasioned by increase of population, which necessitated the cultivation of the less fertile land, it ought to be, not for the benefit of the landlord, but of the increased population.   The juridical origin of rent—and that is what properly concerns the science of Political Economy—is to be found nowhere else than in the right of property, of which rent is a consequence.   If the natural forces of the soil truly co-operate with capital and labour to produce—and in fact these natural forces are the chief co-operators—a part of the products is naturally due to the lawful owner of that land.   To whomsoever the cause belongs, the effect belongs : *res fructificat domino.*

78.   Moreover an estate, unless it be a sandy plain, has natural productions useful to the owner of the soil.

---

as high a price as those who cultivate the worse, and receive something over the value of their produce.   And then many people will be ready to give a premium, more or less, according to the goodness of the soil, for the privilege of cultivating it ; which premium constitutes what we now call rent.   See *Principles of Political Economy*, Part III. Chap. 5. Hence not a few Economists tell us that rent is, after all, a natural monopoly.

Ricardo's theory presupposes the richness of the land first occupied; and that presupposes fruit-trees, pastures, woods, game, fish, more or less, and possibly stone-quarries, gravel-pits, coal-mines, &c. Now, before capital is used and work done, what in themselves are all these gifts of God but rent? They are so everywhere, more or less; and when, besides these agents naturally operating, the other two elements of production, capital and work, are added, the said land will begin to grow abundant crops of corn, &c. Certainly a part of these are due to the labourer, and part to the farmer; but a net part of it will always remain for the proprietor, and ought to be his, because he supplied the chief producer, *viz.* the natural forces inherent in the soil, which is his.

79. It will be objected that the net part remaining is not rent, because rent is the remuneration paid to the proprietor for giving the use of his land.

But why are we to accept this definition? Because Ricardo, McCulloch, Mill, and their followers, do so? It confuses the *rent*, or that which the land *renders*, with the hire, or price received by the proprietor for allowing a man to occupy a part of his land. This confusion arises from the belief that wealth lies in the *value in exchange*, and not in the *value in use*, as Adam Smith would call it; or, in other words, that it consists in the exchangeability of things, and not in their utility—an opinion that we refuted early in this treatise.

80. From all this it follows that Ricardo's definition is to be rejected, and the following, or something like it, substituted : RENT IS THAT WEALTH, OR PART OF WEALTH, WHICH, ANSWERING TO THE NATURAL FORCES INHERENT IN THE SOIL, BELONGS TO THE PROPRIETOR. This definition rests, we admit, on two presuppositions, *viz.* that wealth consists in the sum of useful things, and that natural forces, as far as they are incorporated in a given matter, are appropriable and recognizable; but we have already

proved both these truths. Moreover by this definition
we shut out two absurdities offensive to common sense,
viz. that land, however fertile, gives no rent to the proprietor, unless it comes into comparison with less fertile
land, and that rent is an effect of monopoly—detestable
words that furnish the Socialists with a weapon against
property, and cannot be softened by the epithet *natural.*

Land always gives a rent—i.e. renders much or little,
according to its quality. No one cares for what is quite
unproductive and useless. Such rent may be turned into
hire by letting the land whence it proceeds, and this hire
is metonymically called rent, as we call money wealth—not
that it is so of itself, but because it is equivalent thereto
in virtue of exchange.

In our opinion, therefore, Ricardo's theory is not only
untenable, but also the source of confusion and error.

ARTICLE II.
PROFIT.

81. PROFIT IS THAT PART OF THE PRODUCE WHICH BE-
LONGS TO THE CAPITALIST, *viz.* to the man who provides the
means necessary for working—tools, machinery, wages for
the support of the labourers in anticipation of produce, and
so on. He, too, may be called a proprietor, as owning all
this ; but it pleases the Economists to call him a capitalist,
to distinguish him from the owner of the land that he
works, and because the things that he possesses, constitute
what is called capital. Ricardo says that capital is that
portion of a country's wealth which is employed to produce, and consists in food, clothes, instruments, raw
material, machinery, &c. [1]

82. When there is a question of some enterprise,
agrarian, manufacturing, or commercial, that requires a
special talent, skill, and experience to plan and carry out,

---

[1] *Principles of Political Economy*, Chap. 5.

a fourth person comes on the scene. This is the *entrepreneur*,[1] who forms the conception of it, arranges the means, and directs them to the end intended. Strictly speaking, his is a function by itself: but it has a great influence on the capital employed, because, whether the capital be his own or some one else's, his cleverness and care make it available and productive. A part of the proceeds therefore should be his. In Economy the *entrepreneur's* part of the proceeds is usually called profit, and the part that corresponds to capital simply as capital, is called interest. But we, when speaking of profit, shall intend to express the part belonging to the capitalist.

83. If the proprietor justly receives a rent for the natural agents that he supplies, no less justly does the capitalist receive a profit on the means that he supplies. Indeed, some Economists, thinking with Carey and Bastiat that utility proceeding from natural agents is always gratuitous, are of opinion that rent is lawful as being mere profit. And so, according to them, the proprietor's only claim to receive payment is that he renders production possible by his capital—which amounts to saying that he is simply a capitalist. " Distribution of wealth," says Boccardo, "means the participation of all the producers in the value of the produce. All the producers, however numerous, may be summed up under the two general categories of *capitalists* and *workmen*. The proprietors of the natural agents employed in production do not participate as proprietors in the distribution, because utility is gratuitous. Only by some rare exceptions, as in the case of monopoly, do the proprietors themselves carry away a portion of the produce, which is then called rent. The general rule is that the proprietors enjoy nothing beyond the fruits of the labour, present or

---

[1] I must apologize for using a French word; but I cannot find an equivalent in English. If such there be, ignorance of business terminology must plead my excuse.—*Translator.*

accumulated, by which they co-operate to produce, accelerating and temporarily using the gratuitous forces of nature. Therefore, given the wealth, the selling price of the same is distributed into two parts, wages and profit. Wages go to remunerate labour, profit repays the capital." [1]

This opinion, which, in short, suppresses the proprietor, and consequently the rent, cannot be admitted. It is founded on the false idea of there being no appropriable natural agents; which is neither more nor less than denying the right of property. These worthy Economists have recourse to the sophism that nature gives useful things *gratis*. No doubt they are given *gratis* by nature; but the man who finds himself in the possession of them is not bound thereby to give them *gratis*. By this sophism, therefore, they fall back into the before mentioned error of denying the right of property.

84. But enough of these oddities. Let us go back to *profit*. Profit is contradistinctive from rent and from wages. But, as we said, it corresponds to the appropriated natural agents, and wages are the remuneration of the labourer's toil. Profit lies between; for it answers to the capital employed, in order that the labourer may by his work make the natural agents give the desired produce. If we look for its primordial origin, we can find it nowhere else than in rent. The reason is that profit results from capital, and capital results from saving, and saving supposes rent, because the saving is done on that which the natural agents produced at first, and which was afterwards increased by means of labour.

The first inhabitants could save beyond their daily consumption, and in virtue of that saving they could apply themselves to form or procure tools for working, maintaining, or paying those who were willing to help them in doing the work. Here is the beginning of capital, and the just claim to get a profit out of it as the produce of

[1] Boccardo, *Dizionario*, at the word " Profitto."

what is our own by purchase or inheritance. All the rest is progressive development therefrom in virtue of human ability and civilisation. Minghetti seems to hint at this origin of capital in the following passage : " What is the right of the capitalist ? To understand that we must clearly make out the nature and origin of capital. For most Economists define it as an accumulated work, and thus involuntarily fall back into the error that work is the sole cause of produce. But we, who acknowledge nature with its forces and its materials to be a perennial co-cause, must trace its origin from them ; and consequently, in our opinion, capital might be defined as a natural substance or force transformed by the work of man and employed for reproduction, and is deduced partly from the right of the workman, partly from the right of the landlord." [1]

This again shows that without the right of property and inheritance Political Economy would fall to pieces.

85. Profit is divided into gross profit and net profit. Gross profit is the entire quota gained by the capitalist on the new produce. Net profit is that which remains after deducting the expenses incurred by him for wages and for wear and tear of tools, &c. This excess is what properly constitutes profit. The rest is only reimbursement. If the capitalist could not make a net profit, he would invest his capital in some other way. Evidently such profit is just; for capital, though not, strictly speaking, an agent of production (because the two agents of production are nature and work,) is nevertheless requisite and a means, and therefore deserving of remuneration. The measure of it is difficult to determine; for it necessarily varies according to the variety of places, times and persons, and the plentifulness or scarcity of the produce obtained. In right apparently it ought to equal what he would gain by

---

[1] *Dell' Economia Pubblica*, Lib. V.

any other employment equal to his in facility and safety. [1] In fact it follows the law of proportion between demand and supply. From this it follows that, on the one hand, increase of capital makes profit decrease, not *extensive*, but *intensive*, and on the other hand makes wages increase *extensive* certainly, if not *intensive*, by increasing the demand for labour, that capital may not lie idle. By increasing labour it increases production, so that in every respect that increase is good for the prosperity of the nation, and is of itself favourable to the well-being of the workmen also.

ARTICLE III.

WAGES.

86. The immense majority, three-quarters at least of the population, live on wages. WAGES, as we have said, ARE THE QUOTA THAT COMES TO THE WORKMAN ON THE FRUITS OF THE PRODUCTION WHICH HE HAS PARTLY CAUSED BY HIS OWN LABOUR. This quota is called wages, i.e. pay agreed on for service rendered, usually a remuneration of so much a day according to agreement. Workmen cannot afford to wait for the sale of produce, nor to risk the uncertainty of the event; and therefore they make a bargain with the master, whether proprietor, capitalist, or contractor, to receive a specified recompense, usually in money, for the work that he does. This is advantageous to both : to the workman on account of the advantages pointed out; to the master by freeing him from troublesome duties, and

---

[1] This holds good for capital precisely as capital; but the *entrepreneur* who carries out an undertaking quite at his own risk, may, after paying all who have co-operated in it (workmen, capitalists, and all persons employed therein,) justly adjudge to himself the whole residue of the proceeds. If the undertaking had failed, the whole loss would have been his; and therefore, since it was successful, he has a right to the whole gain.

by the hope of greater returns, in which he is justified by previous outlay and future risk.

Wages are evidently the result of a contract, through which, by mutual consent, the workman gives labour and the master gives pay. Consequently they bring about a transference of dominion. The workman acquires a full right to the pay agreed on, and the master acquires a full right to the labour for which he pays.

87. Proudhon maintains that, besides wages, the workman always has a natural right over the profits of what is produced. But if wages are given to the workman as equivalent to his quota of the profits, how can he have a right to more? Were it so, his quota would be paid twice. Would that be just?

You would be much astonished, if, when you had built a house, the masons or bricklayers, after being paid, wanted to occupy some of the rooms on the plea of having a natural right over the use of the product ; or if a tailor, when you had paid him for making a coat, claimed the right of wearing it once a week. If the workman has given his labour to you for the wages that you pay to him, the fruits of the labour must belong to you. Otherwise you might claim a natural right over his wages. Proudhon's position, therefore, besides being unjust is ridiculous.

88. The truly serious question is this : How much pay is due to the workman? We shall speak of this briefly, setting aside the less important questions.

" Labour," says Ricardo, " like all other things that are bought and sold, and whose quantity may increase or diminish, has its natural price and its current price. The natural price of labour," he says, " is that which is indispensable to the workman generally for their subsistence and for the perpetuation of the species. The current price is the price really paid, as the natural effect of the relation between demand and supply, labour being dearer when

there are few workmen, and cheaper when there are
many."

But he cares not to enquire whether the falling of the
current price below the natural price is offensive to
morality and justice. He is satisfied with saying that
however much the current price may deviate from the
natural price, it will always tend thereto, like all other
merchandise. [1]   Thus, according to him, the natural price
is not a rule for the current price, but only a point round
which it oscillates like a pendulum. This doctrine is
more or less accepted by the later Economists generally.
It by no means pleases us; and therefore we prefer to
treat the question in our own way.

89.   First of all we say that to look on labour as
merchandise, and wages as its price, is a false manner of
considering it, and the source of grave errors, [2] of which
the worst is that it loses sight of the workman's dignity
as a human being.   That such expressions now and then
slip out in a figurative sense by reason of analogy through
the intervention of demand and supply, may be tolerated;
and even Catholic Economists have occasionally used
them.   But analogy is one thing, and propriety of language
is another.   In a proper sense labour cannot anyhow be
called merchandise.   It ought, strictly speaking, to be
called loan of work, and wages therefore, not a price, but
a recompense.   Labour and wages constitute an exchange,
but the formula that expresses the exchange is not *Do ut
des.*   It is *Facio ut des ; do ut facias.*   Merchandise is
regarded in itself simply, according to its usefulness and
rarity, and prescinds from the producer.   When you buy
a thing in a shop, you consider it as it is, without caring
how it came there.   But in the case of labour it is not so.
Labour is a human action; and an action cannot prescind

---

[1]   *Principles of Political Economy*, Chap. 5.
[2]   This was learnedly proved by the distinguished advocate,
Burri, in his excellent pamphlet, *Labour.*

from the agent, nor from the quality of the agent. Labour, therefore, cannot prescind from the man, nor from the consideration due to the man.

It follows that in determining the recompense of labour, we must never forget how, by Divine ordinance, it belongs to man. Now in what respect does it belong to him? In respect of its being a means of providing for his maintenance, according to the manner in which he is naturally constituted. *In sudore vultus tui vesceris pane.*[1] God said man should have bread through the sweat of his brow. The sweat of his brow means labour or work. Bread means all that is necessary to life here below—food, clothes, lodging. Man means the human pair, male and female, and their family: *Masculum et feminam creavit eos. . . . Benedixitque illis Deus, et ait : Crescite et multiplicamini.*[2] Virtually therefore, work is to the workman that which is necessary for the maintenance of himself and of his family. If, therefore, he works for his master, his master should repay to him the equivalent, so as to preserve equality in the exchange, which means justice. *Justitia æqualitatem importat.*[3] We may therefore lay down as a rule that the natural price of a man's labour is the price which, inclusive of the wife's earnings—which cannot be much, because she has the cares of the house—will suffice to maintain him and her and two or three little children, as an average number, considering how many die in their infancy. By such reckoning current wages ought to be regulated. If they exceed that, as indeed they ought in the higher grades of work, so much the better, as giving the workman an opportunity of living in comfort and laying by for his future needs. If they fall below it without any fault of the workman, they will not answer the intentions of nature, nor preserve that equality in the exchange which justice requires.

---

[1] *Gen.* iii. 19.   [2] *Gen.* i, 27, 28.

[3] *Summa,* 2ª. 2ᵃᵉ. Q. LVII. a. 1. ad 3.

90. This opinion, which we always held, even before we had devoted ourselves *ex professo* to economic studies, is, we are glad to see, shared by Steccanella. After discussing the opinions of the principal Economists about wages, he says in his learned work, *On Communism :*

"This is the difference between the opinion of the modern Economists and ours. According to them the price equivalent to what is necessary is the medium price. We call it the lowest ; and therefore we say that to give less is unjust. Demand and supply have, we freely admit, an influence on the price of the same, but not so as to make just what is demonstrably unjust, and for the reasons given it is demonstrably unjust, whether we consider the quality of the personal service done by the workman, or judge it according to the estimate of the Economists themselves, or reckon its value by the intrinsic value of the work to be recompensed. Consequently the regulating principle of payment according to justice is that in ordinary times the pay should at least be equal to what is necessary for the maintenance of work-people.[1] "

Likewise the founder of Political Economy, Adam Smith, seems to teach the same, for he says :

"There is, however, a certain rate, below which it seems impossible to reduce, for any considerable time, the ordinary wages even of the lowest species of labour . . . . A man must always live by his work, and his wages must at least be sufficient to maintain him. They must even upon most occasions be somewhat more : otherwise it would be impossible for him to bring up a family . . . . " And further on he says : " Thus far at least, seems certain, that, in order to bring up a family, the labour of the husband and wife together must, even in the lowest species of common labour, be able to earn something more than what is precisely necessary for their own maintenance." [2]

---

[1] *Del Communismo*, &c. Lib. II. c. 15.
[2] *Wealth of Nations*, Book I. ch. 8.

In practice, however, this is not carried out. In Italy, for instance, most of the workmen have hardly enough to keep themselves alive, and in England the Sweating System is deplored by all good Englishmen. This is a festering sore in the social system, that justifies the murmuring of the poor, and puts into the hands of the Socialists a terrible weapon which they successfully use. Nor can we always blame the masters for this, as if they kept the wages low to fill their pockets greedily. Sometimes it is so; but usually the masters themselves are victims of the economic system now in vogue. Unbridled competition, of which we shall have to speak in the next Chapter, causes an incessant lowering of prices; so that, in order to sell cheap and not be cut out by competitors, the masters are often obliged to fine down the wages. To this is added excessive production by machinery, and in Italy the daily increasing burden of taxes. To remedy this evil, Statesmen should give their utmost attention; private individuals their charitable care; Economists their earnest study. If Political Economy does not succeed in suggesting a remedy for so great an evil, it is an empty and useless science.

CHAPTER VI.

FREE COMPETITION.

REE competition means that every one has full power with respect to trade, commerce, contracts—all, in short, that concerns production and the distribution of social wealth. It might be defined as THE ABSOLUTE EXCLUDING OF ALL STATE-INTERVENTION IN THE FUNCTIONS OF THE COUNTRY'S ECONOMIC LIFE. It is the reverse of the socialistic doctrine that capital, labour and the distribution of produce ought to be under the dominion and management of the executive. The latter is evidently absurd; for it means that all the individual rights and powers of the subjects ought to be absorbed by the State. No man of common sense can seriously entertain such a notion, and therefore to speak of it further would only be a waste of time. We shall go on to speak of the other system, which did, and does, occupy the minds of very many prudent persons.

ARTICLE I.
ITS ADVANTAGES.

92. Even at the dawn of economic science free competition was preached by the so-called Physiocrats. There is the celebrated formula, invented by Gournay: *Laissez faire, laissez passer.* This aphorism was accepted by Adam Smith, and became a common axiom among the later Economists.

The government, they said, should limit itself to securing industry against violence. It should have nothing to do with the rest. The power of using force as we please, in order to procure for ourselves the necessaries and comforts of life, to exchange merchandise, to employ capital, to make bargains by mutual agreement, this power comes by nature. To shackle it is an outrage on the rights of man.

The Economists declaim loudly about this. They represent the intervention of the government in Economy as a tyrannical act. " After all," exclaims Bastiat, " What is competition? Is it a thing existing and operating by itself like the cholera? No. Competition is nothing more than absence of oppression. In what concerns my interest I wish to choose for myself, and not have some one else choosing for me, whether I will or not. That is all. And if any one pretends to substitute his judgment in affairs that concern me, I shall claim to substitute mine for his in the transactions that concern him. Where is the guarantee for things going better so? It is evident that competition is freedom. To destroy freedom of action is to destroy the possibility and therefore the power of choosing, judging, comparing. It kills the intellect. It kills thought. It kills the man." [1] This is an alarming bill of indictment !

He then goes on to magnify the benefits conferred on society by free competition : "Competition," he says, "which we might also call freedom, notwithstanding all the resistance that it arouses, and in spite of all the declamation that pursues it [he alludes to the Socialist writers] is essentially the democratic law. It is the most progressive, the most equalizing, the most humanitarian of all those to which Providence has confided the progress of human society. It is that which successively brings under common dominion what nature appeared to have gratuitously granted to certain regions only. It is that which brings under common dominion for ever all the conquests by

---

[1] *Harmonies Économiques*, X. Concurrence.

which each century increases the treasures of generations."[1]

To free competition he attributes the return of a just equilibrium in value, the impossibility of leonine contracts, monopolies, exorbitant pretensions, inequality in mutual services, inoperativeness of capital, high prices, and so on.

Nearly all the Economists more or less repeat this. Boccardo, for example, says : " What the law of universal gravitation is in Physics, the parallelogram of forces in Mechanics, free will in Morals, i.e. the common regulator and, as it were, the pivot on which all the doctrines comprised in the particular science turn, competition is with regard to the affairs of Economy."[2] From this he proceeds to make known its beneficent influence on the three branches of Economy—production, distribution, and consumption. He also speaks of the struggle which the defenders of this economic freedom had to maintain ; and because the works of certain writers must not be without a sneer (whether to the point or not) against religion and priests, he adds to this: "Often religion served as a mask or a weapon for privilege against equivalence of services. A studious caste,[3] rendered venerable by the marks of the Priesthood, imposed its precept on the prostrate and stupid people, as if it were a divine, fatal, and necessary law,[4] . . . and extinguished in millions and millions of living men the sense of right and wrong, of the true and false."[5] These accusations have been repeated so often, so often refuted, and turn up again so regularly, that we are tired of noticing them.

---

[1] Ibid.

[2] *Trattato Teorico Pratico di Economia Politica,* Vol. I. Della libera Concorrenza.

[3] To call the Catholic Priesthood a caste is down right nonsense. A caste is exclusive : the Catholic Priesthood is open to all. A caste is perpetuated by marriage : Catholic Priests are professed celibates.

[4] We suppose that he alludes to forbidding usury—a prohibition which he fiercely attacks elsewhere.

[5] Ibid.

94. Among the benefits attributed to free competition by its panegyrists there is some truth, as the reader will have perceived : but there is also exaggeration and sophistry. It certainly is a sophism to argue in favour of free competition by comparing it with a despotic protection, that by abuse of power rashly fetters freedom. "Competition," said Bastiat, " is nothing more than absence of oppression;" and if such is its meaning, it is evidently desirable, because nobody likes to be oppressed. But that is not the question. The question is this : Whether free competition, in order to be beneficial, should be left entirely to the choice of individuals, or whether it requires to be tempered and kept within bounds by wise laws. It certainly is an exaggeration to say that the exchange of one country's products for those of another is attributable to free competition. We cannot overstate the benefits of having each nation's wealth accessible to all : but this, properly speaking, is the effect of commerce, not of free competition. Free competition can enlarge and help commerce; but it is one thing to enlarge and facilitate, another to constitute.

95. The true usefulness attributable, strictly speaking, to free competition is the impetus which it gives to production and exchange in every sort of industry and traffic. It awakens and stimulates individual interest, sharpens ability, causes emulation. Agriculture, the arts, trade, owe to it much of their increase. It has given, and is giving, a great impulse to the invention of new instruments and new machines, to the abundance of markets, to the opening of new outlets for the exportation of merchandise, to the discovery of new products. Lowering of prices, therefore, and increase of comforts and luxuries are the certain consequences of it. Moreover it is useful in dissipating the exorbitant pretensions of workmen and tradesmen, and makes unjust privileges generally impossible.

But then, among these and similar advantages, very

grave evils are mingled—evils that justify the aversion of many people, and give us cause to enquire whether instead of free competition unbridled, it might not be better for us and more in accordance with good Political Economy, to have freedom tempered by laws that would prevent its pernicious excesses, and direct it towards the true end of man.

ARTICLE II.

THE DISADVANTAGES.

96. "Though the authority of Adam Smith," says Sismondi, "has not greatly reformed all the facts of economic legislation, the fundamental dogma of a free universal competition has made very great progress throughout civilised society; in such a way, however, that, while prodigious developments have resulted from the power of industry, terrible sufferings have been produced in many classes of the population." [1]

Free competition is helpful, no doubt, to profuse and rapid production, but not so to equal distribution. Its defenders, proceeding in the abstract, consider wealth in itself, but forget for whose use it is. It tends to increase the riches of the millionaire and deprive the poor of a sufficiency. Its inevitable effect is to lower wages.

The Economists try to show that the true cause of this is to be found in the increase of the population. By the law of demand and supply, they say, wages follow the proportion between the working population and capital, or the funds destined for labour. Wages, therefore, cannot fall except through derangement of the said proportion to the disadvantage of the operative class. If this class increases in numbers while capital does not, the supply of work increases, but not the demand for it. The payment,

---

[1] *Nouveaux Principes d'Économie Politique,* Liv. I. Chap. 7.

therefore, that was divided among (for instance) ten thousand operatives, must be divided among twelve thousand, and therefore the rate of each one's pay must be lessened, and cannot rise to the former rate, unless the labouring population decreases, or the capital increases in proportion to the increase of population.[1] From this we might infer that the disturbance of equilibrium between capital and the mass of operatives cannot be lasting. For production, and therefore profit, must increase with the increase of workmen, if new outlets are opened for the products; which can be done by commerce. Increase of profits increases capital; and thus harmony is reestablished between capital and population.

97. This reasoning would be all very well, always supposing that capital and population operate as two physical forces, regulated by dynamic laws. But the fact is that they operate as moral forces, being moved and governed by free will, which is not subject to calculation, but often obeys passions and interests not at all in harmony together. In virtue of that free will the increased capital may be not applied to paying the increased number of workmen: so that the diminished population may still have the reduced wages. The law of demand and supply is often deranged by the acceptance of hard conditions in preference to losing work. The very advantage of low prices in the sale of goods through free competition, is against the workman; for the competition of

---

[1] Stuart Mill tells us that wages depend on the proportion between the labouring population and the capital devoted to paying for labour; and therefore, that if wages are higher in one place than in another at the same time, and the labouring classes more comfortable, it is only because the proportion of capital to population is greater. What is important, he says, to the labouring population, is not the absolute quantity of accumulation or production, nor the increase of funds destined for distribution among the work-people, but in the proportion between these funds and the individuals amongst whom they are divided. See *Principles of Political Economy*, Bk. II. Chap. 2.

the tradesman to undersell implies competition to produce more cheaply, which means paying less to the producers. Hence the horrible maxim : " Get as much work done as you can, and pay as little as you can for it."

98.   It will be said in reply, that what the workman loses in wages he gains by the lower prices of goods.

But this is false. First of all, the one is seldom in proportion to the other. Secondly, the goods cheapened are seldom what the workman wants. Thirdly, that reduction of prices is fluctuating and uncertain through the trickery to which it is liable in the market under full freedom of competition. The chief error of the Economists is their believing that in Economy everything goes by mathematical rules. They think that as there is celestial mechanism, so there ought to be economic mechanism. But the fact is not so, because human will comes in with its long train of human passions.

99.   Bastiat does not disguise this grave difficulty. " They say," he writes, " that the condition of men in this last class is essentially precarious. As they receive their wages for the day, so do they live for the day. For the negociations, which under a free government always precede every contract, they cannot wait. They must find work for the morrow on any conditions, under pain of starvation. If this does not apply strictly to all of them, it does to many ; and that suffices to lower the whole class, because the poorest, being the most urgent, capitulate first, and thus form the general measure of wages. The result is that wages tend to be in proportion with what is strictly necessary to life ; and in this state of things the smallest increase of competition among the workmen is a real calamity, because it is no longer a question of at the least, diminished well-being but of life rendered impossible."[1]

The worthy man undertakes to solve this difficulty,

---

[1] *Harmonies Économiques*, X. Concurrence.

but knows not which way to turn. He first admits the fact, it being undeniable. "There is much truth," he says, "too much truth in the alleged fact. To deny the sufferings and abasement of that class of men who do the material part in the work of production would be shutting one's eyes to the light." And then he adds that he cannot solve so grave a question in one chapter. "As the solution of the social problem lies chiefly in this, the readers will understand that I cannot apply myself to it here." But he does touch on it, and says that he is explaining the laws which he believes to be harmonious in Economics, but has never denied that the action of these laws may be profoundly unsettled by disturbing causes. He reckons among these causes the bad conduct of many workmen, and the vicious institutions of society now-a-days, and then he simplifies the controversy. "The question," he says, "that we ought to propose is this: Abstracting from the good or bad economic institutions, and abstracting from the evils into which the proletarians may fall by their own fault, what, with regard to them, is the effect of competition?"[1]

Well, we have done so precisely, and found that lowering of wages is an inevitable effect of free competition.

But this, he replies, is looking at only one side of the question.

Very well. But that side is so ugly that it cannot be improved by the beauty of the other side.

The beautiful side, he answers, is consumption, which, he affirms, is favoured by free competition.

Yes; but what are these people to consume when they have not money enough to buy the consumable?

Lastly, Bastiat gets into cloud-land. He distinguishes between centrifugal and centripetal competition. He recalls his beloved idea of gratuitous utility in exchanges, which utility, being increased by production, turns out to

---

[1] *Harmonies Économiques*, X. Concurrence.

be good for all and bad for nobody. He maintains that the means tend to equalize themselves, and therefore to be in proportion with the efforts. Society he represents as two strata one above the other, which, being dominated respectively by forces of attraction and of aspiration, mutually seek fusion—and so forth. All this is very fine, and valuable perhaps as an exercise of the writer's fancy; but surely it fails to undo the fact, acknowledged by himself, that free competition not amended by the law is injurious to the operative class.

ARTICLE III.

MONOPOLY.

100. One beneficial effect of free competition is, they say, the exclusion of monopolies—which is true of monopolies given by governments, but not of those that private individuals make for themselves. Before showing this we shall briefly state what monopoly is.

According to its Greek origin, it would mean sale by one person; but in practice it has a somewhat larger signification, being applied to any economic function reserved for somebody, but always with reference to sale. Economists generally extend it to physical and moral worth and the peculiar qualities of a profession. Hence they divide monopoly into natural and artificial. The former, they say, is given by nature, the latter instituted by man. Natural monopoly may be personal or real, according to whether it lies in the singular worth of a person—remark-able ability, for instance, as a scientist, an artist, a man of business,—or in the aptitude of something to produce, as certain vineyards do, products that cannot be got else-where.

Monopolies are called artificial when they proceed from an order of the Government, which can either take the monopoly (of manufacturing tobacco, for instance) or give it to private persons, individually or in partnership, as the monopoly of exporting or importing certain kinds of merchandise.

101. We like not this division; for there is misuse of words, as it seems to us, in the first members of it. " Monopoly " is a word generally understood in a depreciative sense, as attributed to things which, being of themselves common, are more or less arbitrarily put out of competition; and this cannot be said of any one's natural worth or lawful possessions. It would be enough to make a cat laugh to be told, for instance, that Dante was a monopolist, because he alone was able to compose the *Divina Commedia*, or that reserving the copyright of a book is claiming a monopoly.

We think that the word " monopoly " should be restricted to those privileges which the Economists call artificial monopolies, and might be defined as AN EXCLUSIVE FACULTY FOR THE PRODUCTION, TRANSPORT, OR SALE OF SOME MERCHANDISE, IN OR OUT OF THE COUNTRY. But it may be a government monopoly, or a private monopoly, according to whether the government has it, or grants it to individuals or companies.

102. Besides these monopolies, which might be called legal, and in some cases are just, *viz.* when they are based on just reasons and aim at the public good, there are others that may be called unlawful or an abuse—those that private persons procure for themselves without being authorised by the government. Such monopolies may fairly be called artificial, because they proceed from pure artifice. They are always unjust because they are usurped, and because they are injurious to the freedom of others.

Now we say that free competition is productive of these. Competition, when loosed from all restraint of law, puts economic operations in the power of individual tendencies, or, in other words, leaves them to the antagonism of selfishness. It applies in a certain way to wealth what the Darwinists tell us of the struggle for existence, in which the stronger triumph and the weaker go to the wall. In both cases the most powerful will have the best of it. Great proprietors, great tenants, great contractors, great capitalists—those in short who possess the means of doing things on a great scale, will monopolize production, barter, and commerce, dictating laws for the rest. This will bring the distribution of wages into the hands of a few, on their own terms. The leonine contracts of which we were said to be rid, will come in again by the back door.

103. Nor will the labouring class alone suffer from this, but also the smaller proprietors, the smaller traders, and the smaller contractors, who not being able to last out will have to give up. But associations, they say, will set that right. Nothing of the kind. Association would be treated as individuals are. We remember how a powerful company owning steam-vessels competed in lowering fares, till it came to offering free transport of goods and people, so as to make their rivals bankrupt, as in fact it did. Free competition is a terrible weapon, most effectual to crush the weak and reduce whole populations to economic slavery under a rod of iron wielded by the potent rulers of social wealth. This is a monopoly before which all the old monopolies put together sink into insignificance.

It must not be supposed that the outcries of Socialism against free competition left to the arbitrary vicissitudes of demand and supply are to be treated lightly. There is much truth in what they say on this head ; and we must do them justice in that respect, unless we wish them to triumph. ——

ARTICLE IV.
STRIKES.

104. Another corollary of free competition is the introduction of strikes. A strike consists in a simultaneous

cessation from work by one class of operatives at least, for the purpose of making a better bargain with the master especially in respect of wages. It is a phenomenon not unknown in olden times; but in its present form, and particularly in its extent and frequency, it may be accounted as peculiar to our times. Nor is this to be wondered at, for peculiar to our times is the unbridled competition of which it is an offshoot.

Every one knows what disastrous excesses—riots, acts of violence, attempts against public and private security—have accompanied them. In that respect these men are certainly culpable, ought to be put down, and deserve severe punishment. Worst of all is the iniquitous and brutal terrorism by which they compel their comrades to join them. If some workmen think it better to continue working on the same terms as before, what right have the others to force them into the strike by threats, insults and bad usage? Are they not free agents in their own affairs, to act as they think best? This is an unjust claim, an offence against the liberty of the subject, a disturbance of public peace, and deserves the utmost rigour of the law.

105. But, abstracting from these excesses and considering strikes in themselves, we have to say that, given free competition, they are one of the rights of the operatives, and cannot justly be condemned or repressed. A strike is a sort of reprisal. Now reprisals are lawful in war; and a state of free competition is a state of war. Moreover it is the only means at their disposal, seeing that there is no authorized tribunal to which they can have recourse.

They might indeed fall back on arbitration; and we think that even under the present conditions it would be useful to the workmen, who cannot hold out long, having families to provide for. But suppose the master refuses to abide by the award of the arbitrators—what then?

106. But even when there is no violence at all, strikes,

it will be urged, do serious harm. They suspend production, impede commerce, take away the profits of capital, disturb the economic order, and sometimes go so far as to stop the supply of necessaries. Society has a right therefore to forbid them, even under heavy penalties.

All this is true; and society would have an indisputable right to forbid strikes and put them down, if it fulfilled its duty of protection. But the liberalistic fancy for unbridled competition restricts it to the purely negative task of not permitting material violence; and therefore the workman can only be expected to keep within the negative duty of not breaking the law. As to the rest he may use his freedom. If capitalists by refusing may force the workman to compete in lowering wages, the workman by refusing may force the masters to compete in higher wages, because they have no other weapons to fight with. In old times the workman found in the corporations of arts and trades a patron and an avenger; but when Revolution conferred on him the inestimable benefit of what is called freedom, he was left at the mercy of low bidders. With a bitter irony it made him free to starve.

We know very well that capitalists and masters are not always in fault. They are often forced by the pressure of competition to give less than they would. Often, if they gave more, they would get nothing; and they cannot be expected to ruin themselves, and be unable to employ any one. But that is no argument against the strikes. It only proves that the economic system is wrong.

ARTICLE V.
THE ACTION OF THE EXECUTIVE.

107. For the sake of conforming to the common terminology of the Economists, we have hitherto called this competition *free*, unfettered by laws or by government influence; but in truth we ought to call it license rather

than liberty. The epithet " free," as applied to that, came from a false idea of freedom, first put forth towards the end of the last century. True freedom lies in the faculty of using without hindrance *our own right ;* but it then came to mean the power of using *our own strength.* For the idea of right, that traces its origin from reason, they substituted the idea of strength, whose origin is from mere physical being ; and this was in virtue of the liberalistic principle, that man is a law to himself. When this principle is brought into Economy, self clashes with self in free competition, and the strongest have the best of it. In Economy the most moneyed are the strongest ; and so therefore the rest must fall under their yoke—under the despotism of capital, the tyranny of gold.

A certain amount of free competition is unquestionably requisite for the functions of Economy. Without it there would be neither emulation, nor progress, nor new inventions, nor encouragement of industry, nor reward for active ability. But it must not be unlimited. Economic affairs are individual and social. As individual they require freedom, but as social they require the direction of the government. " Experience," says Sismondi, " has made us feel the want of that protecting authority, which we invoke as necessary for preventing the sacrifice of many people to the progress of wealth, in which they will never participate. This authority alone can raise us above the material calculations of how to increase production, and substitute the consideration of how to increase the comforts of all ; which ought to be the aim of every nation." [1]

108. The action of the government in Political Economy comes under two heads : Protection of the weak, Direction of the strong.

With regard to protection of the weak—and therein lies its chief duty—the special object of its care in respect

---

[1] *Nouveaux Principes d'Économie Politique,* Liv. I. Chap 7.

of work, manufactories and workshops, are as follows:

1°. *The Fathers of Families.*—As we said before, the operative's working day should not exceed nine or ten hours. If you want workmen of the right sort, you must not keep them away from their families very long. You must give them leisure for their domestic affairs and domestic duties, and that paternal authority with which they were invested by nature, or rather by God. Above all things, let them have their Sunday's rest, so that they may attend to their religious duties, and go back to their work refreshed.

2°. *The Women.*—The delicacy of women forbids their doing very hard work, and especially working with men. The government should absolutely prohibit such work, when it cannot be well regulated; for the consideration due to women is of the utmost importance in the social system. But over and above the quality of their work, we have to bear in mind the providential mission of the woman. That she it is who forms the family and, like a guardian angel, watches over it, is a fact universally acknowledged. Therefore it never should be tolerated that her home duties as a wife and as a mother should be in the smallest degree interfered with by her work outside. In a recently published course of Political Economy we were glad to find the author advising that women with young children should not work in factories, but only grown up girls and (with due regard to domestic duties) the mothers of older children. [1]

3°. *The Children.*—Another most important point in

---

[1] "Les jeunes mères devraient autant que possible renoncer au travail des fabriques; l'ouvrière d'usine ne serait plus alors que la jeune fille adulte avant son mariage, venant en aide à sa famille et s'amassant une petite dôt, ou la femme ayant des enfants déja grandes et sans détriment grave pour les siens." *Précis d'Économie Politique*, par Paul Leroy-Beaulieu, Membre de l'Institut, Professeur d'Economie Politique au Collège de France. [Paris, 1888.] 1re. Partie, Chap. 8.

the duty of the government is to take care of the children. They should on no account be allowed to begin to work too young, nor to do work beyond their strength. In my opinion, they should not begin to work before the age of twelve years. It is especially important, too, that the workshop and the hours of work do not take them too much away from their parents who ought to form their minds, nor expose their innocence to be corrupted by the words and example of others. To the age of childhood an almost religious reverence is due. At that time of life the future operative takes in the germs, good or bad, that develope later on to bear fruit. Do not delude yourself by hoping that public instruction will do instead of parental care. No school can ever be an equivalent for the family. No schoolmaster can fill the place of a Christian mother.

4⁰. *Precautions against Dangerous and Unhealthy Work.*—We cannot speak too strongly about this. It is a question of health and life—the health and life of the many, who at their own risk labour to procure comforts for others. It makes one shudder to hear of the accidents that might be prevented. The government cannot be too strict about that.

109. Having said this much about protection of the weak, we pass on to the direction of the strong, and fail to see how any one can suppose that to leave everything in the power of individual tendencies can possibly be good. These people want an effect without a cause—order in multitude without an ordering mind. But if the mere shock of private interests can produce order in Economy, one fails to see why it may not do so in other branches of social life, and then anarchy would be the best form of political government. The defenders of un-limited freedom in Political Economy feelingly remind us of the mischief done by fettering the functions of Economy with endless prohibitions and privileges. But

to argue against the use of a thing from its abuse is a very sophistical procedure. If social economy is to be for the common good, it ought not to be cut loose from that authority which has the management and care of the common good. All depends on its regulating those things wisely and justly; but it ought to rule them.

110. The reader will see that what we have been saying generally applies to international free-trade also, in the exportation and importation of merchandise. We are now witnessing a singular phenomenon. After having cried out against protection for more than a century, and in favour of free trade, we see the most liberalistic States in Europe taking the strongest measures against the competition of Asia and America in corn; which means that, taken in an absolute sense, the famous axiom, *laissez faire, laissez passer*, has been found wanting. It is the duty of every State to protect in moderation the home-industry of the country, so that it may not suffer from foreign competition. It should be especially vigilant about the importation of goods that have any relation to public health and public morals. The trifling loss that such protection causes to consumers is not a valid objection. Every one ought to see that we are not justified in being so wedded to our own private interests as to lose sight of the sacrifices that we are sometimes bound to make for the common good—sacrifices, too, that in the long run are for our own good.

I have brought together too many things, each of which would require a volume; but the judicious reader will understand that I have not undertaken to treat economic questions fully. I am only touching on the most important points for the instruction of youth.

ARTICLE VI.

ON A COMMON AGREEMENT BETWEEN THE STATES.

111.   That protection which the Executive owes to the weak, implies, as we have seen, its defending them from an excessive competition by interposing to limit and regulate labour in work-places, especially where there are women and children.   But if this were done by one State alone, there would be a great difficulty about the price of goods, because the producers at home, crippled by the unequal cost of producing, would be unable to stand against foreign competition.   Clearly this ought to be accepted by all civilized nations, their governments agreeing together to lay down general rules on this point.   Nor must we suppose it to be impossible.   We must remember that the social question, or labour question, concerns every government, all of them being bound in duty to satisfy just demands and suitably provide for the most numerous part of civil society.   This reason, at once moral and political, is of such grave importance, that it outweighs all the other economic questions of which we have had to speak.

112.   It seems that some such design is beginning to have a working principle, for in the Swiss Parliament a very learned Economist and an eloquent orator, the deputy Decourtins, seconded by the deputy Favon, proposed that the Government should enter into negotiations about it with the different States of Europe.   The proposal was unanimously accepted by the federal assembly ; and through the different Courts the Swiss Government has already sent out invitations to attend a conference at Berne, for the purpose of coming to an understanding about the following proposals :

1⁰.   To prohibit working on Sundays.

2⁰.   To determine a minimum age for beginning to work in factories.

3⁰. To determine the length of a day's work for young operatives.

4⁰. To prohibit the employment of women and children in dangerous or unhealthy work.

5⁰. To limit the work done at night by women and children.

Decourtins, in proposing this, made a magnificent speech, and argued out each point in detail. [1]

113.   Considering the importance of the question and the powerful support which the authority of such a man gives to what we have already said, we should have thought it well to give an abridgment of that speech, even at the cost of having to repeat ourselves in many things : but we shall content ourselves with his quotation from a pastoral letter of Pope Leo XIII., when he was Bishop of Perugia : " The modern schools of Political Economy," says the Holy Father, " infected as they are with Materialism, regard labour as the supreme end of man, and even level him down to the condition of a more or less valuable machine, according to his aptitude for producing.   Hence the moral value of man is quite forgotten, and the drain on the poor and the children is enormous.   What bitter outcries has it been our duty to hear, even from countries that claim to have reached the summit of civilisation— outcries occasioned by the excessive number of hours during which the operatives have to work in gaining their bread by the sweat of their brow."

114.   After having shown the want of intervention on the part of the Executive to protect labour, M. Decourtins comes to the chief point of his proposal, the necessity of an international understanding, so that the laws passed might not by their differences be injurious to the interests of individual countries.

---

[1] That speech was afterwards printed by the Catholic printing establishment at Fribourg, under the title, *Une Législation Internationale en faveur des ouvriers.*

"The idea," he says, "of international legislation to protect the workman has been widely propagated during the last quarter of a century, and the study of it has called forth in great abundance a literature of its own. We cannot wonder then that such an idea, growing in strength, has found its way into various Parliaments—in Austria through Mgr. Ritter and Mr. Schoenerer, in Germany through Dr. Lieber, in France through the Count de Mun."

ARTICLE VII.

OBJECTIONS.

115. The idea of an international agreement to regulate labour in the great factories by common legislation, though widely spread among Catholics and non-Catholics, is disputed by many as impossible and perilous. They look on it as a concession to the Socialists, who sometimes invoke it in books and speeches. Jannet, in his excellent work, *Le Socialisme d'Etat*, writes as follows : " Good souls are led away now-a-days by the idea of an international understanding, to regulate the conditions of labour. . . . In this there is a chimera and a danger." The proof of its being a chimera is that the wants of the people differ according to locality, climate, difference of food, and the variety of trades in which they are employed, which will not bear identical regulations common to all. A day's work, for instance, is not the only factor in production. Many other elements contribute thereto— machinery, capital, the price of raw material &c. These would prevent equality in products. And then, who will ensure the observance of the compact on the part of the governments who sign it ? We should want international inspectors to watch over that. About the danger he says : " This would be preparing to fulfil the designs of Karl Marx. The International Association of workmen may have disappeared in its original form, but the thought that

inspired it is living still. Secret associations even more revolutionary have undertaken the direction of the labour movement. We must not forget that we are confronted by socialist organizations, which boldly show themselves in public, but obey a secret and a continual direction. Without giving up their principles at all, they are trying to effect by means of conservatives, Catholics, liberals, without distinction, the accomplishment of certain legislative modifications in the present regulation of labour, which are adapted to disorganize the natural order of economy and prepare for the actuation of their designs." [1]

These objections are not to be despised. Some answer must be given to them.

116. Jannet's work is most praiseworthy, and ought to be studied by all who occupy themselves with such questions. It is written in a perfectly Catholic spirit, is full of practical erudition, and contains grave warnings about State Socialism. But he seems to us not sufficiently free from the economic liberalism still in vogue, and therefore too much against government intervention in the industrial order. State Socialism, by which the government makes itself the arbitrary master of the production and distribution of the national wealth, certainly is abominable. If society suffers so much now, as in fact it does, from bureaucratic absorption in the administrative order, what will it be when the economic order has fallen into its clutches? But in considering one excess we must not fall into another. Labour is unquestionably an individual function, not a social one, being the means given by God to man, that man might procure things necessary for his existence: *In sudore vultus tui vesceris pane.* But this function is exercised in the midst of society, and is mixed up with social duties and public morality. In that respect the State has the right of

---

[1] *Le Socialisme d'État.* L'Etat et le régime du travail. § 10.

regulating, harmonizing, and even limiting it, when necessary, for the common good. We must not suppose that
whatever is said or proposed by the Socialists is false *a
priori*. Every false system must, in order to deceive the
unwary, have the support of some truth. Pure error
would find no access to the human mind. The sure way
of overcoming error is to disarm it of this weapon.

Now, when the Socialists tell us of the injury done to
the operative class by unbridled competition, they say
what is undeniably true, and the necessity of finding a
remedy for it is evident. The proposed international
agreement aims at this, respecting the point mentioned in
the preceding article. They may be considered either
in themselves, or as to the agreement about them between
the different States. As considered in themselves, even
Jannet substantially acknowledges them. "We," he says,
"no less than M. de Mun, approve of the provisions
for protecting the woman and the child, and the adult
workman too, within the bounds of justice."[1] And in
§ 16, when speaking about the duty of the State to
enforce the keeping of the Moral Law, he argues for the
obligation of abstaining from work on great Feasts,[2] and
the necessity of regulating the labour of women and
children in factories.[3] He advocates fixing a *maximum* of

---

[1] Ibid., § 8.

[2] "Plaçons nous au premier rang de nos revendications une
loi, qui fasse observer le repos du dimanche et des grandes
fêtes de l'Eglise dans tous les ateliers du travail." And he goes
on to say: "Nous réclamons encore plus, s'il est possible, ce repos
pour les employés des services publics et des grandes industries
placées sous le régime de l'Etat, comme les chemins de fer.
C'est là un droit pour tout homme, et ceux qui font travailler
le jour du Seigneur commettent une faute qui justifie l'action
énergique du législateur."

[3] "Le travail excessif des femmes et des enfants dans les
ateliers doit être réglementé."

work for adults, in case of enormous abuse, [1] and would even allow the State theoretically to determine a *minimum* of wages, as it fixes a *maximum* of interest. [2]

117. If these regulations are good and feasible for individual States, why may they not be the object of a common agreement? Such an agreement would be to each a great comfort and an encouragement to have them carried out. Where is the difficulty? The difference of circumstances, they say, among different peoples. But, if we consider the question, we shall find that these regulations depend very little on such differences, because they answer to wants that are universal and identical. Is not abstinence from work on Sundays a law of religion arising from every man's need of raising his soul to God and resting after the labour of the other six days? Women and children are pretty much the same everywhere. Women everywhere require the same special consideration. Children everywhere have but little strength, and need domestic education. Everywhere fathers of families have the same need of not being wearied by overwork, nor kept over-long away from their wives and children. We must remark that what is here recommended is not an absolute limitation of work, including work done at home, but only what is done in factories, which implies hard labour or monotonous servitude.

---

[1] "Le législateur doit-il fixer pour les hommes adultes un *maximum* à la durée du travail? Son intervention ne nous parait légitime, qu'au cas d'abus énorme." It is true that he does not approve of intervention except in such cases ; but it is something to have the principle conceded.

[2] "Théoriquement le législateur, qui est le gardien de la justice dans les contrats, pourrait fixer un salaire minimum par la même raison qu'il fixe un intérêt maximum."—Ibid., 9.

Part III.—Consumption.

1. This is the last of the three parts into which we divided Political Economy. Pellegrino Rossi, as we remarked at the beginning, would exclude it, believing that production and distribution are sufficient for the integrity of the science. Stuart Mill seems to have agreed with him; for he speaks very seldom of consumption, and then but incidentally. We, however, are in accord with the great majority of Economists, nearly all of whom have made it one of the three members in their division of the science, or at least have written a chapter about it. This appeared to us the more reasonable, as answering better to the idea of wealth, and better adapted for teaching clearly.

CHAPTER I.

THE NATURE OF CONSUMPTION.

IT IS DIVIDED INTO PUBLIC AND PRIVATE CONSUMPTION.

THE ultimate aim of the economic function is consumption. "Consumption," says Adam Smith, "is the sole end and purpose of all production ; and the interest of the producer ought to be attended to only so far as it may be necessary for promoting that of the consumer." [1] To do otherwise would be to busy ourselves about the means without caring for the end.

---

[1] *Wealth of Nations*, Book IV. Chap. 8.

FALSE OPINIONS OF ECONOMISTS REGARDING CONSUMPTION.

3. Unless we are much mistaken, Economists have confused this part of economic science more than a little by the definition which they have given of it, and by the division which they have inferred, *viz.* into productive and unproductive. They have defined it either by the use of an object or by the destruction of a value. McCulloch says that consumption, in the sense in which the word is employed in Political Economy, is synonymous with use.[1] Joseph Garnier says that we make a consumption when we destroy a value. We are told by Say that producing value is producing wealth, [2] and consuming value is consuming wealth, and that production is a gain, consumption a loss.[3] Having this idea of consumption, they naturally divided it into productive and unproductive, because the use and the destruction of a product are either for the purpose of obtaining another product, as when we use a combustible for the purpose of distillation, or they are merely for the satisfaction of a want, as when we put on clothes to keep out the cold.

"As all consumption whatsoever," says Jean-Baptiste Say, "brings with it a loss, a sacrifice equal to the value consumed, it is madness to consume without gaining an advantage which may be regarded as an indemnification for that sacrifice. You must know that we may be indemnified in two ways: either by the well-being that results from a satisfied want, or by the production of

---

[1] *Principles of Political Economy*, Part IV. Consumption of Wealth.

[2] *Elements of Political Economy*, Part II, § 2., Chap. 21.

[3] *Cours Complet*, 7me. Partie, Chap. 21.

wealth equal or superior to the value consumed. Hence there are unproductive or barren consumptions, and reproductive consumptions." [1]

4. But, to say the truth, this idea is inexact; for it does not correspond to what consumption is properly understood to mean in Economy. McCulloch says that consumption is the aim and the goal of human labour; [2] and Garnier says that in the last analysis consumption is the ultimate aim of production. [3] And this way of speaking is common to all the Economists. Now, when you consume a part of your wealth, to obtain another—consume, for instance, a combustible, in order to obtain some spirit by distillation—can you say that such consumption is the goal of your labour, the ultimate aim of the production? Certainly not. By what right, then, do you consider it to be one of two species into which consumption, considered as the third function of Economy, should be divided? Must not the idea of the genus be verified in each of the species? Consumption, in short, when considered as the third economic function, must be the ultimate term of production. But consumption for the purpose of obtaining a reproduction is not that, and therefore does not belong to that consumption which is the third economic function.

5. They would say that in their division of consumption they have added the epithet "productive." We reply that the epithet is absurd, because it carries us on to the idea of capital, which is not consumption, but an element of production. In what does productive consumption, according to the Economists, consist? It consists in the materials employed to obtain a product, in the

---

[1] *Cours Complet*, 7me. Partie, Ch. 2.

[2] *Principles of Political Economy*, Part IV. Consumption of Wealth.

[3] *Cours complet*, 7me. Partie, 1ere Division. Chap. 1. § 362.

instruments required for the working, in the previous cost of labour. All this is nothing else than employment of capital, or, in other words, means of production : and the means of doing a thing cannot be called its goal and ultimate term. The chief defect of our Economists is that very often they are without clear and precise philosophical notions. Hence they are often perplexed in trying to keep the sense of words badly defined at first : and so it is in the present case. "In saying," writes Garnier, "that the word 'consumption' is not a happy one, we are the interpreters of many Economists."[1] There is nothing wrong in the word. The mischief is in the use made of it.

6. Let us say, then, that the functions, or motions, or phenomena (whichever word may happen to please) are three :—Production, Distribution, and Consumption. According to the laws of good division, not one of these three functions must in any way clash with the other two. Therefore, just as distribution cannot become production or a means of production, neither can consumption. Consumption implies the destruction of an object, but does not imply destroying it for the purpose of producing another : its only end is to satisfy some want or desire of ours. Hence it may be defined as THE DESTRUCTIVE USE OF A PRODUCT FOR THE SATISFACTION OF A HUMAN WANT. We say *destructive use*, and not merely *use*, because the idea of use is more general, and simply expresses the employment of a thing, whether consumable or not. You use your intellect when you contemplate a truth, but you do not thereby consume it: but you consume the clothes that you wear, for after a while they become useless, or nearly so. We say the "destructive use of a *product*," instead of the "destructive use of a *value*," because in our opinion the Economists make another mistake when

---

[1] *Cours Complet*, 7me. Partie, 1ere Division, Chap. 1. § 362.

they maintain that in consumption the value precisely is what is destroyed. In fact the thing, not the value, is destroyed. When you order your dinner, you ask for something to eat; and that you consume. You would never dream of asking for a value. The destruction of the value is consequent on the destruction of the thing, inasmuch as the thing destroyed had a value. The above-mentioned opinion of Economists that the value is destroyed in consumption, proceeds from their believing that wealth consists in the value of a thing, not in its utility. This error we refuted at the beginning of our treatise. Lastly we say "for the satisfaction of a human want," because that is the specific difference that determines the notion of consumption as the third economic function.

And this is truly consumption, taken in an absolute sense, because it truly destroys. The other, which takes place in production, is transformation rather than destruction, because the advantage of the thing destroyed remains virtually in the thing produced. You consume the seed to obtain a harvest; flax to obtain linen, iron to obtain steel: but in the harvest, in the linen cloth, and in the steel, the worth of the seed, the flax, and the iron is, as it were, contained. If, on the contrary, you consume wood to warm yourself, you obtain, indeed, the satisfaction of your want, but though the ashes that remain are of some little use, the greater part corresponding to the wood, as wood, is destroyed. This is a true consumption—a real destruction of a thing accomplished in the end for which it was produced.

7. And now, having cleared the idea of consumption from the ambiguities in which the Economists had involved it, we say that the epithet "unproductive" is wrongly applied to it by them. It is extremely productive, because it produces that which all wealth aims at, namely the satisfaction of human wants. This misuse of words was acknowledged by Say when he wrote as follows:

"If we consider the depths of things, we shall find that these denominations are far from being perfect. A consumption that satisfies one of our wants, is neither un-productive nor barren; since it produces a satisfaction which is a real good. On the other hand that consumption which produces, is not at all a reproductive consumption; for, in reality, the productive operations—that is to say, the action of industry, as of the earth's funds of wealth and of capital—are the only means of production."

He proceeds, however, to say: "One is compelled to employ the usual language, because one has to make oneself understood; and the reader must try to enter into the manner in which the phenomenon happens, without quibbling on the words of which the author is obliged to make use."[1]

But what obliges him to do so? Custom and wanting to be understood? But when a custom is acknowledged to be erroneous, it ought to be corrected, not imitated; and he would be equally well understood, if he clearly explained why he corrected it. He would not be quibbling but doing a service by freeing it from a defect of language. Moreover, this is not a question of words, but of ideas.[2]

8. Consumption is not quick or slow equally. A sumptuous dinner may be eaten in less than an hour: but it takes years to use up a carriage, and still longer to wear out a house. Indeed, the consumption of some things is so slow and imperceptible that we can hardly apply the word to them. A diamond, for instance, may last as an ornament through many generations without

---

[1] See his *Cours Complet*, 7me Partie, Chap. 2, in a note.
[2] We must remark, however, that in rejecting the phrase "unproductive consumption," we do not exclude "unproductive consumers," provided that the epithet be applied, not to the consumption, but to the person, as signifying those who, owing to an inordinate love of enjoyment, do no work at all, mental or bodily, but lead an idle time-wasting life.

showing any signs of wear. Nevertheless it is certain that even the diamond will somehow wear out, though insensibly, because no material thing here below is exempt from the edacity of time. But we must never lose sight of what we said in defining consumption, *viz.* that it always is relative to the satisfaction of a want. The greater or less durability of the object, therefore, is of little importance. If the use made of it diminishes its fitness, consumption is verified in respect of such diminution.

ARTICLE II.
COST.

9. What is given for the purpose of obtaining consumable things, is called the cost of them. When, for instance, you pay your tailor's bill, the money that you pay to him is the cost of the clothes charged for in that bill. He might be paid in goods instead of in money; but when money is once introduced, exchanges are usually effected by means of money—by sale and purchase. Hence the cost of a thing is commonly understood to mean the money paid for it.

Since the objects destined for consumption are usually acquired at some cost, the words "consumption" and "cost" are in common parlance used indifferently. Thus any one spending ten shillings a day on his food would be said to consume that much. Properly speaking, he consumes the food, not the ten shillings; but by metonymy the name signifying the end is here transferred to the means. "All our consumptions," remarks Jean-Baptiste Say, "take place in consequence of a purchase, and such purchases form our expenses. This is why the word *cost* has become synonymous with *consumption*." [1]

We have noticed this alteration of words in order to

---

[1] Ibid. Ch. 3.

obviate all danger of misconception, because in the course of this treatise we shall often have to use the one for the other. In this we have imitated Say, who made a like declaration.

We must now point out under their principle heads the prudential rules that regulate consumption or cost, whether in the private or in the public order: but first it seems advisable to say something about prodigality and avarice, the two vicious extremes that have to be avoided.

ARTICLE III.

PRODIGALITY AND AVARICE.

10. Wealth, or abundance of external things, has the quality of a means, being ordained for the maintenance and conservation of human life according to the condition of each person, and therefore its right use consists in a given measure, i.e. in its proportion to that end. "In all things that are for an end," says St. Thomas, "the goodness consists in a certain measure, because that which is ordained for an end should be commensurate thereto . . . . Now external goods have the quality of things useful for an end. Wherefore it is necessary that men's good concerning them should consist in a certain measure, provided that according to a certain measure he seeks to have external wealth as being necessary to his life according to his condition." [1] Now the goodness of a thing consisting in

---

[1] *In omnibus, quæ sunt propter finem, bonum consistit in quadam mensura; nam ea quæ sunt ad finem, necesse est commensurari fini. . . . bona autem exteriora habent rationem utilium ad finem. Unde necesse est quod bonum omnis circa ea consistat in quadam mensura; dum scilicet homo secundum aliquam mensuram quærit habere exteriores divitias, prout sunt necessariæ ad vitam ejus, secundum suam conditionem.—Summa, 2ᵃ. 2ᵃᵉ. Q. CXVIII. al.*

a just measure, i.e. in its correspondence to the end, may be corrupted in two ways, *viz.* by defect or by excess. Hence there are two opposite vices with regard to wealth —prodigality and avarice.

11. Avarice may be defined as immoderate love of wealth *(immoderatus amor habendi)*, and especially of money, which is the equivalent of all wealth. It is practised in two ways—by acquiring and by keeping. The miser seeks to accumulate money, without ever being satisfied; and in order to keep it, he will deprive himself even of necessaries. It implies a great deformity of mind, for the lower the thing is that we inordinately love, the greater is the moral turpitude of that inordinate love; and material goods are the lowest with respect to man. Cicero justly said: "Nihil est tam angusti animi tamque parvi, quam amare pecuniam." [1]

Many are the vices that avarice brings with it; but the worst of all is that hardness of heart which it engenders, and which extinguishes every sentiment of beneficence. Hence a miser is deservedly disliked and despised by every one.

12. Prodigality is less disgraceful, but still vicious. As to the effect, it sins by excess, by unmeasured spending of money, whereas avarice sins by defect. But as to the affection it is just the reverse; for avarice sins by excess in immoderately loving wealth, and prodigality sins by defect in not taking sufficient care of it.

"Avarice and prodigality," says St. Thomas, "differ according to excess or defect in different ways. For in the love of riches the miser superabounds by loving it more than he ought: while the prodigal man fails by not having sufficient care of the same, as duty would require. But about the external things, it is the part of prodigality to give in excess and be defective in retaining, while on

---

[1] *De Officiis*, Lib. i.

the contrary avarice fails in giving, and exceeds in receiving and retaining."[1]

13. Prodigality must not be mistaken for liberality, which is not a vice, but a virtue, and a very splendid virtue. The evil of prodigality does not consist in giving much, nor in spending much, but in giving and spending against the dictates of reason in a mad way and without a praiseworthy aim, or in favour of unworthy people. Often the liberal man gives and spends more than the prodigal; and yet he deserves praise, not blame, because in doing so he not only does not fall into the faults of the prodigal, but acts according to the suggestions of a noble mind, with a holy purpose, and without injuring in any way the rights of any one, but distributing that of which he is the absolute master. He, therefore, who with the intention of following Christ dispossesses himself of all that he has, giving it to poor relations or, failing such, to strangers in need, is certainly not prodigal, but eminently liberal. And here we have to complain of M. Say for speaking of Christian poverty without understanding it. *Sutor, ne ultra crepidam.* In the first chapter of the fourth part of his course of Political Economy, he quotes in a note a fine passage, where Socrates says that happiness does not consist in multiplying one's wants and satisfying them by enjoyments of every sort, but in restricting as much as possible the compass of our wants. And then he tells us that " the ancients had no idea of the nature of

---

[1] *Differunt avaritia et prodigalitas secundum superabundantiam et defectum diversimode. Nam in affectione divitiarum avarus superabundat, plus debito eas diligens: prodigus autem deficit, minus debito earum sollicitudinem gerens. Circa exteriora vero, ad prodigalitatem pertinet excedere quidem in dando, deficere autem in retinendo et acquirendo; ad avaritiam autem pertinet e contrario deficere quidem in dando, superabundare autem in accipiendo et retinendo.—Summa,* 2ª. 2ᵃᵉ. Q. CXIX. a. 1.

wealth and the manner of multiplying it. They believed,"
he says, "that it was never obtained otherwise than by
fraud or rapine, because they knew not how the art of
creating it could be reducible to rules. For them the
most sublime effort consisted in doing without it. From
this arose the doctrine of the early Christians on the merits
of poverty." Now the doctrines of the early Christians
about the merits of poverty, like that of the later Christians
(for they had a common Master), was not derived from
the teaching of Pagan philosophers, but from the teaching
of Christ. The Pagan philosophers praised poverty for
bringing peace in this life—*O vitæ tuta facultas pauperis !* [1]
—but Christ praised it for bringing peace in the future
life. *Beati pauperes, quoniam vestrum est regnum cælorum.*
Hence the great multitude of those who, not being poor,
make themselves poor. Touching which, it must be remarked that this spontaneous poverty, so meritorious
among Christians, belongs to the perfect life. There are,
as our Lord Himself teaches, two perfect lives, the one
common, the other of *perfection*. The perfect life common
to all of us consists in keeping the Divine precepts: *Si
vis ad vitam ingredi, serva mandata.* [2] The life of perfection consists in giving up all temporal things to follow
Christ : *Si vis perfectus esse, vade, vende quæ habes, da
pauperibus . . . et veni sequere me.* [3] He that loves the
latter, must profess poverty; and this, besides bringing to
the individual person immense wealth in Heaven, is of
immense advantage to society in this world, as we could
easily prove, if this were the right place. But he who is
contented with the former, may justly acquire wealth, provided that he does so without offence against God or against
his neighbour. Nay, he does well by acquiring it, where
he honestly can ; for besides helping him to have the

---

[1] Lucan, *De Bello Pharsalico.*
[2] *Matt.* xix. 17.
[3] Ibid. xix. 21.

comforts of life, which assuredly are not forbidden by any
divine precept, and besides enabling him to fulfil the duty
of providing for his children, wealth is available as an
instrument for the practice of many virtues, especially for
the good of our neighbour. The poor man has not sufficient for himself; but the rich one, if he is virtuous, may
help and support many.

<hr>

ARTICLE IV.
PRIVATE CONSUMPTION.

14. All of us are consumers, but not all are producers.
We are all consumers, because every human creature, so long
as he lives here, requires food, clothing and lodging, at
least, as necessaries. But we are not all producers in the
economic sense, because all are not engaged in agriculture,
trade, or commerce. Were it otherwise, there would be
none to do anything else; and society, which cannot go
on without difference of duties and conditions, would
break up, or be reduced to the lowest degree of human
civilization.

15. Since consumption is common to us all, it requires
care and forethought in practice. The Economists generally give good instructions and good rules about that.[1]
For us, writing compendiously, it will suffice to say that
in this we have to avoid the two vices before mentioned,
viz. avarice and prodigality. In general the regulating
measure of consumption for a private person or for a
family is given by the proportion between the true wants

<hr>

[1] Say speaks as follows: "Consumption better understood,
will be:—1°. That which satisfies real wants.... 2°. That
which is slow rather than quick, preferring products of better
quality ... 3°. That which is in common. 4°. Consumption
rightly understood is that which sound morality approves.
Finally, that, on the contrary, which outrages morality and is
injurious to the nation and to private persons.—*Traité
d'Économie Politique*, Liv. III. ch. 4.

and the means of supplying them. The real wants are not the same in all people, nor are their incomes the same. Every one ought to acquire the art of so adapting the means to the wants, that the wants may be sufficiently satisfied and the means not exceeded by the expenses. Nor is that enough. It is better, if possible, to lay by for the uncertain future, and in order to improve one's condition. He who spends his whole income, remains in the same state. He who spends more, is on his road to ruin. He only who spends less, can form capital out of the balance in hand and thereby increase his property.

16. In doing this, however, we have to guard against falling into avarice by excess of saving to the prejudice of what is right and necessary. Avarice, as we said before, concerns two acts, acquisition and retention. In two ways, therefore, we may be avaricious through excess of saving : by greed of acquiring more wealth, and by love of hoarding it. There are people who live miserably and impoverish their families through a bad inclination for risky speculations from which they expect vast profits. Immoderate love of riches is contrary to the Christian spirit. The apostle St. Paul, writing to Timothy, said : *Qui volunt divites fieri, incidunt in tentationem et in laqueum diaboli, et desideria multa inutilia et nociva, quæ mergunt hominem in interitum et perditionem. Radix enim omnium malorum est cupiditas ; quam quidam appetentes, erraverunt a fide, et inseruerunt se doloribus multis. Tu autem, O homo Dei, hæc fuge.*[1]

Still more blamable is that other species of avarice which makes a man save in excess, not to employ his money in acquiring more, but simply for the pleasure of having it. In this there is not even the social advantage of increasing wealth, but only a disgraceful stinginess originating from mere cupidity.

---

[1] *Ad Timoth.*, vi. 9, 10, 11.

17. The opposite vice, prodigality, consists in waste by excess of spending and giving. It leads without fail to poverty. He who buys too much to-day, said Franklin, will sell to-morrow. We might put it thus: He who gives immoderately to-day, will be a beggar to-morrow.

Aristotle said that a prodigal man is vain rather than bad—" Prodigus magis dicitur vanus, quam malus," [1]— and this is true when prodigality is kept within limits. But when it goes so far as to use up capital, it cannot be excused, especially if a man has wife and children, for whom he is bound to provide, not only at the present time, but also in the future. In that case he sins doubly. He sins towards himself by dissipating the goods on which he ought to live, and he sins towards his family by rendering himself incapable of permanently supporting them. *Prodigus peccat in seipsum, dum bona sua consumit, unde vivere deberet ; peccat etiam in alterum, consumendo bona ex quibus aliis deberet providere.* [2] Still worse is it when he squanders his goods in leading a bad life.

Any one who wishes for more particular precepts may consult Agnolo Pandolfini's very famous treatise, *Del buon governo della famiglia.*

Article V.

Public Consumption

18. The expenses of the State for the good of the Community are called Public Consumption. Civil society constitutes a true collective being, a moral body, which has its own existence, its own end, its duties to be fulfilled, its rights to be protected, and consequently its wants to be satisfied. It requires an army to defend it from external attacks and guarantee it against internal

---

[1] *Ethicorum,* Lib. iv. c. 1.

[2] *Summa,* 2ª. 2ªᵉ. Q. CXIX. a. ?. ad 1.

commotions, magistrates to maintain justice and peace, and various officials for other branches of public administration. It requires encouragement of national industry, protection of science and art, schools for the people, external manifestations of religion, and so on. All these different wants assuredly cannot be supplied without cost, which means consumption of produce; and that necessitates taxes, of which we shall have to speak further on.

19. Say remarks that the same rules hold good for public as for private consumption. "The consumption," he says, "or if you prefer it, the expenses of which the object is to satisfy the wants of the public, are precisely of the same nature as the wants of private persons. The nature of riches, the laws that preside over their formation and their consumption, do not differ in virtue of the use that is made of them. In this they are like the laws of hydrostatics, which remain the same whether they are applied to the construction of machines for individuals, or for the State. To have put this truth beyond question is one of the latest advances in Political Economy."[1]

Though this be true as regards the object, it cannot be denied that, if we look at the subject, and the end and the means of the one consumption and of the other, great differences appear. Consumption in the private order concerns the interests of a private person, or of one family considered within its domestic limits; but in the public order it concerns the common interests of the whole nation, or of the same individuals and families, not as such, but as united to form one social whole. In the private order he decides on the expense, who feels the want, and in doing so disposes of his own. In the public order the wants are felt by the people; but the decision about providing for these wants is made, not by those who

---

[1] *Cours Complet, &c.*, 7me. Partie, Ch. 3.

feel, but by those who learn the wants, and who supply
them, not with their own money, but from the pockets of
the tax-payers. Hence the public consumption is by far
the most difficult and troublesome, requiring much more
wisdom and virtue and sincere love of the common good.
To bring these things under rules is the business of
science other than Political Economy restricted to
general principles in the abstract. We must confess that
the practical application of those principles, even from an
economic point of view, is beyond us. It would require
experience in finance.

20. We may however point out that what we said
about the avoiding of prodigality and avarice in private
consumption, is proportionably applicable to public consumption. A government is a miserly one, that underpays
its servants through inordinate love of saving, or has
fewer of them than the public service requires, or cares
not to supply the real and sometimes urgent wants of the
people, or by administrative centralization—in which, by-
the-by, there is even more injustice than avarice—turns
the most and best of everything to the advantage of the
metropolis and its neighbourhood, treating the rest like a
conquered and tributary country under Proconsuls.[1] But
a government is prodigal, that keeps up an enormous army
of officials, most of them superfluous,[2] or favours its own

---

[1] This administrative centralization is one of the fatal
legacies left by the Revolution of '89, whose centenary is about
to be celebrated in France—a sad instance of a noble nation
gone mad through the influence of madder sectarian rulers.
[The original of this translation was written before the
centenary.—*Translator.*]

[2] The other continental States took the French type as their
model. There is a general outcry against it now, but no one
does anything to amend it.

"The National Assembly of 1850," says Boccardo, "did not
dare to decree, as proposed by the Representative Randet, that
the statistics of the bureaucratic staff should be printed, because

supporters with employments and contracts burdensome
to the exchequer, or squanders the national wealth in useless expenses or mere embellishment, instead of in works
for the common advantage, such as roads, bridges, canals,
railways, harbours, industrial and artistic establishments,
&c. Worst of all is the prodigality which throws away
considerable and even vast sums in exciting enthusiasm,
that few feel and no one regrets to have not felt. The
effect of that is afterwards the reverse of what the government expected ; for people are justly indignant at seeing
such waste of public money, which might have been
employed in relieving the destitute.

Some Economists, following Say's example, go on to
discuss national defences by land and sea, administration
of justice, legislative power, public instruction, forms of
government, and I know not what besides. This comes
from their confusing Political Economy with Social Science
in general—a conception that we rejected at the beginning
of this treatise.

In the next chapter we shall complete this one by
speaking of luxury.

---

the printing would have cost 572,000 francs [£22,880], and
would have formed more than twenty-five quarto volumes."
—*Trattato Teoretico Pratico di Economia Politica*, Vol. III.,
p. 54.

224

CHAPTER II.

LUXURY.

CLOSELY connected with the idea of consumption is that of luxury; for, however luxury may be explained, the conception of it is inseparable from that of excessive consumption. That is why we said that the last chapter would be completed by what we should have to say in this about luxury.

Three things have to be done about it. First of all we must show what it consists in, because among ordinary thinkers and even among Economists, there are various opinions about that. Then we must determine whether, as some say, it is good, or, as others more rightly say, it is bad. Lastly we have to inquire whether it can be remedied by laws. The conception, the moral quality, the sumptuary laws—these are the three points with which we are now concerned.

ARTICLE I.

THE CONCEPTION OF LUXURY.

20. James Stewart defined luxury to be *the use of the superfluous*. Say will not allow this definition, and his reason is that the superfluous cannot easily be distinguished from the necessary. "Luxury" he says, "has been defined as the use of the superfluous. I confess that I know not how to distinguish the superfluous from the necessary. Like the colours of the rainbow, they melt into each other by imperceptible gradations." [1] We reject Stewart's definition and Say's reason.

Luxury means more than prodigality. How then can it be defined by the idea of use, when that idea will not even suffice to define prodigality, seeing that prodigality is not use of wealth, but waste of it? Nor would it have sufficed in our opinion, if instead of "use" he had said "abuse." Luxury always implies a notable excess, and abuse, or consumption beyond what is fitting, is not always a notable excess. Would you call a man luxurious for spending a little too much on his clothes, or his table, or the furniture of his house? Luxury is not only wasteful, but extremely so.

The reason given by Say is not a good one, because in distinguishing one thing from another we are not required to discern the precise term that separates them. Let us take the example that he gives. You can distinguish very well the green from the blue in a rainbow, though you cannot show exactly where the one ends and the other begins. In like manner, though we cannot point out where necessary expense becomes excessive, we can see clearly in the extent of the one and of the other the difference between them.

21. But setting aside this incidental consideration, Say rightly rejects that definition, as we do, by reason of its ambiguity. In defining it himself he considers the heavy amount of the disbursement. "It may be affirmed in general," he says, "that luxury is the use of things which cost much." [2] This definition is better as being less indeterminate; but we are not satisfied with it, because if the use of costly things corresponds to the goodness of the object and the social grade of the person, it is not luxury, but magnificence, which is reckoned among the

---

[1] *Traite d'Économie Politique*, Liv. III, Ch. 5.
[2] Ibid.

virtues. *Magnificentia nominat virtutem.*[1] Thus it is praiseworthy in a king to have magnificent furniture, thereby honouring the nation, and still more to spend money on magnificent Churches and vestments to the glory of God. Therefore in defining luxury we must bring in some element that separates it from magnificence, restricting it to private persons and private ends; for as Aristotle observes, the magnificent man is not bountiful towards himself. *Magnificus non est sumptuosus in seipsum.*[2]

Finally, Say thinks that living a soft and sensual life is not properly included in the idea of luxury, but love of show and grandeur. The word "luxury," he says, "awakes in us simultaneously the idea of ostentation rather than that of sensuality. Luxurious clothes do not indicate that the clothes are more comfortable to the wearer, but that they are made to strike the eyes of those who look at them. A luxurious table recalls the

---

[1] *Summa,* 2a. 2ae. Q. CXXXIV. a. 1.

[2] *Ethicorum,* Lib. IV. Cap. 2. St. Thomas gives the reason of this, when he says : *Ad magnificentiam pertinet facere aliquid magnum, quod autem pertinet ad personam uniuscujusque, est aliquid parvum in comparatione ad id quod convenit rebus divinis vel rebus communibus, et ideo magnificus non principaliter intendit sumptus facere in his quæ pertinet ad personam propriam : non quia bonum suum non quærat, sed quia non est magnum.* Sometimes, however, things are done on a great scale by private persons, in certain cases, such as those that happen once in a way, a wedding, for instance, or when the thing paid for has a sort of perpetuity, like a dwelling-house. In such cases, the extra expense, if it does not exceed the means of that person, is magnificence, not luxury. *Si quid tamen,* says St. Thomas, *in his quæ ad ipsum pertinent, magnitudinem habeat, hoc etiam magnifice magnificus prosequitur ; sicut ea quæ semel fiunt, ut nuptiæ, vel aliquid aliud hujusmodi, vel etiam ea quæ permanentia sunt, sicut ad magnificum pertinet præparare convenientem habitationem.—Summa,* 2a. 2ae. Q. CXXXIV. a 1. ad 3.

sumptuousness of a great banquet rather than the delicate food of an epicure." [1]

This may be usually true; but we think that luxury may also be charged with love of dainties. The rich man in the parable, who was clothed in purple and fine linen, and feasted sumptuously every day—*Induebatur purpura et bysso, et epulabatur quotidie splendide* [2] —seems to have cared for pleasure more than pomp. This we gather from Abraham's reply : *Fili, recordare quia recepisti bona in vita tua, et Lazarus similiter mala : nunc vera hic consolatur, tu autem cruciaris.* [3] The word *cruciaris* is in contradistinction, not to pomp, but to pleasure. This therefore seems to have been the sin of the rich man ; and certainly he lived a luxurious life.

For these reasons it seems to us that luxury might be defined as THE USE OF RARE AND COSTLY THINGS ON ONE'S OWN ACCOUNT, FOR THE PURPOSE OF OSTENTATION OR SENSUALITY. In this all the elements that constitute the idea of luxury are included. By the words " rare and costly things " are expressed the excess over what is necessary and becoming. It is distinguished from magnificence as being on one's own account, which is the reverse of what the great objects are, such as divine worship and national splendour. Lastly the words " ostentation and sensuality " mark its twofold motive, proud sensualism, and unrestrained sensualism.

---

[1] *Traité d'Économie Politique*, Liv. III. Ch. 5.
[2] *Luke* xvi. 19.
[3] Ibid., 25.

ARTICLE II.

THE BADNESS OF LUXURY.

22. There are Economists who praise luxury; but most of them condemn it. We adhere to the latter opinion, because luxury is pernicious in its effects, and because it is intrinsically bad. It naturally tends to ruin families, however wealthy, by consuming capital. Luxury means consumption on a great scale,—consumption always increasing, because it has no fixed limit, but is always struggling to outdo competitors, and be looked at and admired by others. Now consumption means destruction.

While ruining the rich, luxury does not benefit the poor, but, on the contrary, makes them poorer. De Montesquieu said that if the rich do not spend much, the poor will die of starvation; but the reverse is true of luxury. The poor will starve, if the rich are luxurious. The funds of the poor are two—their own labour and the beneficence of others, both of which diminish with increase of luxury. Luxury is not benevolence, but selfishness, and therefore dries up the sources of beneficence. By absorbing the wealth of the rich it leaves them without means wherewith to relieve the indigent. By diminishing capital it gradually diminishes labour, which capital supports. Say wisely remarks that want always follows the footprints of luxury, and that a rich man gives to display, spends on precious jewels, sumptuous banquets, and the rest, money which, productively invested, would give necessaries and comforts to many who have no work and are destitute.[1] Hence the rancour of the destitute classes towards the enjoyers of wealth, whose display seems to insult them. That a certain splendour, according to the rank or position of the person, may rightly be kept

---

[1] *Luke* xvi. 19.

up by those who can afford it, any one who thinks may
see ; nor does it excite any irritation in reasonable people.
But immoderate and scandalous pomp, excess of delicacies,
having no reason of being except vanity and self-
indulgence, exasperates the minds of those who possess
nothing, arouses in them contempt, envy, anger, desperate
and subversive thoughts. The glitter of luxury attracts
the eye, misleads the mind, inspires people with love of
pleasure, generates a longing for enjoyment. A state of
society in which all wish to possess, and few can, must
sooner or later bring the country into a state of war,
or, rather, make it a hell upon earth.

23. There is another effect of luxury, very bad and
not unfrequent. It tempts people to make money by any
means, however dishonest. Say remarks on this : " When
the love of luxury," he says, " inspires a man with a longing for gain, will the slow and limited means of true
production satisfy the craving of his wants ? Will he not
rather reckon on the quick and shameful profits of
speculation—a trade ruinous to a nation, because it produces nothing, but only takes from what others have
produced. The rogue then puts in practice all the re-
sources of his despicable mind. The pettifogger schemes
in the obscurity of the law. The man in power sells to
folly or iniquity the protection that he owes freely to
worth and right. [1] 'I have seen at a supper,' says Pliny,
' Paulina covered with a net-work of pearls and emeralds
worth forty millions of sesterces, as she could prove, she
said, by her account-books. This she owed to the plunder-
ing practices of her ancestors. In order that his grand-
daughter (adds the Roman writer) might appear at a
banquet laden with jewels, Lollius was contented to spread
desolation in several provinces, have a bad reputation

---

[1] To this last accusation we cannot plead guilty in England.
—*Translator's Note.*

throughout the East, lose the friendship of Augustus' son, and at last die of poison. ' " [1]

24.   But apart from its bad effects luxury condemns itself as being intrinsically bad.   It is a perversion of order in the matter of morals, because it contradicts the end for which the use of wealth is given by nature.   It employs external goods for the satisfaction, not of real human wants, but of sensuality or ostentation.   It madly squanders the superfluous, which nature has ordained for the relief of the poor.   Doubly, therefore, it perverts the order of nature, and is doubly opposed to the morality of human actions.   St. Thomas teaches us that the superfluous is by the right of nature *owed* to the poor for their relief : *Res, quas aliqui superabundanter habent, ex naturali jure debentur pauperum sustentationi.*[2]   And the reason is that the appropriation of external things, which is of *secondary* natural right, cannot nullify for the use of any man what is of *primary* natural right, *viz.* the right of getting from those external things what is necessary to maintain life.   Property is required by nature, because it is required for the permanent security of individual and domestic subsistence.   But an essential condition of it is that the owner should give to the poor what is more than necessary and suitable to his wants.   Now luxury annuls this condition by excessive dissipation of that superfluous money.   It therefore truly implies a violation of nature's meaning, and from that point of view would justify Proudhon in saying that property is a theft. " La propriété c'est le vol."   This formula is blasphemous as referring to rightful property rightfully understood, which proceeds from God because it proceeds from nature made by God ; but it is partly true, if applied to the property of a man who misuses it by luxurious pomp, withholding and wastefully spending the superfluity which he owes to the poor.

---

[1]   *Traité d' Économie Politique*, Liv. III. Ch. 5.
[2]   *Summa*, 2ª. 2ᵃᵉ. Q. LXVI. 7.

ARTICLE III.

A DEFENCE OF LUXURY.

25. We shall invite Mr. McCulloch to defend the cause of luxury. His opponent will be Jean-Baptiste Say, who is quite worthy of being his antagonist.

M'Culloch says that society owes every improvement to the desire of rising, of bettering our condition, of having useful things and articles of luxury in ever increasing abundance. He tells us that with the love of luxury the abundance of products, not only necessary, but useful and pleasing, greatly increases, and the population is better provided for, and increases rapidly.[1]

First of all, we must observe that here he falls into confusion by mixing up different things. With the desire of bettering our condition (which of itself is not blamable), and with abundance of necessary and useful products which may be rightly and even virtuously sought, he puts the love of luxury, which, as we have shewn, should be reprobated and avoided as a vice. It is rather startling, too, to be told that love of luxury enables the population to be better provided. Better provided with what? The population cannot live on articles of luxury.

Perhaps he thinks that luxury gives an impulse to the production of other things, which are wanted by the population: but Say thinks differently. " Production," he says, " cannot increase otherwise than by means of capital ; and capital does not increase without saving. Now what sort of saving is to be expected from those whose only inducement to produce is their desire to enjoy ?"[2]

Saving implies moderating one's expenses ; and moderating one's expenses excludes luxury. To grow rich you must produce much and consume little : but luxury does

---

[1] *Principles of Political Economy*, Part IV.
[2] *Traité d'Économie Politique*, Liv. III. Ch. 5.

wonder, then, that slavery was abolished, though it was said to be a right of nations as to the fact—a fact generally admitted in heathendom, through want of clear ideas about human personality.   In short, the right to deprive the conquered of their freedom was conceived as resulting from the rights of war.   Now the rights of war are rights, not individual, but social, and therefore subject in many of their consequences to the national will.   Not so the rights of property ; for they, as we have said, are individual, as resulting from the right that every individual person has to secure permanently his own maintenance and that of his children.

The writer's remark that no objection was made by the Church against the abolition of slavery, is curious.   How could the Church object to it after having helped and inspired it by her preaching, by her law, and by her example ?   The same cannot be said about the abolition of private property ; for the Church has never been adverse to its possession, but, on the contrary, defended the right of Clerics to have it, as a guarantee of their not being obliged to depend on the civil power.

Article III.

A Doctrinal Summary.

35.   In conclusion we shall sum up under distinct heads.

1⁰.   The *jus gentium*, according to Catholic Theologians, is midway between the *jus naturæ*, strictly so-called, and the *jus civile ;* for its dictates come from the natural law as consequences, more or less mediate,—not as determinations of general principles.

2⁰.   When the Catholic Theologians called the *jus gentium* positive, they spoke of Positive Right in contradistinction to Natural Right strictly so-called, whether

induced by love of enjoyment, refined or otherwise—in fact, by love of luxury. He had never heard it inferred, he tells us, from the principles laid down, that the stimulus given to industry and the spirit of invention by love of luxury is the best stimulus. Certainly, he says, it would be better if the money wasted on frivolities were applied to some useful art or science, or industrial' undertaking, or employment for the relief of those who through accident or misfortune are a prey to unmerited misery. But he holds to his opinion that in such matters it is useless to consider what men ought or ought not to be, since we have to do with them as they are, and not as we would wish them to be.[1]

This is a detestable maxim, suited only for sending the human race headlong down the precipice of inordinate appetite and vicious tendencies. The contrary is true. The worse people are in habits and morals, the more we ought to raise our voices in reproof, so that those who are contaminated thereby, may at least feel ashamed. What would have been the result if the Apostles had followed such teaching? We should now be floundering in the mire of paganism.

Say is wiser than McCulloch, and deservedly attacks this disgraceful pandering to the customs of the many. " It is a sad truth," he exclaims, " that the customs and habits of the country to which one is bound by birth, by fortune and by affection, draw under their influence even the wisest and those who are in a position to weigh the danger and foresee the deplorable consequences. Few men are strong enough in mind and independent enough in position to behave according to their own principles, and not take other people as their models. Most of them even against their inclination follow the senseless crowd, who, through want of reflection, do not perceive that when the

---

[1] *Principles of Political Economy*, Part IV.

ordinary wants of life are satisfied, happiness is not found
in the vain enjoyment of luxury, but in the moderate
exercise of our physical and moral faculties.   Those
persons who with great power and great talent seek to
disseminate a taste for luxury, conspire against the
happiness of nations." [1]

28.   McCulloch, wishing to explain in an acceptable
sense, De Montesquieu's proposition that, if the rich do not
spend much, the poor will die of starvation, speaks of it
thus: We need not, he says, wonder at its being impugned,
because it may be true or false according to the way in
which it is understood.   If, he says, you mean that a rich
man, spending his income on sumptuous furniture, may
directly employ more servants and work-people than by
applying part of it to improve his capital and in saving for
his children, the proposition is clearly erroneous.   The
demand for labour cannot sensibly increase without
increase of capital; and those who spend all their income
on immediate pleasures cannot accumulate capital; they
consequently cannot employ even one workman more.
But De Montesquieu's proposition, he tells us, should be
interpreted, not in this restricted sense, or as referring to
the influence of the rich man's expenses, or the quantity of
work required by them on their own account, but as
relating to the influence thereof on the demand for labour
in society; and he thinks that if we so understand the
proposition, and suppose it to mean that excessive
expense and luxury on the part of rich people is of great
use to the poor, by exciting the emulation of those who
cannot hope to spend as much, except by redoubling their
economy and activity, the proposition will be found
most correct.

The argument of this well-known Economist comes to
this: Luxury excites the emulation of those who cannot

---

[1] *Principles of Political Economy*, Part IV.

practise it with the means which they possess. These, then, will take to economy and harder work for the purpose of gaining the wealth which luxury requires. Luxury, therefore, is helpful to labour and industry, at least by reaction.

To say the truth, we have no faith at all in this species of antiperistasis. We believe rather that the emulation excited by luxury, instead of inclining people to economy and work in order to enjoy afterwards at some time or other, inclines them on the contrary to rival the rich as soon as possible. Just consider. When a man through bad example has acquired an excessive relish for enjoyment and ostentation, is it probable that he will devote himself to saving money and working hard, instead of seeking immediate enjoyment? We are told that he will do so, in order to procure the means of enjoyment. Our answer is that he will find the means in other ways—first by squandering the whole of his superfluous income, then by borrowing on heavy interest, lastly by selling his capital and going to rack and ruin, as experience but too often proves. Say notices this : "I could easily prove," he says, "that the extravagance of the rich is the cause of extravagance in the moderately well off, and in the poor, who come sooner to the end of their incomes. Thus the general extravagance increases rather than diminishes the inequality of fortunes. Moreover the extravagance of the rich is always preceded or followed by the extravagance of governments, whose only resource is taxation, which always presses more on small than on large incomes." [1]

---

[1] *Traité d'Économie Politique*, Liv. III., Chap. 5.

ARTICLE IV.

SUMPTUARY LAWS.

29.　Often, in ancient and modern times, the Executive has tried to check luxury by laws. Such laws were called Sumptuary from *sumptus* "expense," to restrain which they were made. The Economists, whether friendly or hostile to luxury, despise these laws as senseless, unjust and impotent. McCulloch tells us that although they were long popular in Rome, and were in force in England and in many other European countries, they never produced any good effect, and are a manifest violation of the rights of property. [1] Boccardo says that, besides being erroneous and absurd, they are unjust and immoral, because civil society is founded on the right of property—that right in virtue of which every one freely disposes of himself and his substance. [2] Minghetti dwells more on its inefficacy. " The laws of the twelve tables," he says, " retrenched the cost of funerals, and determined the number of mourners and of musicians. By the Oppian law variety of clothes, abundance of golden ornaments, and the use of carriages in the city were forbidden to matrons. The Orchian law came in to limit the cost of banquets, the number of guests, the quality of the dishes. But the rigour of the laws and the severity of the censors did not at all restrain luxury. It increased with the increase of wealth acquired by plunder, till it reached the extreme of refinement and corruption in the days of the Empire, which excites our horror and indignation. In modern times the sumptuary laws had a political, rather than an economical, purpose. They chiefly aimed at preventing confusion of classes and show of

---

[1] *Principles of Political Economy*, Part IV.
[2] *Trattato Teoretico Pratico di Economia Politica*, Vol. I., Lib. III., Cap. 2.

power in men of ignoble birth.[1] But even with these
limits they had no real efficacy.[2]

30. Our own opinion is this : First of all, though
sumptuary laws are very difficult to carry out, it is an
exaggeration to call them absurd. Certainly it is a most
arduous task to lay down general rules about a matter that
varies beyond measure, being of itself relative to the
various conditions of families and individuals. Nevertheless it does not seem impossible to aim at checking the
enormities among them, which are generally vicious, and,
as vicious, capable of being repressed by law, when they
begin to spread too much, gravely injuring economy and
morals. And, besides, there is an indirect way of making
sumptuary laws, by taxing objects of luxury.

---

[1] Ludovico Bianchini, in his book *De' reati che nuocciono
all' industria e alla circolazione delle richezze*, speaks as
follows about the economic regulations in the kingdom of
Naples under the Spanish rule : "Another evil, not unim-
portant to our manufactories, was occasioned by the laws called
sumptuary, by which, from 1559, at different epochs (we
read of twenty-nine pragmatic ones under the title of *Lex
sumptuaria*), the legislator thought to regulate the manner of
dressing among different classes of persons at different times
and in different cases ; the manner of conducting funerals,
giving wedding presents, fitting up houses and carriages,
keeping and clothing footmen, coachmen and other servants.
Luxury was considered bad, and the principle of encouraging
the national manufactures was professed : yet at the same time
those laws prohibit—these are the precise words of the pro-
clamation—'Ogni sorta di broccato, brocatello, tele e telette
d'oro ed argento, velluti alti e bassi, ed ogni altra cosa dove
entri oro o argento tessuto e ricami e frangie, cordoni, cordon-
celli e qualsivoglia altra cosa d'oro ed argento filato, cosi vero
come falso ; e che nulla persona di qualsivoglia grado e con-
dizione, cosi mascolo come femmina, le possa portare nè vestire.
Et medesimamente si proibiscono tutti ricami di seta, trine,
trinette, cátinelle, cordoni e frangie di seta, che non si possono
fare sopraveste, robe e saji di velluto, nè d'altra seta, &c.' "

[2] *Dell' Economia Pubblica*, Lib. III.

31. It is also an exaggeration to say that sumptuary laws are in themselves a violation of the rights of property. In fact, they simply restrict them. Natural rights cannot by human authority be extinguished or lessened as to their substance; but they may be put in order and modified, and sometimes even restricted, as the common good may require.

32. There is some force in the other objection : *viz.*, that laws are impotent against the evasive artifices of sensuality and pride. Minghetti justly remarks that moral feeling has more power than law to restrain luxury. But then it must be added that to produce the moral feeling there is no effectual means except religion, without which true morality has no place. "If luxury," says Taparelli, "is an excessive expense against the purpose and the order of the means in relation to the individual and society, it evidently is a social evil also, against which society has the right and therefore the duty of defending itself by all the means that prudence suggests and justice approves. Certainly among these religion, which has been so much inveighed against for being hostile to luxury, is the most effectual, and at the same time the gentlest means of defence that society could have. By inculcating a horror of voluptuousness, a contempt of ostentation, the fulfilment and the inviolability of duties, it roots out luxury and establishes within the domestic walls the reign of a wise economy, fertile in supplying present wants and provident for the future.[1]

---

[1] *Saggio Teoretico di Diritto Naturale*, Dissertazione IV. Cap. III., Art. 2.

CHAPTER III.

IMPOSTS.

ENRY STORCH alone among the Economists denied that imposts are matter of economic science. "Analysis," he says, "of the effects of imposts on the price of merchandise, and consequently on their production and consumption, does not come within the sphere of Political Economy, but belongs to financial legislation, and forms one of its most important objects." [1]

But Jean-Baptiste Say contradicted this assertion, remarking that in the study of economic phenomena imposts cannot be ignored, because they are closely connected with the production, distribution and consumption of wealth. "A financial legislation," he says, "not illumined by the light of Political Economy, would be worthy of Bedouin Arabs." [2]

Indeed, the writers on Political Economy speak of it at considerable length; and we, though writing much more briefly, feel that we ought to say something.

---

[1] *Course of Political Economy*, by H. Storch, with notes b Jean-Baptiste Say. Part I. Bk. IV. Ch. 3.
[2] See his note to the passage just quoted.

ARTICLE I.
THE LAWFULNESS OF IMPOSTS.

34. Imposts are THAT PART OF THE STATE'S WEALTH WHICH IS TAKEN FROM THE TAX-PAYING CLASSES TO SUPPLY MONEY FOR PUBLIC EXPENSES. They are also called taxes, tribute, duties, &c. But, whatever its name may be, the thing is the same, i.e. money paid by the subjects to supply the economic wants of the State.

This simple definition will suffice to shew that they are lawful. He who has a duty to do has a right to the means without which it cannot be done. Now the State has the duty of keeping public order, which requires expense. The mere machinery of government is very expensive; and the expense is greater in proportion to the advance of civilisation. Where is this money to come from? The State, as such, is not a producer. It is neither an agriculturist, nor a manufacturer, nor a merchant, and, as a State, is not even a proprietor. The land belonging to the government is mostly not productive, and, where it is so, would not suffice to pay a thousandth part of the State expenses. The only funds of the State are the pockets of the taxpayers. Taxes, therefore, are a just institution, and, as such, the Apostle St. Paul commands the faithful to pay them : *Reddite ergo omnibus debita : cui tributum, tributum; cui vectigal, vectigal : cui timorem, timorem : cui honorem, honorem.*[1]

35. The justice of this is the more apparent when we remember the great advantages conferred by the State in return for the contributions received. St. Paul, writing to the faithful in Corinth, said : "If we have sown unto you spiritual things, is it a great matter if we reap your carnal things !" *Si spiritualia nos vobis seminavimus, magnum est, si nos carnalia vestra metamus ?*[2] And the

---

[1] *Rom.* xiii. 7.
[2] 1 *Corinth.* ix. 11.

State may justly say to the taxpayers: "If I ensure the safety of your persons and your possessions, if I secure you in the exercise of your rights, defend you against foreign invaders, have the law administered justly, furnish instruction for your children, facilitate your commerce, and so on, is it unreasonable that you should give me a little of your substance for the purpose of enabling me to live and act? The sacrifice that I require from you, is well repaid."

36. It is not worth while, however, to say more about a self-evident truth. Rather let us point out the limits within which taxation is truly lawful. We can find these limits by considering the subject of the tax, and the end for which it is paid. The subject should be in proportion to the economic ability of the same. Taxation is a burden and is even called so; and, being a burden, it must not exceed the strength of those who have to bear it. But most governments forget this, and incline to increase the taxation; so that he who is the sharpest in getting money out of the taxpayers, is reckoned as the best financier. Hence the payment of taxes has come to be generally considered, not as a duty binding in conscience, but as an oppression, from which any one may lawfully escape if he can.

37. There are people ready to defend anything; and of these there have been some who said that enormous taxation is not burdensome, because the State gives back with one hand what it takes with the other. The Economists justly reply that the State does not give back gratuitously, but receives in exchange for what it gives. It pays workmen, but receives their labour. It buys from tradesmen, but receives their merchandise. It pays officials, but receives their services. If this is restitution, any man who robs a tradesman and spends the money at his shop, may be said to restore it.

38. The other point that we have to keep in view in

considering the lawfulness of a tax that falls on all without distinction, is whether it answers to real wants of the State, and tends at least indirectly to benefit all, rich and poor. To raise taxes for the purpose of employing the money, not in works of general utility, but in grand buildings, theatres, public gardens and pompous monuments, while the greater part of the population is in want of the necessaries of life, is bad. Jean-Baptiste Say asks whether any one will venture to maintain that a father should lessen the food and clothing of his children for the sake of public monuments? " Qui osera soutenir qu'un père doit rétrancher un morceau de pain, un vêtement chaud à ses enfants, pour fournir son contingent au luxe des monuments publics?"[1] " If the executive," says Taparelli, "takes its right of taxing from the obligation to combine for the public good, the *right* ceases when there is no *obligation* on the part of the subjects. Now their *obligation* extends to what is necessary. The surplus, which concerns comforts and neatness, they may *lawfully* spend in the absence of more urgent duties; but they are not obliged to do so. Therefore, when there is *necessity*, the Sovereign himself may fix the rate of taxation, but when it is a question of mere polish, the superior ought to tax those only (individuals or corporations) who, desiring to obtain those advantages, voluntarily consent. It must be clearly understood, however, that society, no less than the individual, regards as necessary not only that without which it could not exist, but also that without which it would exist needily."[2]

---

[1] *Traité d'Économie Politique*, Liv. III., Ch. 9.

[2] *Saggio di Diritto Naturale*, Dissertazione V., Cap. VI. Art. 3.

ARTICLE II.

DIRECT AND INDIRECT TAXATION.

39. Taxes affect every one's income, whether it be from land, or from interest of capital, or from payment for work. But how can the income be exactly ascertained, so that it may be taxed in just proportion? "If we were able to count on the good faith of the contributor," Say remarks, "one way alone would suffice. We should only have to ask each man what his income amounts to. No other basis would be wanted for determining his share. There would only be one tax; and none could be more equitable, nor cost less to collect. This is what was practised in Hamburg before the disaster that befell it, and cannot be done except in a republican State of small extent, where the citizens know each other, and where the contributions are moderate.[1] "

40. Setting aside this way as impracticable in great States, especially where they are far gone in modern corruption, the work of exactly fitting the tax to the wealth of individuals is most difficult, or rather impossible. To meet the difficulty, various expedients are tried, which are reducible to the two classes of direct and indirect taxation. The former comes directly from the people, whether it be levied on permanent or moveable wealth. The latter is levied on consumable goods, necessary or otherwise, and falls on the purchaser by raising the price. The producer, says Stuart Mill, or he who imports merchandise, is bound to pay a tax for it, not for the purpose of levying a particular tribute on him, but in order to tax through him the consumers of that merchandise from which he is supposed to recuperate the expense by increase of price.[2]

41. At first sight it would seem that by direct taxes

---

[1] *Traité, &c.*, Liv. III., Ch. 10.
Principles of Political Economy, Bk. V. Ch.

equality in the taxation could be attained, especially in the case of real property, which can be easily known and valued by the government. And yet it is not so even with respect to that, owing to its continual variations in value by reason of improvements and deterioration, and the many vicissitudes of production and price. As to the proceeds that constitute what is called moveable wealth, formed of those very mutable elements, the profits of capital, and the money made in commerce or by different professions and trades, it is impossible to find accurately a common measure; and therefore a tax on them is equivalent to a capitation tax.[1]

42. Still less can equality be attained by means of indirect taxation, though it is easier of application. An indirect tax is proportionate to the consumption, but the consumption is not always proportionate to the wealth.

43. Its other fault is that it is burdensome, because it presses on things that we make use of, and therefore

---

[1] By the capitation tax people were taxed *per capita*, according to their presumed wealth or social rank. It was given up as evidently bad; but now it seems to have revived in the shape of taxes on moveable wealth. "Capitation taxes," says Adam Smith, "if it is attempted to proportion them to the fortune or revenue of each contributor, become altogether arbitrary. The state of a man's fortune varies from day to day, and without an inquisition more intolerable than any tax, and renewed at least once every year, can only be guessed at. His assessment, therefore, must in most cases depend upon the good or bad humour of his assessors, and must therefore be altogether arbitrary and uncertain.

"Capitation taxes, if they are proportioned, not to the supposed fortune, but to the rank of each contributor, become altogether unequal; the degrees of fortune being frequently unequal in the same degree of rank. Such taxes, therefore, if it is attempted to render them equal, become altogether arbitrary and uncertain; and if it is attempted to render them certain and not arbitrary, become altogether unequal."—*Wealth of Nations*, Bk. V. Ch 2. Part ii., art. 4.

absorbs a great deal of one's income. Nevertheless, being confused with the price of the goods, it is less noticed than direct taxation.

ARTICLE III.
RULES TO BE OBSERVED.

44. All Economists, when treating of imposts, have more or less laid down laws to be followed, in order that they may not prove intolerable to the payers and insufficiently profitable to the State; but in our opinion no one has put them so concisely and clearly in short formulas, as Sismondi. They are as follows:

1°. Every impost ought to be a charge on the income, not on the capital. In the former case the State spends only what the individuals would spend: in the latter it destroys what ought to maintain the individual and the State.[1]

2°. In establishing a tax the annual raw produce must not be confounded with the net return; for the former includes, besides the return, all the circulating capital also; and a part of this product should remain to keep up or renew all the fixed capital, all the accumulated labour, and the lives of all the productive workers.[2]

3°. A tax, being, as it were, the price paid for social enjoyments, cannot be demanded from those who have them not. Therefore it ought not to be charged on that part of an income which is necessary to the life of the contributor.[3]

4°. A tax ought never to use up the wealth on which it is charged; and therefore the more transient the nature

---

[1] The capital becomes less, if the production is less.

[2] Only the net profit is really profit. Of the gross profit the greater part is merely a repayment of expenditure.

[3] Hence those taxes are unjust that press chiefly on the poor.

of the wealth is, the more moderate should the tax on it be. It should never touch that part of the income which is necessary for the preservation of the income.[1] To these rules he adds in the following chapter the directions given by Adam Smith, and sums them up thus: "Any tax whatever is worse in proportion to the degree in which the sacrifice to which it subjects the people, exceeds the income that it procures for the Exchequer: and the more economically it is collected, the better it is. It is worse in proportion to the amount of inconvenience brought on the contributor by the time of its payment, and better in proportion to the convenience of the time.

"The more it requires vexatious inspection in collecting it, and the more it results in violation of prudence, the worse it is. The less it tempts to fraud, the less inspection it requires, and the more voluntary its payment appears, the better it is."[2]

45. We insist on two rules only.

The first is that taxation generally should be as light as possible. This, it was thought, would be more easily secured by the institution of representative government; but experience has shown the contrary. Under no absolute government has taxation [in Italy] become so oppressive as under the new representative government. Taxes have so increased and extended, that now it is nothing less than pillage of private property; and the worst of it is that you cannot make any one responsible, because a representative government is, as they say, impersonal. The parliament that makes the laws is an abstraction; the ministry that carries them, resigns, and so ceases to be.[3]

---

[1] This rule refers chiefly to profits that proceed from capital, particularly circulating capital.

[2] *Nouveaux Principes d'Économie Politique*, Liv. VI., Chaps. 2, 3.

[3] Any one who knows how things are in "regenerated" Italy, will know that this is the bare truth.—*Translator's Note.*

The increase of taxes has made commodities and house-rent so enormously dearer, that poor people can hardly live, the better off sink into the ranks of the poor, the middle class tends to disappear. Society, unless the Providence of God intervenes, will before long be divided into millionaires and owners of nothing—plutocracy and pauperism.

46. This leads to the second rule, which is one of Sismondi's already quoted, viz. that taxes should never be levied on the necessaries of life. Therefore very small owners ought tó be free from direct taxes. It is horrible to see how often such proprietors are driven to sell their little property [in Italy], because they cannot pay the imposts on it. [1]

Indirect taxation ought to exclude as much as possible all those means of subsistence that are of the first necessity, such as flour, vegetables, oil, salt, fuel, the common wine of the country, &c. Taxes on such things often deprive of necessary food a great part of the population : and therefore the " grinding tax " [in Italy], which most of all presses on the poor, because they live chiefly on bread, is considered to be the most iniquitous.

Owing to the enormous expenses of modern governments, indispensable articles of general consumption cannot be quite exempted from paying taxes, because the taxes on things that are not necessary bring in little ; but at least we may try to make them as little burdensome as possible to the poor. [2]

---

[1] The well known "three acres and a cow" would have verified this in England on a great scale, and left no one to pay wages for agricultural labour.—*Translator's Note.*

[2] Which in fact we have done in England.

ARTICLE IV.

WHETHER TAXES OUGHT TO BE PROPORTIONAL OR PROGRESSIVE.

47. Proportional taxation keeps the same proportion to the wealth taxed, however much the wealth may increase. Thus, if the tax were two per cent, an income of three hundred a year would pay six pounds, five hundred a year ten pounds, and so on. Progressive taxation varies by increasing with increase of wealth, as for instance, if it were two per cent up to three hundred a year, four per cent up to a thousand, five per cent up to two thousand, &c. Evidently neither proportional nor progressive taxation can be applied to indirect taxes, unless the tax on certain manufactures were raised when their production exceeded a given amount. In that way there would be some progression, *sui generis*, of an indirect tax.

48. The Economists differ in determining which of these ways is best. Adam Smith seems to prefer the latter; for after remarking that, if the house-tax were paid, not by the proprietor, but by the occupier, it would be heavier on the rich than on the poor,[1] he adds : " In this sort of inequality there would not, perhaps, be anything very unreasonable. It is not very unreasonable that the rich should contribute to the public expenses, not only in proportion to their revenue, but something more than in that proportion." [2] Jean-Baptiste Say is more explicit. " I am not afraid to affirm," he says, " that progressive taxation only is equitable." [3] And this opinion is supported by an eminent philosopher, Taparelli, who says : "Another important deduction from the principle

---

[1] It would also do away with the enormous injustice of charging, as some governments do, on houses that are unlet.

[2] *Wealth of Nations*, Bk. V. Ch. 2, Part ii. Art. 1.

[3] *Traité, &c.* Liv. III. Ch. 9.

here laid down is the injustice of the simple proportion of weight and forces; for society ought to secure the good of each person according to the importance of that person's rights; and therefore the right of the poor to subsist comes into collision with the right of the rich to his super-abundance. Therefore progressive taxation is just." [1]

49. Boccardo denies that Adam Smith approves of progressive taxation, and thinks that all who take his words in that sense are light-minded. "To say the truth," he says, "I wish that Adam Smith had not let slip those rather imprudent words, on which light-minded men have founded this opinion as coming from so great an authority."[2] We can hardly suppose that he means to include Say among the light-minded men; but Say does certainly attribute to Adam Smith the opinion in question. He says: "De Montesquieu accepts it fully as being the only equitable taxation; and Adam Smith, who had much juster ideas about the true interests of society, approves of it no less."[3] But a great number of Economists reject it as unjust and injurious. Stuart Mill says that he desires as much as any one to moderate the inequality of wealth, but not so as to stop labour and the accumulation of capital. To put a higher rate of taxation, he tells us, on large incomes than on small ones, is to lay an extra tax on industry and economy, and inflict a penalty on people for working hard and saving more than others. It is, he says, a partial tax, a sort of theft.[4] Other writers of no less authority say the same in different words.

50. We cannot venture to give a definitive judgment in a question so knotty and so much controverted; but

---

[1] *Saggio di Diritto Naturale*, Dissertazione V. Cap. VI. Art. 3.

[2] *Trattato Teoretico Pratico di Economia Politica*, Vol. III. Sect. iii. Cap. 3.

[3] *Cours Complet*, Partie VIII., Ch. 4.

[4] *Principles of Political Economy*, Bk. V. Ch. 2.

we allow ourselves to say that the reasons urged by the adversaries of progressive taxation seem to us insufficient. Why does Mill call it a sort of theft? Because, he says, it inflicts a penalty on people for the economy and industry by which they have accumulated their wealth. But, setting aside the fact that some of them, especially among the Jews, have not acquired their vast wealth by honest industry and saving, certain it is that if his reasoning were valid, it would also apply to proportional taxation. "Why," it might be said, "do you want so much from me and only a tenth of it from So-and-so?" The answer of course would be that So-and-so's income is only a tenth of the grumbler's income. But the grumbler would reply that his having ten times as much was due to his own industry and economy or to that of his progenitors. "You are punishing me," he would say, "for being industrious and careful. This is a sort of theft."

51. Surely all this is beside the question. What has to be considered in taxation is the wealth of the payers; not as to its origin, but in accordance with their duty of contributing to the public expenses. Non-progressive taxation appears, when so considered, not as a theft, but an act of distributive justice. Taxation is, as we said, a burden and a compensation. As a burden, it is just that some extra weight should be borne by the stronger shoulders. As a compensation, it ought to increase or decrease in proportion to the advantages gained by the contributors. Now the State is evidently more advantageous to the rich than it is to the more or less poor. The State gives many advantages. Protection of property, for instance, is more important to the rich than to the poor, for such protection is of comparatively little importance where there is little to lose. *Cantabit vacuus coram latrone viator.*[1]

---

[1] See Art. ii. § 42, of this third Part.—*Translator.*

CHAPTER IV.

THE NATIONAL DEBT.

EVERYWHERE in these days there are three heavy burdens on the Exchequer—a countless number of officials, an enormous army, and an immense national debt, which perhaps is the most destructive of the three, because it absorbs the greater part of the State's income, and threatens with bankruptcy the richest of nations.[1] Of that, as belonging to consumption, we must now speak; and firstly we have to make the nature of it clear.

ARTICLE I.

THE NATURE OF THE NATIONAL DEBT.

53.   Extraordinary cases arise—as, for instance, a war, or a famine, or some immense public work urgently required—in which the State wants money that cannot be got out of taxes, because they are not sufficient for the purpose, or would furnish the supplies too slowly, or cannot be much increased.   In such a crisis there is nothing for it but a loan.

Formerly such cases were met by accumulated treasure saved in prosperous times: and that custom continued almost up to our own days, as, for example, when Napoleon

---

[1] In England we have been paying some of it off, as the Fund-holders know to their cost.

used for the campaign of 1813-14, the four hundred millions of francs, that he had stored up at the Tuileries. But this method was given up as bad, because the money so kept was often wasted by the government in gifts or useless expenses ; and moreover those vast sums of money locked up might have been profitably employed. It was considered safer and more advantageous to borrow what was wanted at the time, rather than keep unproductive money in readiness for an occasion ; and so the State assumed the responsibility of paying and giving annual percentage to the lenders as long as they are its creditors : and the State's obligations to them constitute the national debt, which may therefore be defined as THE AMOUNT OF THE STATE'S PECUNIARY OBLIGATIONS FOR LOANS RECEIVED.

54. There are two species of national debt. The one includes a promise of repayment : the other does not. The one is a temporary, the other a permanent loan. In the former case the State, besides paying the interest, binds itself to repay the principal within a given time, either all at once to all the creditors, or successively to each by a periodical allotment. This is the most reasonable way of borrowing, and is practised in the United States. In the latter species of national borrowing the State restricts its obligations to paying an annual interest. It does not engage to repay the capital lent, but reserves the right of paying it off. This latter species of national debt is more like a buying and selling, in which the lenders buy and the State sells. The State offers an annual interest of so much per cent on a nominal capital. The customers come in : but they offer eighty or ninety for a hundred pounds, and certainly try to make as good a bargain as they can according to the law of demand and supply, which obtains in purchase and sale. But then owing to the power, reserved by the State, of paying off the capital if, and when, it wills to do so, the contract is not a true purchase and sale, but a loan with interest.

55. Either of these two species of loan can be raised in two ways—by subscription, or by adjudication. In the former case the State deals directly with the lenders. In the latter it deals with them indirectly through a company of capitalists, or a bank, and the company or the bank buys the whole interest, engaging to pay the individual fund-holders, just as a tradesman buys wholesale and sells retail. This method is generally preferred by governments now, to avoid the risk of not being able to get the whole sum wanted, and also in order to secure the amount at once. But the State loses much by the transaction; for the said company or bank, having to make money by it, will not pay the interest at the nominal value, or a little below, but with a discount of twenty, thirty, or even forty per cent, according to the credit of the government, which nevertheless has to pay the interest of this discounted sum, just as if it had received the whole.

56. Besides these two there is the forced loan, so called from being forcibly imposed and collected. But this is an extortion rather than a loan. It is thoroughly odious, being against freedom, injurious to industry by taking away capital, dishonourable to a government by shewing that it resorts to extortion because nobody has confidence in it.

ARTICLE II.
CONSOLIDATED DEBT AND FLOATING DEBT.

57. In France, and also in Italy, the loans contracted by the State at a fixed percentage are inscribed in a public register that goes by the name of the *Great Book*, extracts from which are given to the creditors. Formerly they were in the names of certain persons, individual or associated; but now, to facilitate their circulation, they are made due to the bearer. The State's debt for such loans is called consolidated, by reason of its permanence and solidity. "When we say *consolidated debt*," writes

Pellegrino Rossi, "we mean a debt regularly inscribed in the registers of the State, known, determined, not alterable except in virtue of a law."[1] In other words the consolidated debt is the debt of the State, with a fixed interest, which debt is either not repayable, or repayable by slow degrees through a sinking fund.

58. Just the opposite of this is the floating, or, more correctly, the fluctuating debt, so called from being, not fixed, but transient and extremely variable. Cases occur, unforeseen and impossible to foresee, in which the government has temporary need of capital without having the power or the right to contract a permanent debt. To supply this want the government puts itself in communication with some banker or private capitalist, and opens a running account with him for the sums wanted, giving for it bills, called Treasury Bonds, Treasury Notes &c., payable at a short date, which are like so many promissory notes for which the State makes itself responsible, and which it must pay off within the year. This would seem more like an anticipation of the next year's income than a loan: but let us see what Pellegrino Rossi has to tell us about it:

"It is very difficult," he says, "for the Treasury to have always in readiness the precise amount of money required for use day by day in every place. We cannot expect that revenue and expenses will combine in such a manner as to free us quite from moments of difficulty and stagnation. It may very well happen that, when the government has to spend two millions of francs at Bayonne there are two millions in the coffers of the custom-house at Havre or Marseilles. It is a question then of balancing the expenses by receiving the money in different sea-port towns.

---

[1] *Cours d' Économie Politique*, Fragments: deuxième Fragment, Première leçon.

" Likewise the expenses of the government are not fixed. If the Minister of Finance had only to pay the army and the officials, the rate of whose pay and the time of payment are known beforehand, he could easily put the expenses in perfect harmony with the revenue. But there are expenses that cannot be calculated beforehand; and therefore in the balance-sheet there are those entries which are called *crédits extraordinaires et crédits supplémentaires.*

"Also circumstances may arise that make the revenue less abundant than usual, or at' least not so readily got.

"In all this one clearly sees how the Treasury may need a temporary credit of 2, 3, 4, 5, 10, or 15 millions [of francs] for the time being. Well, it does not contract by this a true loan, an addition to the debt inscribed in the *Grand Livre.* It does not thereby create an additional revenue. It asks capitalists to lend a certain amount of capital, a certain sum of money. It becomes a monthly debtor, and like a bank issues notes that, as they say in ordinary parlance, circulate.

" Well then, these Treasury bonds, these promissory notes bearing interest, which are not written down in the *Grand Livre,* but are sold in the streets to owners of money, who keep as payment the interest of their money, form what is called a floating debt.

" You see then that the floating has not the characteristics of the consolidated debt. It is not written down in the *Grand Livre,* nor does it constitute stocks. It is not absolutely determined; and therefore it is called floating, because the sum of it is sometimes higher and sometimes lower. At times we have had a floating debt of nearly 400 millions of francs, and at other times the Treasury was embarrassed by the enormous sums that it had." [1]

---

[1] *Cours d'Économie Politique,* Fragments: Deuxième Fragment, Première leçon.

It may happen that the floating debt exceeds the power of the government to pay it. In that case the only remedy is a law authorizing a loan to pay it off; which transforms the floating debt into a consolidated debt.

ARTICLE III.
SINKING AND CONVERSION.

59. The State, which is a moral person, should, like a physical person, do its best to pay its debts. This is understood in the very idea of debt, because it is immoral to borrow money, if we know that we cannot at any time repay it, or that we care not to do so. Hence the Sinking Fund, which consists in an accumulation of money by the government for the purpose of paying off a debt contracted by itself. The State receives a loan, and gives up the use of a small part, which, being profitably invested, so increases that in a given time it suffices to extinguish the whole debt. Calculations first made by Dr. Price prove that by putting out at interest the hundredth part of a capital, and getting interest on the annual interest of it, you can re-make the whole sum in thirty five years. By means of this operation, then, the government may in that time be in a position to pay back what it had borrowed.

60. But the Economists remark that, although the effect of this operation is indisputable in theory, being founded on arithmetical calculations, it never is obtained in fact; for in fact the State has dipped into the sinking fund, in order to supply social wants ever recurring. Therefore many Economists, with Say at the head of them, have proposed to abolish it as a thing that only multiplies the expenses of administration. They suggest that, by means of economizing (which, after all, is the only means of extinguishing debt), the State should keep its expenses

within its revenue, and that the excess be applied at once to the payment of the debt, buying, on account of the government shares in the public income, so that after a certain time all the obligations would come back into the possession of the State, and the State be freed from paying any interest. Say writes as follows: "For a State, as for a private person, there are no two ways of paying one's debts. The only one is to devote thereto the surplus income. If the expenses equal the income, the debt will not decrease, whatever you may do; but it will increase, if you spend more than you get. If the income exceeds the expenses, the quickest and cheapest method is to employ the surplus in redeeming a part of the State's obligations. The trick of compound interest is mere quackery. When the State is so fortunate as to have a surplus of twenty million francs, and consequently redeems a million of interest, has it not a million less to pay in the following year? And if its income and its expenses remain in the same proportion, would not the surplus for the next year be also twenty-one millions, which would take off a million and a half? Is not this result all that we could expect from compound interest? Evidently the essential condition of extinguishing a debt is simply to restrict the expenses and employ the surplus in payment of it." [1]

61. Modern States have another way of dealing with debts, not by paying them off, but by lightening the weight of them; and this is called conversion. This means that the government, taking advantage of a fall in the interest of capital, offers to the fund-holders the choice of either receiving back the principal, according to its nominal value of a hundred for every five, or whatever the percentage may be, or else be satisfied with less interest. It is probable that most of the fund-holders,

---

[1] *Traité d'Économie Politique*, Liv. III. Chap. 11.

considering the difficulty of getting a higher interest, will accept the reduction, especially if the government binds itself to abstain from another conversion for a given number of years. Thus the burden on the Exchequer is lightened.

This financial operation, though unfortunate for those who lose by it, is not at all unjust in itself. Every debtor has the right of repaying, whenever he likes, the money that he has borrowed. Much more, then, has the government that right, seeing that it represents the interests of the whole country, which is weighed down by a debt greater than it can bear. On the other hand, the holder of the securities gains by receiving the nominal value of a hundred, when he perhaps bought in at eighty or ninety pounds.

To find the money for this repayment, the government raises a loan at a lower rate, which, owing to the low rate of interest offered by good investments then, is taken up. The profit on that pays off the people who prefer to get back their capital, instead of accepting a lowered percentage, and the surplus is employed in buying up bonds on the old debt.

By virtue of this financial operation several times repeated, the United States of America have reduced their debt from six to three per cent.

ARTICLE IV.
STOCK-JOBBING.

62. The place authorized by the government for negotiating, by means of brokers, the purchase and sale of government stock and all sorts of negotiable things is called the *Bourse* [in England the Stock-Exchange], and the name applies also to the assemblage of capitalists, brokers, &c.

So far as the public funds are concerned, this word

" stock-jobbing " means the infamous traffic of speculators on the rise and fall of the public funds by a fictitious purchase or sale of shares, which rise and fall are often brought about dishonestly by themselves. [1] For instance, one of the said speculators pretends to sell a certain amount of stock at the current price, binding himself to buy it back at the end of the month, i.e. the time of liquidation, at whatever price it would then fetch in the market. This, too, is a pretence; but if the price has risen, the pretended purchaser pays the difference to the pretended seller, and receives the difference if the price has fallen. There are many accidental differences in these contracts; but substantially they are all reducible to this, which, as any one may see, is but a game of chance or cheating, in which the competitors bet on the rise and fall of prices.

63. The ruinous consequences of this now fashionable gambling and the abuses to which it tempts people, not excluding members of government, would seem incredible. Droz says : " Dishonesty is a natural result under the rule of debt. Stock-jobbing is the child of borrowing. Shares rise or fall according to the confidence of the public in the government; and therefore it is advantageous to sell them at one time in order to buy at another. But this game, so circumscribed, appeared to be limited too narrowly. A man who really has no shares at all offers

---

[1] Stock-jobbing is not exclusively practised on the public funds. "The interest on the State's debt," Say remarks, " is not the only matter of stock-jobbing. People speculate on brandies, oil, coffees, soaps, &c. That is to say, they undertake to consign or accept a certain portion of such merchandise at a certain time. This does not imply the intention of really buying or selling. It means that when the time comes they dissolve the contract by paying or receiving the difference between the price agreed on and the current price."—*Cours Complet, &c.*, Partie VIII. Chap. 15.

to sell some, at a given price at a given time, to another who wants to buy them. It is a bet on the rate of interest at that given time. The loser owes a sum equal to the amount about which he was mistaken. The *Bourse* then becomes a gambling-house, all the more dangerous because the players are not required to limit the points. But the most disgraceful part of it is that men in the government can be suspected of mixing themselves up in such gambling transactions, being sure of their game because they have the earliest information about the circumstances that make the interest rise or fall.[1] Thanks to our financial inventions, the administrators of the public fortune, who ought to give an example of scrupulous honour, can make money on their own account, and afterwards become bankrupt on account of the State."[2]

ARTICLE V.
THE GOODNESS AND BADNESS OF LOANS.

64. We can now see whether a national debt is good or bad for a nation. Some people have thought it good, but their sophistries are so miserable that we should only waste time and ink by refuting them. Any one who wishes to see them refuted, had better read Say. Others have thought it bad, as being a burden that presses not only on the present generation, but worse on future generations that have to pay for it. And so it is, no doubt, if we look at the debt absolutely. To be in debt is in itself bad for governments, as for a private person. In this there is no difference between the one and the other. But the national debt when considered relatively may show opposite moral qualities according to the end

---

[1] To this England cannot plead guilty.
[2] *Économie Politique, &c.*, Liv. IV. Chap. 3.

for which it is contracted. Assuredly, it may sometimes be a lesser evil, which under some contingencies should be accepted in order to avoid a greater.

65. It seems to us that the following general rules may be laid down.

The debt, if contracted for some useful purpose, not permanent, but only for a time, and really conducing to benefit the community, may be said to be lawfully contracted, perhaps even laudably so, provided that the State is sure of being able to pay it off shortly, so as not to burden posterity with any part of it.

It may be even indispensable, if contracted to defend the national independence against unjust aggressors. In that case the question is one of life and death. For the independence of a nation is its life as a nation; and since life is the foundation of every good, the preservation of life is more important than the avoidance of any evil in the purely material order. But this is a very rare case.

The debt may be considered useful, if it be contracted for undertakings that are of great and permanent utility to the whole nation, and whose economic advantages exceed the disadvantage of paying for it. Posterity has no right to complain of that; for the benefit received therefrom greatly outweighs the transmitted obligation of paying it off.

But the worst of all national debts, and utterly detestable, are those contracted for expenses of a frivolous kind, or for party purposes, or for unjust or risky enterprises, or for useless and ostentatious armaments that give a false appearance of military greatness when the country is not in a position to have the reality.

66. Some people think that debts contracted in foreign countries are bad, because the interest on them is taken out of the country; but the Economists rightly consider this to be a mistake. A loan contracted abroad does indeed take the interest out of the country; but it

leaves the capital which otherwise would be given to the government to consume, and which, being applied to industry (always supposing that the capital is there, and really is so applied), may give a great impulse to industry, and bring much greater profits; which, however, as Italy shows, does not always happen. So that a debt contracted abroad may sometimes be more useful than one contracted at home, or, at least, not so unfavourable.

In conclusion, we have to say that great care should be taken not to increase the debt, so as to make it intolerable, and that somehow it ought to be extinguished gradually. In these days national debt has reached such colossal proportions, that national bankruptcy seems inevitable, and not far distant. One shudders at the thought of what that means. The following figures are taken from Otto Hubner's statistical and geographical tables. Last year [1888] the national debt in France was 37,800 millions of francs, with an annual interest of 1,302 millions. In England it was 17,897 millions of francs, with an annual interest of 699 millions. In Russia it was 18,597 millions, with an annual interest of 1,125 millions. In Austro-Hungary it was 11,345, with an annual interest of 550 millions. In Italy it was 11,515 millions with an annual interest of 505. [1] The approximate figures given by M. Leroy-Beaulieu differ little from these. He says : " One cannot reckon the French national debt at much less than 32 or 33 milliards. The national debt of England, which is the most heavily burdened of the other powers, only comes to 18 milliards of francs. That of Russia, with its population of a hundred million souls, amounts to 18 or 19 milliards of francs. That of Italy is 11 milliards. The German Empire and all the States that compose it have only a debt of 9 milliards. The debt of Austro-Hungary comes to a dozen milliards." [2]

---

[1] Otto Hubner's *Geographical Statistical Tables of all the Countries in the World* ; 1888.

[2] *Précis d'Économie Politique*, Partie V. Chap. 3.

A SUMMARY.

I**N** concluding this treatise it seems advisable to epitomize briefly what we have said in the foregoing pages, so that the reader may view it as a whole and see the connecting links. The treatise contains an introduction and the three parts into which Economists usually divide Political Economy, i.e., Production of wealth, Distribution, Consumption. We thought it unnecessary to add circulation separately, for, inasmuch as circulation consists in exchange, it may well be considered in production. Our Summary, likewise, will be in four parts.

I.—The Introduction.

2.   Man does not consist of spirit only, which lives on truth and virtue, but also of a body, which requires material means to preserve it. He has need of food, clothing, shelter : and besides those three primary and essential wants, many are caused by the habits and culture of civilized life. Therefore, as there is speculation about what is good for the spirit, so is there speculation about what is good for the body ; and since that is called wealth, speculation there is about wealth, a speculation which is called Economy, and moreover Political, because it regards wealth, not as individual and domestic, but as public and national.

3. Strictly speaking, Political Economy is a science ; for although it may also be called an art, because it furnishes precepts about what is feasible (which the attainment of wealth is), it nevertheless reasons on those precepts and looks upwards to their causes, even to their supreme

causes. But it is a practical science, because it aims at action, *viz.* production, distribution and consumption. It is subordinate to Political Science, because it regards a part only of the aim of Politics. It is subordinate to Moral Science, because the latter subordinates to itself and governs all the other sciences that regard proximate and particular ends. As being subordinate to Political Science it is subject to the regulation of the State. As being subordinate to Moral Science it is subject to the regulation of the Church.

From this it follows that Political Economy might be defined as the science of public wealth as to its right regulation and as a means for the promotion of the common well-being of the society or country.

II.—PRODUCTION.

4. Producing a thing signifies making it exist ; and therefore to produce wealth is to make wealth exist. But before we say how it is produced, and what are the agents of its production, we had better pause awhile to make our conception of it quite clear.

Economists generally do not use the word " wealth " in its ordinary sense. In its ordinary sense it means an abundance of goods ; but Economists mean any useful object, if it be only a pin. Preferring to follow the common usage, we mean by wealth a comfortable suffi-ciency of goods, and call the elements that compose it elements of wealth, or objects, or products, or merely goods. The common use of words ought not to be changed without necessity ; and in this case the necessity is not apparent.

5. In the elements of wealth two things have to be considered, *utility* and *value.*

Utility is the aptitude of an object for satisfying some want, as bread, for instance, has an aptitude for nourishing us. Everything in this world is either useful or may become so through the industry of man; but we must distinguish between them. Some things are given by nature alone, such as air, light, &c., and so profusely as to be within the reach of all. Nor can they be exhausted, however much they are used. These, not being appropriable, do not constitute wealth. A man is not said to be rich because he has plenty of air and light. Other things there are, which, though supplied by nature, are limited and cannot be at the service of every one, such as the tillable soil, animals, mines, and so on. These are appropriable, and constitute wealth.

Appropriable goods and their fruits, as being useful, are commutable with other goods, and are adapted for sale and barter. This aptitude of a thing to be exchanged for something else constitutes its value. Value, therefore, is the aptitude of things to be exchanged for other things. It lies in the commutability of products.

6. Does the nature of wealth consist in utility, or in value? We say that it consists in utility. Wealth consists in abundance of those things that make life comfortable by their utility, not by their value. Indirectly they do so by their value, because their value enables us to procure, by means of exchange, what we want.

Though metaphorically we give the name of wealth to immaterial goods—as, for instance, when we say that some one is rich in virtue, or rich in knowledge,—properly speaking the word is restricted to mean material goods; for so it is conceived in economic science, which otherwise would be confused with other sciences. Materiality is an essential characteristic of wealth as the object of Political Economy.

7. Since wealth consists in the utility of things, producing wealth is equivalent to producing utility; and this may be done either by production of a useful thing, as when the soil produces a crop of wheat, or by transforming a thing in order to make it useful or increase its utility,

as when linen is spun out of flax. In the former case the thing is made by nature ; in the latter by the work of man. Therefore nature and work are the two factors of wealth. These help each other, inasmuch as labour employs natural agents in transforming objects, and nature in producing requires to be put in suitable conditions by labour. The soil, for instance, must be worked and sown to produce corn.

A third factor is generally brought in by Economists, *viz.* capital, which is the result of having saved, being formed from a part of wealth not consumed—a part kept in reserve to be used for the purpose of production. It cannot, however, be a factor of wealth, because of itself it has no action for that ; but it may be called an auxiliary, or an instrument, or a means.

8. Human labour applied to production constitutes industry. There are three species of industry, *viz. extractive*, which is employed in getting goods from nature ; *manufacturing*, which modifies or transforms raw material got from nature ; and *commercial*, which transports and exchanges products, natural and artificial.

9. Machinery and division of labour are two great helps to production, the former by organizing the forces of man, the latter by organizing the forces of nature. This organization has caused prodigious effects, but also grave evils. These cannot be removed ; but they ought to be lessened, and we have pointed out the remedies.

10. The passing of goods from hand to hand with increase of value till they come to the consumer, constitutes circulation. It is accomplished by means of exchanges, and exchanges are accomplished usually by means of money, which was introduced precisely to facilitate them, and in civilized countries is made of gold and silver with a stamp to certify its quality or weight. Exchanges of thing for thing could hardly be effected ; but money is the substitute for them all, measuring their

value in money as their equivalent. This equivalence forms the price, which therefore is nothing more than the value of the goods calculated in money. The price rises or falls according to the demand and supply in the exchanges, and the result is what is called the current price or market price, which, however, is always tending towards the natural price, or that which answers to the cost of production.

11. Paper is a substitute for money, as its representative. This is in virtue of credit, or confidence in other people as to the fulfilment of an obligation assumed. Hence banks come to be, and bank notes, cheques, &c.

12. From this we passed on to consider production with regard to population; for clearly, the former ought to increase with the increase of the latter, seeing that it supplies the necessary means of subsistence. Malthus says that production cannot accord with increase of population, because the population increases in geometrical progression, while the means of subsistence increase in arithmetical progression. To make the two correspond, he says, obstacles to the multiplication of the people must intervene; and these obstacles must be either preventive or repressive. The former diminish the births by abstinence from marriage or, at least, from too early marriages. The latter increases the deaths by poverty, and by the physical and moral ills that are consequent on it. Therefore, if we wish to keep off these latter obstacles, we must choose the former, which he calls moral constraint. And so he inveighs fiercely against the marriages of the poor—that is, of those that are not in a position to maintain a family—and blames charitable institutions as encouraging people to marry without means of support.

We deny the progression supposed by Malthus. In plants and in the lower animals generation is much more prolific than it is in man. Moreover there is land in Europe still uncultivated and immense tracts of it

in North and South America, Africa, Australia, New
Zealand, New Guinea. The land will never fail to give
nourishment for man, if the soil be duly cultivated and
the sheep and cattle duly attended to. To say the contrary is to blaspheme God, Who commanded men to
multiply and to subdue the earth. *Replete terram, et
subjicite eam*, are two terms of the divine formula that
will always be in proportion. Enforced celibacy of the
poor cruelly violates the first rights of man. Certainly a
man should, before he marries, put himself in a position
to maintain a future family, but this is a dictate of
prudence, not an absolute precept of nature. If sometimes
for the strongest reasons the poor fail to follow that
dictate of prudence, we have no right to accuse them of
committing a crime. Malthus's moral constraint is preg-
nant with evil consequences.

13. Lastly, we spoke of the three economic systems—
the mercantile, the agrarian, and the industrial. The
mercantile system, also called Colbertism, because Colbert
applied it to France, supposes that abundance of money
makes the wealth of a nation. Therefore he recommended
commerce, but so that exportation should exceed importation, because then the excess of the former over the
latter would have to be paid for in money. So he ruled
that manufactures must be preferred to agriculture and
importation of raw material, which, if worked up at home,
would be afterwards exported much increased in value.
This system is justly ridiculed by the Economists. Its
chief defect is, that it ignores the function of money,
which is to serve as a vehicle for the exchange of goods.
Wealth does not consist in abundance of money, but in
abundance of those things that make the comforts of life.
If there is too much money in a country, it must be
exported to prevent fall in its value.

The agrarian, or physiocratic, system supposed wealth
to be in the products of the earth, as giving an excess on

the expenses of production, and therefore the physiocrats ruled that agriculture is the true worker of wealth. All other industries, they said, are barren, because they only reimburse expenses. But if the mercantile system ignored the office of money, the agrarian system ignored the nature of economic produce. In Economy the production of wealth means, not merely producing the useful thing, but also giving utility to a useless thing, or making it more useful if it was useful before. This is done by manufacturing and commercial industries ; and therefore they are not barren, but productive of wealth.

The industrial system lays down the axiom that labour is the source of wealth. This system, which we owe to Adam Smith, has much truth in it, because all production of wealth requires the labour of man ; but it errs in exalting labour too much, forgetting nature, and enabled Sismondi to say : " We profess, with Adam Smith, that labour is the *sole* origin of wealth." No. The principal factor of wealth is nature, which furnishes labour with the materials and forces that it employs in its operations. After all, every useful product is but an effect of the active and passive qualities of bodies, which are given by nature to be employed by the mind and hands of man.

III.—DISTRIBUTION.

14. The division of products among those who contributed to form them, constitutes the idea of distribution. But we must speak first of property, which it presupposes.

Property means exclusive possession of a thing with power to dispose of it at will. The right to such possession is the right of property, which may be immoveable (real property), or moveable (personal property), and may be private or public.

15. Against private real property the attacks of Socialism are directed, and yet most evidently it is in accordance with the designs of nature, as being necessary

for insuring order, peace, and abundant production in society, and also as being a natural consequence of man's right to provide for his own future and that of his children. It has, however, a necessary modification in the proprietor's duty of giving the surplus to the indigent. St. Thomas says that we must distinguish between the possession and the use of property. As to the possession of it, it may be private ; and, indeed, private property ought to be, as being useful to human life. But as to the use, it ought to be common, in the sense that the owner should make the needy participate in what exceeds his just requirements.

The old Doctors said that the right of property is not a natural right, but a right of nations, because they distinguished the *jus naturale* from the *jus gentium* as being an absolute and primary dictate of nature, while the *jus gentium* is a relative and secondary one, and therefore proceeds from discourse of reason. Closely connected with the right of having property is the right of inheritance either by will or *ab intestato*.

16. The proprietor's duty of giving the surplus to the poor, or, in other words, to those who cannot support themselves, constitutes the duty of beneficence, which is gravely binding on conscience, and as to its fulfilment under certain circumstances may even be subject to the action of the ruler. The Executive cannot abolish private property, because private property is founded on a right anterior to society and independent of it, but can regulate it and harmonize it with the right that all have to live on the fruits of the earth. *Secundum naturalem ordinem ex divina providentia institutum, inferiores sunt ordinatæ res ad hoc, quod ex his subveniatur hominum necessitati.*[1]

17. This being presupposed, wealth is naturally divided between those who have co-operated to produce it. They

---

[1]   *Summa*, 2ª. 2ᵃᵉ. Q. LXVI. a. 7.

are, the proprietor who supplied the natural agents ; the capitalist, who supplied the instruments and paid the wages; and the workman, who gives labour. The proprietor's quota is called rent, the capitalist's quota profit ; the workman's quota wages.

18. To explain the origin of rent, Ricardo invented his theory about superior land and better situations. As long, he says, as there was plenty of fertile land near a market, there was no rent ; but when, through increase of population, less fertile and more distant land had to be cultivated, the price of the produce necessarily rose, to pay for extra expenses. Then, of course, the produce of the better land rose in price; and that rise in the produce of the better land constituted the rent of it. This theory is ingenious, but not consistent ; for the produce of land, setting aside its price, is of itself rent, being wealth, which is a store of useful things. Property is the origin of rent. He who has the right of possessing land has a right to have the fruits of it. *Res fructificat domino.* Ricardo confuses the landlord's rent with the tenant's renting; and this confusion comes from believing that wealth consists in the value, not in the utility of things.

19. If the proprietor has a right to have recompense in the shape of rent for having supplied those natural agents of production that are incorporated in the soil, the capitalist has a right to recompense in the shape of profit for having supplied instruments and other aids to production. Profit is midway between rent and wages. Its origin, like that of rent, is to be found in property ; for it results from capital, and capital results from rent, because it was originally formed out of the savings on that which the earth in the first place produced, and labour increased.

20. The contractor may be classed as a capitalist because by capital supplied by himself, or procured from others, he carries out some industrial enterprise, which he has either originated or agreed to manage. To him also

a recompense on the produce is due ; and if the undertaking was at his own risk, he has a right to the net
profit, or what remains after paying all who co-operated
in it.

21.   Wages are not a price, because labour is not a
commodity but a producer of commodities.   They are a
recompense for a loan of work as being the workman's
quota of the produce, for his having by the use of his
powers co-operated in producing.   Since the workman,
being usually a poor man, can neither wait till production
is completed, nor be liable to its risks, he agrees to do so
much work for so much pay ; and this is settled by mutual
contract.   But in the order of nature it has a limit that
cannot lawfully be passed.   It cannot lawfully be less than
will suffice to provide necessaries for him and for his
family.   The reason is, that according to justice the virtue
of the wages ought to equal the virtue of the labour.   Now
in nature's ordering labour is given to man as a means of
procuring what is needful for the support of life.   By
saying " man " we mean the human pair and their family :
by "the support of life " we mean all that life requires—
food, clothes, and lodging.   Therefore, wages ought to
contain these things virtually for those who devote all
their labour to the service of others.   You cannot contract
to give less than that without offending against justice,
because justice requires this equalizing of wages and work.

22.   Even at the outset of economic science free competition was proclaimed.   The *Laissez faire, laissez passer,*
of the Physiocrats became a common aphorism.   Men
were never weary of persisting upon its benefits to business and its encouragement of ability.   But if it does
some good, it also does much harm.   It is helpful to profuse and rapid production, but injurious to its equitable distribution.   It has been the means of lowering wages and
impoverishing operatives.   It originates artificial monopolies, and furnishes a reason for strikes.

23. A certain amount of State-intervention in the economic affairs of society is indispensable. Leaving them at the mercy of selfishness in conflict is applying to industry the Darwinian idea of the struggle for existence, in which the strongest has the best of it by survival of the fittest.

The duty of the government in this matter is to protect the weak and direct the strong. To protect the weak, the Executive should by law regulate in manufactures and workshops the quality and quantity of the work and the length of the working time, especially for women and children. In directing the strong it ought not to leave industry without regulation, exposing it to the shock of private interests in conflict. Economic science is, as we said at first, subordinate to Political Science; and therefore industrial movement is subject to the direction of the government. This extends to external commerce, in what concerns exportation and importation of merchandise. Wherever there are different tendencies, a regulating principle is needed. To expect order without a reason of order is to suppose an effect without a cause. Economic liberalism brings into the industrial world the cosmic system of Epicurus.

24. In order that the measures taken for the protection of labour in factories may not injure individual countries in their competition abroad, it would be well for civilized nations to agree about this and establish common rules. The labour question interests all States, and all feel the necessity of solving it in a way that would be just and acceptable. It has been said that by so doing they would favour Socialism, but we have shown this to be false, and why.

IV.—CONSUMPTION.

25. The ultimate aim of economic functions is consumption. Men seek wealth to enjoy it, save money to spend it. Therefore in Political Economy it must have a distinct place, whatever Pellegrino Rossi may say to the contrary.

Economists generally have defined consumption either as the use of an object or the destruction of a value, and also have divided it into productive and unproductive. Neither the definition nor the division will hold. The idea of use is more general than the idea of consumption; consumption implies destruction, but destruction of an object, not of a value. Destruction of a value is a consequence of consumption, inasmuch as the thing consumed had a value. Value is understood to imply exchange; and if there were no exchanges at all, there would be consumption—that is to say, destruction of useful things.

And then, productive consumption is not properly consumption, but employment of capital, which is an element of production. Consumption, properly so called, must be destruction of a product for the satisfaction of a want; and that is its definition.

26. The words "consumption" and "expense" are very often used as convertible terms. Expense does not, of itself, truly mean consumption, but means that which is given for obtaining things to be consumed. Nevertheless by metonymy the one is put for the other. The means are made to signify the end, and the end is made to signify the means. Thus a man is said to consume the money that he spends on eating and drinking.

Consumption may be either public or private; and the rules for moderating the one and the other are nearly the same. It may be said generally, that the two excesses of prodigality and of avarice ought to be avoided. The former sins by excess of expenses, the latter by defect.

27. With the idea of consumption, the idea of luxury is connected. Luxury was defined by James Stewart as the use of the superfluous; but that definition is evidently false, because luxury implies the idea, not of use, but of abuse, and of abuse in an excessive degree. Say defined it as the use of things that cost much: but that definition also is wrong, because, when costly things are used for a noble and high end, such as the worship of God or the national splendour, the use of them is not luxury, but magnificence, which is not a vice, but a virtue. Luxury is always attributed to a private person, and is intended either for showing himself off or for self-indulgence. Therefore it may be defined as the use of requisite and costly things on one's own account, for the purpose of ostentation or of pleasure. It is blamable, because it is opposed to the end for which wealth is given. It squanders the capital that might be usefully applied to production, ruins families, and scatters the superfluous which by natural right is owed to the poor. *Res, quae aliqui superabundanter habent, ex naturali jure debentur pauperum sustentationi.*[1] Some Economists have defended luxury, but Say justly contradicts them, and refutes all their arguments.

28. Often in ancient and modern times attempts have been made to restrain luxury by laws, which from *sumptus,* "expense," were called sumptuary laws; but these attempts failed. An indirect restraint by heavy taxation of luxuries would seem to be a surer remedy; but this, too, is insufficient, if it be not a stimulant to the appetite for luxuries. The *only cure* is Religion, which inspires temperance and the love of doing good.

29. To public consumption all taxes and State-debts are reducible.

---

[1] *Summa,* 2ª. 2ᵃᵉ. Q. LXVI. a. 7.

Taxes are that part of wealth which the State takes from the tax-payers to supply money for public expenses. In order to be just they should correspond with the true wants of the State and the means of the payers. They are direct and indirect. The former are directly paid on real or personal wealth by individuals. The latter are paid by the same indirectly; for they are put on goods, and, by reason of the extra price consequently added, the buyer is caught by them. Direct taxation should spare those incomes that hardly suffice to maintain the individual and his family. Indirect taxes ought to weigh as lightly as possible on the necessaries of life.

30. But inasmuch as taxes are not always sufficient (for instance in the case of war), the State is sometimes compelled to borrow money, paying so much per cent for it. This percentage is often nominal; for the bonds are often sold at ninety.

The sum of all these obligations form what is called the national debt. It is written down in a public register, called in France *Le Grand Livre;* and the debt is called *Consolidés,*—in English " Consols."

Sometimes the State contracts another sort of debt, which is called floating or fluctuating, because it is not fixed, but variable. It is contracted for a short time, to pay temporary and unforeseen expenses.

31. Sometimes, for the purpose of extinguishing debt, the State establishes a sinking fund, and sometimes resorts to conversion, in order to lighten it. The former plan consists in subtracting a small part of the money borrowed, putting it out at interest, and, being left so to increase, it suffices to pay off the whole debt. The latter consists in offering the creditors the alternative of getting back their money or accepting a smaller interest for it, which, if the rate of interest in safe investments is low at the time, most of the fundholders accept.

32. This leads to the question of whether it is good or bad for the State to borrow money. Running into debt is in itself an evil always to the State as well as to individuals. Nevertheless there are cases in which a State loan is the lesser evil and unavoidable. It may even be beneficial, if the purpose of it is a very useful one, and if there is a fair prospect of paying it off. But the national debt has reached such frightful dimensions everywhere, that now it unquestionably is a very grave and dangerous evil, which if not checked will prove ruinous to society.

CONCLUSION.

In Economy, he who undertakes to combat the errors of liberalism runs the risk of falling into the opposite errors of Socialism.

Incidis in Scyllam cupiens vitare Charybdim.

We, if we are not mistaken, have by God's help so steered between the rock and the whirlpool that we have avoided both. Liberalism boasted of having introduced into the economic world two grand ideas, freedom and property; but, to say the truth, instead of introducing, it falsified them, desiring freedom without any restraint and property untempered by its duties. We have attacked each of these errors. We have shown that unlimited competition is bad, and we have shown that the rich are bound to give their surplus to the poor.

Socialism mainly rests on the following assumptions: Firstly, that labour is the only source of wealth. Secondly, that the right of having property is dependent on the State. Thirdly, that the State, therefore, has a right to alter the foundations of it and make it collective, instead of individual. We have shown that the principal factors of wealth are natural agents, which are incorporated in matter and are an object of appropriation; secondly, that the right of the individual man to have property is a natural right independent of the State ; and, thirdly, that the State cannot touch its essence.   Private property cannot be justly abolished, even by agreement of all the States together.

Having thus kept equally free from anarchical liberalism and Socialism, we conclude this treatise.

———

APPENDIX.

WORKMEN'S ASSOCIATIONS.

I.

AMONG the difficulties that now have to be faced, there
is none more formidable than the labour question, or, as
some call it, the social question; for it threatens not only
private property but even the political order. In virtue
of principles put forth by the Revolution and promoted
by perfidious agitators, a fierce antagonism has arisen
between capital and labour; and the antagonism is
growing. The workman looks on the capitalist as a
usurper, fattening on the fruits of labour; and the
capitalist looks on the operative as a disturber, who covets
other people's goods. Till this antagonism comes to an
end, there will be no peace, no security. Economists and
governments have tried to find the means of curing the
disorder; but, whatever they may think or do, it seems
evident now that the one practical remedy is to restore
the old corporations of arts and trades (in English, Guilds)
with such modifications as the altered conditions of the
times might require. And this is precisely what the
great Pontiff, Leo XIII., suggested in his memorable
Encyclical *Humanum Genus*. "There is an institution,"
he says, "wisely instituted by our ancestors, and in process of time discontinued, which may serve in these days
as the model and form of something similar. We mean
the Guilds or Corporations of arts and trades, to protect
the material and moral interests of its members, under the
guidance of Religion. ... We should exceedingly like to
see these Guilds everywhere restored suitably to the times,

under the auspices and patronage of the Bishops, for the salvation of the people.[1] *Una quædam res est, a majoribus sapienter instituta, eademque temporum cursu intermissa, quæ tamquam exemplar et forma ad simile aliquid valere in præsentia posset. Scholas seu Collegia Opificum intelligimus, rebus simul et moribus, duce religione, tutandis ... Collegia illa magnopere vellemus, auspiciis patrocinioque Episcoporum, convenienter temporibus, ad salutem plebis, passim restituta.*

II.

THE OLD SOCIETIES OF ARTS AND TRADES [GUILDS].

OUR forefathers were not slow to understand that association is the only means of insuring for the workman stability of life, and the only means of defending the master against the excesses of competition. Corporations were multiplied in the threefold character of civil, professional and religious. Every Corporation had its own particular laws, its elected heads, its assemblies. It made its own rules, had jurisdiction in the trade, administered its property and its income. Having a life of its own, its own privileges, its own organs, its own syndics, it formed a perfect corporation in the urban community, which was not then, as it is now, composed of detached individuals with equal rights, but resulted from a social union, varying in importance according to the class or profession of its members.[2] Thus juridically organized, labour flourished for nearly six hundred years, producing those wonders of art that still are objects of admiration and proofs of a glorious past.

These associations were the offspring of Religion and

---

[1] Domini Nostri Leonis Divina Providentia Papæ XIII. Epistola Encyclica, Die XX. Aprilis, Anno MDCCCLXXXIV.

[2] L'Association Catholique: *Revue Mensuelle*, &c., Tome XXVIII. No. 3. P. 153. [Paris, 1889.]

mutual benevolence. They were based on the Confraternities, with which they are often confused even in name. They had their feasts, their pious exercises, their works of mercy, their Institutes for relieving the spiritual and temporal wants of the members. Each was under the protection of a Saint. St. Joseph was the Patron Saint of the carpenters ; St. Cecilia of the musicians ; St. Crispin of the shoemakers. Each had the portrait of its Patron Saint on its banner. Divided into three orders—masters who were also workers ; fellow-craftsmen, who having finished their time of novitiate had given proof of their ability ; and apprentices who were beginners in their art —it kept up a hierarchy in the trade, excited an honourable ambition, guaranteed the skill of the workman, and the goodness of the work. The modern strike, now so destructive to industry and order, were, in those days, almost unknown. Wages, prices of goods and hours of work had their judge and their rules. Under that system cheating, which is now so common, was almost impossible, for it would soon have been discovered, would have been against the interest and decorum of the Corporation, and was liable to heavy penalties.

We are not meaning to imply that the old Corporations were free from defects. *Vitia erunt donec homines.* The chief point in the bill of indictment against them are these : Impediments to freedom of labour ; monopolies ; length of the novitiate ; arbitrary power of the masters ; continual disputes through the limiting of the different professions ; difficulty of entering and leaving ; overcharges for passing from one grade to another.[1]

---

[1] The faults of the old Guilds are greatly exaggerated by the defenders of economic liberalism. In their eyes there was nothing in them but privileges, often bargained for, selfishness, extortion, oppression of the consumers, impediments to the progress of industry, and so forth.

III

THE HARM DONE BY ABOLISHING THEM.

INSTEAD of remedying whatever defects the Guilds might have, the Revolution of '89 did away with them, and forbade their restoration.[1] The Revolution proclaimed that the only legitimate association is the State, in whose presence there should only be detached individualities. This was a flagrant violation of the rights of man, who is by nature qualified for accomplishing, by means of union with others, a just purpose which by himself he could hardly effect, or not at all. His being associated in a political unity for a general purpose does not extinguish within him the power of associating for particular purposes, which he has as much right to seek with the help of others as by his own powers alone. But the Revolution under the disguise of freedom aimed at absorbing into the State all the rights of man : which is political Pantheism.

From that time the Guilds disappeared in France, and by degrees in other countries, according as the principles of the Revolution penetrated therein. The workmen were isolated, each under the authority of his own advice and his own power. But woe to him that is alone ! *Væ Soli.*[2]

Free competition, by unlimited lowering of prices, compelled the master to diminish wages, thereby impoverishing the workmen. But the worst consequence was the moral destitution that followed. The introduction of machinery, having once opened the doors of factories and workshops

---

[1] A few years before, *viz.* in 1776, the Minister Turgot suppressed the Corporations ; but after his fall they went on again till the Constituent Assembly of 1791 definitely abolished them.

[2] *Eccles.* iv. 10.

to women and children, loosened and often broke up family ties, by keeping the members of the family away from home and separated from each other. Great businesses, requiring many hands, attracted great numbers of work-people to the same spot, and, what is worse, without distinction of sex or age, men, women, boys and girls were brought together. Such a mixing up without precautions, provision and safeguards has produced a frightful relaxation of morals. "In all operative agglommerations," Harmel says, "great factories, mines, foundries, industrial centres of all sorts, vice exercises an unlimited oppression. If the associations do not bring to bear against it the only efficient resistance, it leads to fearful crimes, which the Socialists point out in print, and which cannot be denied. We, who know what these places are, do not hesitate to affirm that those who describe the degradation produced there are always within the mark. Some realistic novelists of these days are the only people who have dared to sound its depths."[1]

The cause of all this is clearly to be found in the imprudent abolition of the Guilds, which broke the moral connection between the master and the operative. It became a mere question of buying and selling, by which the workman sells the commodity, labour, and the master buys it by paying wages. This paid, all relation between them ceases. They are governed by the law of demand and supply, which regulates purchase and sale. The master, therefore, no longer sees in the workman anything more than a means of getting profit for capital by moving a machine, which is regarded as the factor of production. For this task he pays him so much; but the man, as a moral being, as a neighbour, as ordained for a supermundane end, as labouring to supply the means of suitably maintaining himself and his family, disappears

---

[1] *Catéchisme du Patron Préliminaire*, § ii. L'Ouvrier.

from the eyes of the master, who remains as the master only, before him, enclosed in his individual interest. Can we wonder at the ill-feeling which has resulted from such a state of things?

Nothing but a return to the old Corporations can remedy the disorder. It would take the workman as he is—a man composed, not of mere body, but of body and spirit, a man bound by family ties, a man wanting spiritual as well as material food. It would bind him to the master in fraternal friendship, unite their interests, bring them permanently together, and form, as it were, the organization of mutual good will.

IV.

ATTEMPTS AT RECONSTRUCTION.

Nil violentum durabile. The abolition of the Corporations was an open violation of the rights of man, against the natural inclination that human beings have to seek in union with others a help to the weakness of their own powers. The effect of such a cause could not be lasting.

In spite of the prohibition, a certain common understanding went on, more or less in secret, among the workmen, till at length it showed itself openly. The first manifestation of this was in England under the name of *Trades' Unions*, which, after being forbidden, were made legal. They fell into the defects attributed to the old Corporations. They are often too minute in their prescriptions, restrict overmuch the number of apprentices, and forbid their members to practise a trade other than their own. Moreover, in some places they have not hesitated to promote and maintain strikes, thus embittering the struggle, instead of helping to restore peace.

After these came the Syndicates in France, which were unions either of masters or workmen, or of masters and workmen together, and therefore called mixed Syndicates.

These also, after having been tolerated for twenty years, had a legal sanction at last. The law of March 21st, 1884, confirmed the freedom of labour, and stopped all obstacles to professional association. The Syndicates composed of masters only, or of workmen only, do not properly constitute an organic body, because they disjoin the head from the members, and instead of uniting their interests put them in opposition. The Syndicate of masters aims chiefly at defending the masters against the excessive pretensions of the workmen. "Il faut l'avouer," says Claude Jannet, "la raison qui trop souvent a provoqué les patrons à former des Syndicats, fut la nécessité de résister aux grèves. C'est seulement par cette union étroite que leur résistance a pu être efficace."[1] The Syndicates of workmen were organized mainly to protect the workmen against the masters, and help them to keep up the struggle. "Leur premier et principal but," says Jannet, "a été généralement d'organiser la classe ouvrière contre les patrons ; ils sont nés de l'antagonisme social."[2] The mixed Syndicate is the only sound one. By uniting masters and workmen it paves the way for a true Corporation. Similar societies under different names have arisen and multiplied, not only in Europe, but even in America ; so that the tendency to associate in the economic order may now be called universal.

But without a Christian spirit these associations instead of being useful will only do harm. They easily become the prey of the Sects, who make use of them as a powerful means of carrying out their dark designs. Unhappily the

---

[1] *Le Socialisme d' État*, VI. La loi du 21. Mars, 1884, sur les Syndicats professionels. The whole of this Chapter ought to be read. It contains not only an exact account of the origin and development of Syndicates, but also excellent remarks on their nature and influence.

[2] Ibid.

result is to a great extent justifying the worst apprehen-
sions; for not a few of these societies are, in fact, so
many centres of Socialism and anarchy.

Besides these associations which have a certain generality
of scope, there are others that aim at some particular purpose, and are called co-operative, because they unite the
forces of individuals for some common advantage. Of
these the most important have to do with credit, production, or consumption. "The object of these societies,"
says M. Leroy-Beaulieu, "is either to amass capital, for
the purpose of lending money to affiliated workmen who
want it and offer security, (co-operative societies of credit);
or to organize a common purchase of goods for the purpose
of selling them afterwards by retail to the associates,
(co-operative societies of consumption); or to establish
groups of workmen of the same trade, who produce without the direction of a master, and sell their products in
common. The latter is called a co-operative society for
production." [1]

The two first of these are sure of success, and, if well
organized and well administered, must be advantageous
to the members. The first protects the workmen against
the money-lenders: the second enables him to buy
necessaries at a reduction of ten, twelve, or (if they had
come directly from the producers) even forty per cent.
This however is injurious to the class of small tradesmen,
and, if extensively practised, would destroy one of those
independent economic existences that deserve to be
supported and encouraged. To have advantages and disadvantages is proper to every human thing: and in this
case the bad consequences might be much lessened by
restricting the co-operative supplies to certain necessary
commodities.

The third-mentioned Co-operative Societies, _viz._

---

[1] _Précis d'Économie Politique_, Deuxième Partie, Ch. VII.

societies for production, have mostly come to nothing, by reason of the grave obstacles that stand in their way. "Intelligent, economical, and very laborious workmen," says Leroy-Beaulieu, "can, no doubt, when they have united their savings, agree among themselves to set up a small commercial or industrial establishment. If they are very prudent, persevering, and well disciplined—if they can choose a good manager, pay him well, follow with docility his directions, be contented with moderate wages, and apply the rest of their gains to increasing their capital—they may in time succeed, especially in a small way of business. Nevertheless, it is very difficult for these associations to achieve a lasting success. The usual causes of their failure are jealousy, want of discipline, difficulty of finding a good director, and also, (but this is the least of the obstacles) want of capital. Those Co-operative Societies for production that have been successful, have effected a great concentration of directive power. They have gradually reduced the number of their active members, and they employ a certain number of non-associated workmen, to whom they give the usual wages. In short most of these happy little societies end by becoming, as in the cotton trade in England, mere joint-stock companies—that is to say, associations of capital, in which paid workmen, not associates, are almost exclusively employed." [1]

V.

THE CHRISTIAN CORPORATION.

We understand a Christian Corporation to mean a society of masters and workmen, mindful of their common prosperity, material and spiritual, but especially their spiritual welfare. It must be formed of masters and workmen together, because otherwise their antagonism

---

[1] Ibid.

would continue. Associations of masters only, or of
workmen only, tend rather, as we have seen, to confirm
their separation and hostility. To heal this division, you
must bring the two classes together. You must make
them known to each other, make them unite, make them
look on themselves as if they were members of one
family. In no other way can prejudices be removed,
suspicion silenced, hearts united in mutual good will.
Its advantages to the associates ought to be, not merely
material, but also, and principally, spiritual; for thus
only can it improve the whole man, who is composed of
body and soul. And since the soul is superior to the
body, the interests of the soul come before the interests of
the body.

We are considering Corporations in their ideal form,
proceeding from the different applications that circumstances may happen to require. Thus considered, it
seems to be principally marked by the four properties of
being freely undertaken, of being founded on religion, of
seeking to restore the domestic relations, and of being
fruitful in producing economic institutions.

First and foremost is the condition of being freely
undertaken, so that each man may enter or leave it by
his own free will; for working appertains to the individual, and therefore the individual ought to have the
power of choosing what work he will take to, and when
and where he will do it. As a member of the association
he is justly bound by its rules, but always under the
condition of having freely accepted them. If he agrees
to work in community with others, and enjoy the advantages of union, rather than take his chance by himself, it is only just that he should keep the rules laid
down. The faults attributed to the old Corporations
chiefly proceeded from want of freedom.

Austria followed the opposite method. It restored the
Corporations, but in a compulsory manner. Any one

there, who wishes to practise a trade, must, as in olden times, be enrolled in its Corporation and contribute to the support of the institutions established for the common benefit of the members. This method is not objectionable there; for the spirit of personal independence is not so strongly marked in the Austrians, nor in the Germans generally, as it is in the Latin and Anglo-Saxon races. Association under orders from superiors is almost natural to them; and therefore no violence is done by imposing it as a law. Moreover, those Corporations, though they might be improved, have done much good, and particularly by having protected the working classes from the influence of Socialism, which in the North, more than anywhere else, is making every effort to get hold of them and rule them.

Clearly Corporations ought to be founded on Religion. Their chief purpose is to improve the morals of the workmen; and this can only be done by Religion, because Religion, and Religion only, has power to keep bad inclinations in check. A Corporation should subsist in virtue of mutual benevolence: and Religion alone can infuse into man's heart the true love of his neighbour. Man is naturally selfish. To love another effectually he must get out of himself; and he cannot do that for the sake of his neighbour, unless he rises up to God by love, and from God descends to his neighbours, whom he recognizes as a child of God and his own brother. All this is an effect of Religion and of nothing else. Divine Charity alone warms the heart with a heavenly fire, makes people forget themselves, makes them ready to sacrifice themselves for the good of others. By zeal for the glory of God, by desire to do what is pleasing to God, we are led to consider our neighbour's interest apart from our own. *Qui diligit Deum, diligat et fratrem suum.* [1]   Brotherhood supposes a common Father; and this Father can only be God.

Here the Austrian Corporations are wide of the mark, being compelled to admit *oves et boves universas, insuper et pecora campi.* [2]   Catholics, Protestants, Jews, and even Atheists are indiscriminately brought together therein; so that the basis of those societies is not religious, but purely economic. This is the result of the compulsory system, which is also against harmony of thought and feeling. But the defect is imposed by circumstances : for prudence dictates that when we cannot obtain the whole of what is desirable, we should try to obtain a part of it. The danger of intimacy between people of different religions may be much obviated by instituting for the Catholics pious congregations to serve as an antidote and bind them together in a separate unity. Thus, whereas in former days Corporations arose out of Confraternities, Confraternities would now come out of Corporations.

The third condition is that the Corporation ought to keep an eye on the domestic relations. The Corporation receives the man, not in the abstract, but in the concrete. Now the concrete man either is the father of a family, or belongs to a family ; and as such he should be considered. The greatest harm done by abolishing Corporations was the breaking up of domestic unity. Father, mother, and children go to different factories where they happen to find employment, stay there all day, and come back to their home, as if it were a lodging house. Thus family duties are forgotten—the duties of the husband to the wife, of the wife to her husband, of the father to his children, of the children to their father. This immense evil the Corporation should remedy by endeavouring to

---

[1] 1 *John* iv. 21.
[2] *Psl.* viii. 8.

re-establish home life in its due order. It should limit the hours of work, so that the father and mother may have time for attending to home duties, and the children have time for instruction, religious and secular, for which purposes schools and pious congregations are required.[1]

Lastly, a Corporation ought to be fruitful in producing economic institutions. The workman has many material wants, and the Corporation should relieve them. His strength, which is his patrimony, may diminish through illness or old age; and work may fail owing to an industrial crisis or some other cause. The Corporation should help in such cases by means of Savings banks and other co-operative institutions, which would not be impossible when the Corporation had progressed and formed a corporate patrimony by help from the masters, regular payments from the workmen and donations from benefactors, who would not be wanting.

And so in fact have Corporations been formed, and are forming now, in different countries, among those workmen who are men of good will. Jannet, speaking of France, writes as follows: "The Catholic trade associations, or Corporations, as they like to be called, have everywhere multiplied, thanks to the active labours of the workmen's clubs, founded on the ruins of the Commune in 1871 by Albert de Mun, with some admirably zealous men, foremost among whom was his brother, Count Robert de Mun, likewise a man of very high character. Everywhere this work has met with a reception that will be singularly honourable to France in the history of these latter years. In Angers, Nantes, Toulouse, Caen, in Paris, and in many other cities it has

---

[1] The limitation of the working hours is one of those points in which the government should intervene, so that free competition may not make it impossible. Indeed, as we said before, there ought to be a national agreement about it.

created Corporations of trades in the form of mixed Syndicates, or unions of masters and workmen. The basis on which these Corporations are, as it were, seated, is always a Confraternity, that prepares their foundation and remains as their real bond of union. Societies for mutual help, retiring pensions, co-operative societies for supplying consumable things, add material interest thereto. Those sentiments of a Christian Apostolate which M. de Mun so powerfully put forth before a select assembly of workmen in clubs and in rising Corporations, lead us to hope for a happy solution of the problem on which depends the future of society, and the return of the masses to the Religion that freed their forefathers and ennobled labour during the ages of Faith.

"At Lille, which is a most active autonomous centre for every Catholic work in the northern part [of France], an association of Christian masters, recruited from among the great men of business, and presided over by a Priest of great mental capacity, inculcates in the workshops all the most practical means of securing for the workman moral and material prosperity. Its influence is not confined to its members: through the work that it does many local abuses gradually disappear."[1]

The same things are done in other European countries and in America. In Italy the Corporations, generally speaking, are not taken from Confraternities, but are constituted in the manner of Confraternities. They have their patron Saints, whose name they usually take, their banner with the effigy of their Saint, their feast; pious exercises, frequenting of the Sacraments, religious assemblies under the direction of Ecclesiastics. They establish professional schools and doctrinal instruction for young men and girls. From the smaller contributions of

[1] *Le Socialisme d'État*, VIII. Les associations professionelles Catholiques.

the workmen, the larger offerings of the masters, and the gifts of beneficent people, they form the corporate patrimony for the common expenses, help the sick and the old, found societies for the relief of accidental wants.

VI.

THE AUTONOMY OF A CHRISTIAN CORPORATION.

The Christian Corporation, so far as its organizing and its internal administration are concerned, should be formed and maintained independently of the State. This is essential; for the State, separated from the Church and without God, would influence it badly. A Christian Corporation should be professedly and thoroughly religious, faithfully keeps the laws of the Church, and obey devoutly the Vicar of Jesus Christ. How then can it accept the interference of governments that are either hostile to the Catholic Religion, or at least indifferent to it. The Corporations must keep clear of rulers whose touch defiles. "May God preserve us," says Claude Jannet, "from seeing the modern State add this social policy to its other numerous invasions of the rights of the individual and of the family."[1]

What the Corporation should accept from the government and claim as a right, is legal recognition and perfect personality as to the possession of its own property. Any association for a just purpose has a right to exist and act, and therefore has a right to insure the means.

By the French law of 1884, the right of the associated workmen, as such, to have real property is limited to the places necessary for their meetings, their libraries, and their professional courses. This is unjust. A moral person has a right to have property no less than a physical person, and more so in a way, because the moral person

---

[1] *Le Socialisme d'État*, VIII.

has the rights of all the individuals that compose it. Such a limitation, we think, will certainly disappear.

But beyond this legal recognition of personality and of the society's rights to hold property, the government has no right to intervene, unless the common interests of society are concerned. In all that belongs to the internal affairs of the association, such as the appointment to offices, the regulations about work, the management of the property &c., the State has no right to interfere.

But this does not take away the right and duty of the government to lay down general rules connected with public morality and the protection of the weak, such as prescribing rest from work on Sundays, &c., fixing a limit to the hours of work, determining the age at which children may be admitted into the factories, and excluding women from work done at night and from work above their strength.

Whilst the interference of the government in the internal affairs of the Corporations is bad, it is well that the individual members of a Guild should have a voice in the management of it. That each of them should, in one way or another, participate in the government of it is according to reason, because nothing is more likely to make people look on the well-being of a society as their own, than having a share in its administration. This, however, must be understood in the hierarchical manner; so that the highest places be filled by the masters, who are superiors born of the Corporation; the next by the principal and best workmen, the lowest by the whole multitude, as having the right to select their representatives, and thus by means of them watch over the management and distribution of what is owned in common.

These remarks on the organism and relation of Christian Corporations are but light touches. Those who wish to go deeper will do well to read that most excellent book, *Manuel d'une Corporation Chrétienne*, written by the incomparable Léon Harmel. There they will find a minute and perfect legislation, tested by him in his vast works at Val-des-Bois. It more particularly concerns industries on a great scale, but supplies many ideas that are applicable to a smaller way of business, and also to associations of arts and trades properly so called.

THE END.

INDEX.